The
LONELY WARRIOR
The Life and Times of Robert S. Abbott

Robert S. Abbott

The
LONELY WARRIOR

The Life and Times of Robert S. Abbott

BY

ROI OTTLEY

Chicago • HENRY REGNERY COMPANY • 1955

For

MYRTLE AND JOHN H. H. SENGSTACKE III

IT IS NOT SURPRISING if the Negro turns with more than ordinary devotion to the printed page. To him it is an institution peculiarly embodying his group life, something like his church or his lodge, but even more like some public work of art symbolizing his aspiration.

—FREDERICK G. DETWEILER, *The Negro Press in the United States,* 1922.

FOREWORD

I NEVER MET OR SAW Robert S. Abbott, the subject of this biography. I knew him only by his reputation, which was in full flower when I worked as an editor for New York's *Amsterdam News,* a Negro newspaper. This fact, I believe, has given me enough objectivity toward the man to see the lights and shadows. What is described in this book has been gathered from a multitude of sources—principally, his writings, interviews, fragmentary papers he left, and of course the columns of the Chicago *Defender.*

Son of ex-slaves, Abbott passed from small-town obscurity to national preeminence, due neither to great wealth nor hereditary status, but by sheer character, determination and imagination. He was a crusading journalist, who ultimately developed into a national leader, and, *in the process,* became a millionaire. As a newspaper editor, he influenced and molded the opinions of millions of Negroes in the United States, and therefore his career is of unique interest—indeed, his extraordinary achievement is a triumphant American success story.

The roots of greatness should be sought in a man's formative years. Until now, most Negroes who have achieved anything noteworthy seemingly have no traceable background—notably Booker T. Washington and George Washington Carver—and like Topsy seem merely to have "growed up." But Abbott's accomplishments represent continuity of family enterprise and perseverance. However, the purpose of this volume is not at all genealogical. Essentially, this is a *biography of a people,* for Abbott's life and times spanned the most triumphant period of the Negro in the United States. Born three years after the promulgation of the Emancipation Proclamation, he lived to see and chronicle the spectacular progress of his people.

The idea for this book belongs to John H. H. Sengstacke III, now the editor and publisher of the Chicago *Defender,* who more than anyone else wished to see the achievements of his uncle, Robert S. Abbott, placed on the record. He wanted the true and unvarnished story told, for he recognized his uncle as a human being as well as a public figure. Consequently, he was not only generous with his own time, but he placed at my disposal the facilities of his organization and all the documents, photographs and papers in his possession.

In a sense, then, this book is his monument to a man who unselfishly championed the cause of his people.

As this biography evolved from the research to the writing stage, I became increasingly more conscious of a rapidly growing debt to a multitude of helpers and advisers. I therefore wished to acknowledge the personal help of Robert S. Abbott's sister, Rebecca Sengstacke, who provided me with a mass of family letters, documents, and diaries. Without her collection, it would have been virtually impossible to reconstruct her brother's childhood and youth. I must mention the energetic cooperation of President Alonzo G. Moron and W. Barton Beatty, Jr., of Hampton Institute, Hampton, Virginia, and that of Henry D. Middleton, Phil A. Jones, Agaliece Westbrook Miller and Esther Talley. Many astute insights were given me by Dr. Charles S. Johnson, president of Fisk University, Nashville, Tennessee. Allison Davis read and criticized the first four chapters with considerable profit to me.

Metz P. T. Lochard, Frank Young, Alfred E. Monroe and Enoc P. Waters, executive editor of the Chicago *Defender,* not only cooperated cheerfully, but they gave me much valuable information. I wish to express my sincere appreciation to Inez Smith for her secretarial assistance, and to Gloria Gras who typed the manuscript. I also thank most cordially such institutions as the Georgia Historical Society, Savannah, Georgia; the American Missionary Association, New York; and the staffs of the George Cleveland Hall Library, Chicago, Illinois; Georgia State College Library, Savannah, Georgia; Atlanta University Library, Atlanta, Georgia; and the Schomburg Collection, New York City. My wife, Alice, contributed in no small measure to the completion of this manuscript, giving advice, criticism and encouragement.

ROI OTTLEY

Chicago, March 1955.

CONTENTS

CONTENTS—*continued*

ILLUSTRATIONS

The

LONELY WARRIOR

Before I started on my life's work—journalism—I was counseled by my beloved father that a good newspaper was one of the best instruments of service and one of the strongest weapons ever to be used in defense of a race which was deprived of its citizenship rights.—ROBERT S. ABBOTT, Chicago *Defender*, 1930.

CHAPTER I

Sincerely, "Georgia Boy"

ROBERT SENGSTACKE ABBOTT, temperate and imaginative, was one of the first Negroes in the United States to become a millionaire—and, in the process, he revolutionized the Negro press, today the greatest single force in the Negro world. He became a rich man purely by accident. He wanted money enough to support a wife and perhaps indulge a few quiet luxuries; but he neither sought nor ever hoped to be as rich as he became—indeed, the idea of becoming well-to-do was inconceivable to a Negro of his day. Wealth was thrust upon him as a by-product of his crusading journalism. For Abbott no amount of material comfort and well-being could compensate for the denial of equal citizenship to his race. Consequently, in his labors he was passionately, perhaps fanatically, obsessed with the social emancipation of his people. He was often a solitary man in fighting for his principles.

Now, with the perspective of history, Abbott ranks as a leader with the giants of his time: Booker T. Washington and W. E. B. Du Bois.

1

Yet he was strikingly different.

The Tuskegee educator was eloquent. Abbott was almost inarticulate. Du Bois was brilliantly intelligent. Abbott was intuitive. Washington was pliable and rational. Abbott was uncompromising. Du Bois was an egotist. Abbott was a humble man. Washington was a solitary drinker. Abbott was abstemious. Du Bois was impulsive. Abbott was cautious. Washington was light-hearted. Abbott was somber. Du Bois was hastily critical. Abbott was sympathetically patient. Washington was superficial. Abbott was methodical. Du Bois was individualistic. Abbott possessed the self-control needed for teamwork. Du Bois was a master of prose. Abbott had a pedestrian style.

Yet he shared their passion for the Negro race and, like them, acquired the power to influence great masses of people.

Dr. Charles S. Johnson, president of Fisk University, Nashville, Tennessee, who was closely associated with the publisher when both were members of the Chicago Commission on Race Relations, offers an astute appraisal of the man. He says, "My personal judgement at the time was that the progress of the racial movement, supported by the *Defender*, exceeded the *Defender's* own calculated designs; that, paradoxically, if Mr. Abbott had had more of the discipline of formal education, he would have achieved less, because he would have been restrained by history and precedent."

Gunnar Myrdal, author of the monumental *An American Dilemma,* pronounced Abbott as the greatest single force in Negro journalism, and indeed the founder of the modern Negro press. The publisher's newspaper contemporaries as well have acknowledged his significant role in the development of Negro newspapers.

This reputation was erected upon uncompromising racial idealism, a policy pursued with such vigor that the man was excoriated as a "yellow journalist" in the Hearst tradition. During World War I, he was charged with publishing editorials destructive to Negro morale, a fact that caused him serious difficulty with the Federal government and brought threats of reprisal from the Attorney General. To be sure, he loved his country and served her as willingly and faithfully as any—but he refused to say all was well with her Negro citizens.

He stood squarely on principle.

The strange thing is that he was not characteristically a ruthless or violent person. He was in fact a mild man who liked flowers and poetry. He was indeed absurdly timorous. Those who had read his flaming editorials and were awed by the power he held in his hands were quite disappointed when they saw him. Maybe they were surprised to meet not a wild-eyed radical but a polite, soft-voiced man, even given to kissing ladies' hands. Seen in a different context, he would have been mistaken for a petty bookkeeper suffering from occupational myopia, or, perhaps, for an inoffensive professor from a Southern state college.

His life was shot full of such paradox.

The blood coursed in the man's veins was pure Negro. He was in fact distinctly black—a fact of profound meaning to his story. He was slightly bulky but erect, with silky skin and bland features. He carried himself with a curious elastic grace, but, at the same time, stiffly. Of medium height—five feet some six or seven inches—but rather long-legged, he liked to be photographed wearing a top hat, cutaway coat, striped trousers, spats and carrying a gold-headed cane. His eyes were remarkable: shrewdly luminous, and never at rest. Both his face and his speech seemed somewhat arid until the eyes lighted them up. His voice was high-pitched but not unpleasant. But among the character traits of Abbott we must mention first, and above all, his stubbornness, his tenacity.

He chain smoked cigars. He never learned to drive an automobile, though he had several. He remembered the names of few people. He referred to one woman twenty years in his employ as "that girl in circulation." He forgot even his

3

secretary's name. But every staff member bears witness to the fact that he never forgot an order he had given. If he gave instructions for a story to be written, he afterwards carefully perused the paper to find that particular article, and if it failed to appear he was quick to call the culprit to account. He was in fact shrewd, suspicious and calculating and not above the use of guile, but his moral courage was indisputable.

He was a gentleman, high-minded and nearly puritanical, but he never forgot any injury done him, particularly racial, no matter how slight. His manners were impeccable, almost courtly. He had a great sense of dignity, even nobility. His sports editor, Fay Young, declares, "He made you feel you were talking to a spiritual person." Yet he was not a religious man in the accepted sense, though a regular churchgoer. He had in fact a peculiar kind of mysticism. He was, too, a very orderly man and often unconsciously rearranged things on his desk while talking. He rarely showed emotion. He seldom laughed and only infrequently smiled, though he had, at times, a droll sense of humor.

Though sensitive and sometimes standoffish, he had a magnetic personality and could be conspicuously urbane. He was basically a friendly person with a touch of the common man. He talked with every and anybody. He had no hobbies, no relaxations, except entertaining friends by singing. He played bridge and attended the opera, but really liked neither. He rarely read books, though he had an extensive library and felt "no time was lost reading." His idea of a good time was to walk the streets of the South Side and watch his people. His appearance of humility, bordering on the apologetic, was disarming to whites as well as Negroes. But few people ever reached him sufficiently to develop any intimacy. Underneath he was often tense, uneasy and aloof.

One interesting sidelight on the man is the fact that he never acquired a nickname, though he himself was gifted at giving colorful labels. To acquaintances and cronies alike he was known simply as "Mister Abbott" and sometimes, for precise identification as "black Abbott," but not even the irreverent curbstone pranksters ever thought of calling him by a nickname. Few felt close enough to refer to him as "Bub" or "Bob." Even his two wives never got beyond calling him "Mister Abbott." His early staff members, who often chummily shared food and carfare with him, sometimes referred to him as the "chief" or the "Old Man"; but in his presence, they could never bring themselves to call him by anything but his surname.

His nurse before his final illness, a Daisy Dickerson, was seemingly the only one to break through his reserve, and she labeled him "Sir Robert," which in itself is significant. He was no rabble-rouser or backslapper, but he deeply loved the rank and file of his race, and conceded, though he did not wish to have intimate associations with them, "It's the little man who digs ditches in the streets, who is paying me my salary." Nevertheless, he had no intention of sacrificing his own personal integrity to become a popular leader; nor would he submit himself to the dictates of the mass. He never frequented barbershops, saloons or cabarets—in his day the centers of Negro social life. He was in fact that peculiar but no less genuine product, a self-made aristocrat. He had all of the aristocrat's instinctive dislike of the mob with, at the same time, all the aristocrat's sense of public duty and willingness to serve—and, in Abbott's case, a racial loyalty to boot.

The man was also an incredible combination of showman and black parson. He was a salvationist and messiah as well as a super-opportunist and pragmatist. His penury was legendary. Yet he gave away thousands and was swindled out of thousands more. He had a love of travel and an unusual capacity for work. To some he was a demagogue; to others, the anointed leader. To Julius Rosenwald he was "like a monkey with a shotgun, who will hurt anybody"; but to Dr. Johnson, he was "a man with a sense of crisis." To all, though, he was

5

a thoroughly engaging personality, whose incorruptible dedication to the cause of his race won the respect and admiration of black and white alike.

Robert S. Abbott was the son of slaves, and was reared on the outskirts of Savannah, Georgia. Born on the heels of the Emancipation Proclamation, he grew up under a pattern of color—white, mulatto and black—which even as a boy frustrated his aspirations. He developed deep resentments against whites but, curiously, not against mulattoes, though he frequently was a victim of their cruel color discriminations—one of the social realities of those days. His resentments were to be translated into the cardinal principles of the newspaper he would establish—indeed, his odyssey began, at the age of nineteen, as a search for a way to escape color prejudice.

His wanderings led him to Hampton Institute, Virginia, where his racial bitterness was somewhat softened and channelized. He studied the printing trade and came under the influence of Booker T. Washington, who frequently returned to his alma mater to deliver addresses and mingle with the students. The Tuskegee principal, whom Abbott worshipped, became his hero. His visions were also expanded by tours with the Hampton quartet in which he sang tenor. One such trip took him to Chicago, where Colored American Day was being celebrated at the World's Columbian Exposition. The young man was inspired by the speech of the ex-slave and distinguished Negro spokesman, Frederick Douglass, and by the account of the anti-lynching crusader, Ida B. Wells, who described how a white mob destroyed her Memphis newspaper and drove her out of town.

Upon his graduation, Abbott returned to Chicago where he lived unobtrusively for several years trying unsuccessfully to obtain work as a printer. He briefly toyed with the idea of a legal career, and did indeed attend law school, but he was advised that he was too black to make any impression on the courts. He learned what it was to stand in the breadline of a prominent white church and be told to step aside and make way for a white man; and, again, to make way for a white man while looking for work, even though the latter was an immigrant who could speak no English. He became acquainted with people in similar straits, and he listened while they angrily described the desperate meanings of being a Negro. Like himself, they had no vehicle for articulating their racial grievances, no public defender.

The American attitude toward Negroes smelt to Heaven!

Abbott recalled how his stepfather, Rev. John H. H. Sengstacke, had insisted that a newspaper was one of the strongest weapons a Negro could have in the defense of his race. This, plus Abbott's observation of the Negro's melancholy condition, were the twin inspirations for starting a weekly newspaper in 1905—the Chicago *Defender*. His capital totaled twenty-five cents. Nearly eight years had elapsed before he had taken the plunge—in fact, he was a late starter in everything he did: he did not graduate from Hampton until he was twenty-seven; he launched his newspaper when he was thirty-seven; not until he was fifty did he marry, and indeed was nearly seventy years old when he took a second bride.

The idea of a paper had natural roots in the depths of his personal experiences, but the decision to publish was made in the face of every advice to the contrary—indeed, he stood in lonely isolation with his project. With unquenchable faith and perhaps the most unflinching will of any contemporary Negro, he had set himself to the task. It was his good fortune that a social change, for which he was not accountable, occurred just at a time when his own personal revolt against old forms of life and thought found itself aligned with the major forces driving society along new paths. His purpose was revealed in the nakedly simple slogan he adopted: *American race prejudice must be destroyed!* His passion for journalism often out-

7

ran his capacities, but he persevered and spent more than twenty dreary years giving the project a sound footing. He eventually established an organ that was to be published without a break in continuity for fifty years. It reached a peak circulation of 230,000 nationally—until recently, with the exception of the Bible, no publication was more influential among the Negro masses.

There were very few trained Negro newspapermen in those days, and few places for them to gain the apprenticeship. Consequently, Abbott was forced to recruit personnel from the ranks of Pullman porters, barbers, hoofers, waiters and bartenders and train them himself. When special talents were unavailable, he sometimes assisted young men financially to secure the necessary training, as he did with Dan Day, a cartoonist who studied at the Chicago Art Institute. If Negroes were unable to acquire the skills, as was the case with the printing trades, he had no reluctance about employing white men, as he did when he purchased the paper's first presses. The mechanical department, headed by a white foreman, was afterwards manned by white linotypers, pressmen, stereotypers and mailers, since their skills were possessed by no more than a handful of Negroes throughout the country.

The key to Abbott's successful operations was the fact that he recognized his own limitations and recruited people accordingly. "Mr. Abbott," Dr. Johnson observes, "was a shrewd publisher, who had the wisdom to engage sagacious and highly literate editors to interpret the significance of events, and alert news editors to select and project the news." He had indeed an extraordinary ability to choose talent. For example, Wayland L. Rudd, whom Abbott hired as a reporter, became a poet of distinction. He personally chose Willard Motley as a boy to edit the young people's Bud Billiken pages. Motley afterwards became a best-selling novelist with *Knock On Any Door*. He insisted upon publishing the first seventy-five poems of Gwendolyn Brooks, when she was a youngster. Now a Pulitzer prize winner, she says he provided her with the needed incentive to continue writing poetry.

The man's crusade to bring Southern Negroes north was perhaps the most gigantic project he attempted and his most notable achievement. Nearly a million migrated on his urgings. Carl Sandburg, who closely observed the movement, credited Abbott with almost single-handedly setting the migration in motion. "Whether with or without his planning," says Dr. Johnson, "the *Defender* became one of the most potent factors in a phenomenal hegira that began to change the character and pattern of race relations in the United States."

The reason for his success as an editor-publisher was this, briefly: his remarkable headlines, satirizing cartoons and direct style of appeal, caused Negroes to see their image in the *Defender*. For he was so thoroughly a Negro himself, that everything he said and did was a reflection of the mass mind. He had as well an unusual capacity for judging both the Negro and the white man. He knew what the Negro wanted and what the white man would accept, and in this sense he had something of the genius of Booker T. Washington. Moreover, while he himself was a Republican, the paper was politically independent and supported only those candidates, white or Negro, who were aggressively in favor of Negro progress. He himself had no political ambitions, and rejected a plan to run him for Congress. He had in fact little confidence in politicians. His most caustic rakings were reserved for the way in which they applied democratic principles: "When you consider the fact that few men in responsible political positions are in love with great principles that are vouchsafed by that historic document, you may not wonder that the Constitution has become more of a reference than a philosophy of action."

By 1918 the Chicago *Defender* was a triumphant success, despite the fact that the publisher had little business acumen. Roscoe Conkling Simmons, a *Defender* columnist and personal friend, explained the publisher's disinclination to pay close attention to the business operations in this florid language: "Details he left to minds that delight in detail, but his soul, his idea could not be confined to ledgers." One of his editors, Julius J. Adams, declares: "As a publisher, he seemed to have less greed than other Negro publishers. He was in the old tradition: he placed emphasis on journalism. He was not primarily concerned with building a financial institution." He opposed, for example, the opening of a branch office in one city, because he did not want to hurt a competitor—a fact that caused one man to remark, "He was a poet-philosopher with the weaknesses of both!"

Even so, Abbott was the only Negro publisher to become an eminent financial success in Chicago. Exactly thirty-two newspapers failed during the thirty-five years he was at the *Defender's* helm, and not one which began during his long regime is in existence today.*

Yet, according to Claude A. Barnett, director of the Associated Negro Press, he had the ability to step into a crucial situation and get things going with some variation of the snappily delivered phrase, "Let's put some juice in this!" He was wiser than his modes of expression indicated, though. He did in fact have a faculty for synthesizing his ideas by the use of proverbs, idioms, humorous anecdotes or epigrams. For example, he used to say, "Never let anybody know what card you hold in your hand; maybe, you might let them peep at the end of one, but never let them see it completely." And he often said: "Throw the rock—but hide the hand!", a saying which gives a revealing insight into his character.

He may have been no business wizard, but he was a flaming success as a missionary and teacher, which was logical in view of his missionary childhood and youth. Essentially his

---

* Prominent among these were: *Whip, Bee, Broad Ax, Conservator, Idea, Bulletin, Appeal, Searchlight, Advocate, Enquirer, World, Fellowship Herald, Enterprise, Metropolitan Post,* and *News-Ledger.*

program was to uplift his people. Enoc Waters, now the *Defender's* executive editor, recalls how Abbott constantly admonished him, "Elevation of the race is our job!" He did launch the first campaign in a Negro newspaper to improve the public conduct of Negroes. Until this campaign, incidentally, Negro newspapers had been apologetic, or had attempted to explain away offensive behavior—buttressed of course by the view of social psychologists that Negro aggressions were merely outlets for their frustrations.

Unaware of such abstractions, Abbott insisted, "If we act like decent people, the chances are we shall be treated decently." As violently critical as Abbott was of the society that hurt him, his analysis of what was wrong with Negroes was even more harsh. "When I consider the whole range of our social behavior," he remarked in a moment of despair, "I am almost tempted to say that we are just a little more than educated apes." Thus, for him "polite society," "fine manners," "correct usage," finishing schools for girls, the acquisition of culture, and the learning of foreign languages became of great importance in the Negro's progress.

His experiences in Europe and Latin America, which he always recalled with sentimentality, inspired this trend in his thinking and reinforced his own ambitions to be a cultivated person. Perhaps his proudest moment was when he was given permanent membership in the Literary and Artistic Institute of France.

He spent the summer of 1929 abroad, which marked a turning point in his outlook. Yet, in all his European experiences he seems never to have been very sensitive to esthetic emotion or interested in the spiritual aspects and currents of the European past. Chartres had stirred him as little as had the Sistine Madonna. When he stood at Wenlock Edge gazing over mile on mile of exquisite Shropshire landscape to the blue hills of Wales in the hazy distance, it was not to yield himself to the influence of beauty but to ponder the race problems of Britain. Suddenly, however, he began to see America with fresh eyes, and this, upon his return, resulted in a new approach to his crusades for racial equality.

Abbott, the racial reformer, was also a psychological puzzle. His associates regarded him as an enigma. His curious background may have been the reason. Yet he was fortunate in having had vigorous and enterprising ancestors, healthy and thrifty parents, a rearing in a pleasant home in rural Georgia, a group of sisters and a brother to teach him the give-and-take code, and attendance at a school and church that provided mental and moral training. His surroundings were physically ideal: a farm, the river, and the woods afforded ample opportunity for bodily development. But in the midst of these natural blessings, he was surrounded by poverty-stricken, ignorant, shiftless, superstitious ex-slaves, whose broods were his only playmates, and he was unconsciously swept into the backward undertow.

For example, Abbott was labeled a "Geechee," a term implying certain primitive qualities of mind and behavior. He had, in truth, absorbed many of the supersititious beliefs of coastal Georgia. Toward the close of his long life he suddenly began talking about "spells" and "fixings"—which was a reversion to the so long forgotten superstition of his early environment. He could hardly have escaped its pervasive influence, for sorcery was practiced extensively in the old days. The old root doctors, visited by superstitious clients, used to perform mystic rites and promise to work miraculous cures. Many Negroes who lived in the area of Abbott's upbringing viewed adversity not as the workings of fate, but as the revenge of a personal enemy. The supernatural was a significant part of life among the people whom Abbott knew as a boy.

He often used the term "Georgia boy"—referring to the folkways of the section. He himself was a "Georgia boy" to the core. And yet, though born in a slave context, he achieved the extraordinary feat of functioning successfully in a modern society. But he never was quite able to escape his background. Negroes in Savannah, for instance, placed a premium on a complexion approximating that of a Caucasian. Thus from birth, Abbott's own color became a cross for him to bear within his own race. He protested against racial discriminations, not because he felt himself different, but because he wanted to be similar and was forcibly held to be different—not only by whites, but by the mulattoes of his own group. The problem of color was to shadow his footsteps as closely as the black dog shadowed Faust, and do much to twist and misshape his outlook.

He came to hate the color black—indeed, I suspect he was afflicted with a case of self-hate. He avoided black as a color for clothes and rarely appeared in public accompanied by a black woman. He even had an aversion to the term "Negro." He was, however, fiercely loyal to any man who was black, as distinct from those who were brown or fair of complexion. He kept notoriously incompetent black workers in his employ simply because he felt society offered them no social mercy. He once retreated sufficiently to observe: "Black isn't a bad shade; let's make it popular in complexions as well as clothes." His eccentricities about color made him object to the use of the term "blackball" by Negro fraternities, and urge instead the use of "whiteball," as a term for denying aspirants membership. Thus the slogan emerged: "Blackballs elect; whiteballs reject!" This preoccupation often produced constructive ideas, such as his campaign, "Go to a White Church Sunday."

The man's endless search for racial peace led him finally to the Bahai faith. This is not as sensational as it sounds. As with everything else, Abbott judged a religion by the degree to which racial equality was practiced; moreover, like the Chinese, Negroes care little for religious stratifications. Abbott had been brought up in the Congregational church in

13

which his stepfather, Rev. Sengstacke, was a missionary. When the publisher reached manhood, he turned to the Episcopal church and then the Presbyterian church. In both he was a victim of color discrimination by mulattoes. He retreated to the teachings of Christian Science, but withdrew when this group established separate places of worship for whites and Negroes. Before he died in 1940, he embraced Bahaism.

The repeated assaults on his color developed in him a persecution complex which sometimes became so strong as to indicate morbidity. As he went on, he began to reveal a tendency to over-dramatize himself and to exaggerate the color aspects in every situation, intensifying in his own mind the odds against which he had had to struggle. Circumstances that may have opposed his plans were not accidents; they were insidious conspiracies on the part of enemies to thwart him. Ultimately he came to feel that anyone who criticized him must be a scoundrel.

This aspect of his mentality was characteristic of the German-reared stepfather who had such a profound influence on his life. Rev. Sengstacke, a mulatto who had married Abbott's ebony-skinned mother, Flora, after the death of her husband, was a remarkable man. He was the only male parent the publisher ever knew, since his own father died during his infancy. The clergyman, a highly controversial figure in the tiny Negro community of his day, was well educated, spoke several languages fluently, and was in general a cultivated person. He became a missionary to educate and uplift his race, a purpose he bequeathed to his children with stern admonitions. His immigrant background, plus his lack of racial experience as known by Negroes born and reared in the South, complicated his social relations. Consequently, he became embittered when he labored unselfishly and his efforts were not only rejected but met open hostility. The belief that the world was against the Sengstackes became characteristic of the family and Abbott was naturally caught up in its current. The logical response was family unity, as a defensive measure. In any case, the clergyman's unhappy experiences created a fierce loyalty and solidified the family with Rev. Sengstacke as the idolized family symbol. Consequently, though Abbott was no relation to them, he embraced his stepfather's white German relatives as his own. He regularly assisted them financially, and helped educate their children—Hitler's denunciations of the Negro notwithstanding.

Himself childless, Abbott educated his brother's son, John, and afterwards made him his heir and successor as editor and publisher of the Chicago *Defender*. In fact, no Abbotts shared in his will—only his wife and the Sengstackes. For Abbott felt deeply indebted to Rev. Sengstacke, of whom he wrote: "He was one of the dominating influences in my life. . . . It was his teachings that gave me a lust for travel, that developed in me an avid desire to know more than just what appeared on the surface. He fed my cultural nature while my mother endowed me with practical common sense, and kept my feet on the ground." But the singular love and veneration he held for this man was especially revealed during the twenty-fifth anniversary celebration of the *Defender*, when he composed a moving racial testament which might stand as his epitaph to his stepfather.

He wrote: "For twenty-five years I have hearkened to the sacred advice of my [step] father, and have endeavored to give expression to my love for him, my Race and humanity through the columns of The Chicago *Defender*. I have been accused of red journalism, of insincerity, of incompetence, but in spite of all adversities I have faithfully and diligently striven to make known and alleviate the suffering of my people.

"I have endeavored to bring to the attention of the reading public all the inhuman treatment, discrimination, segregation, disfranchisement, peonage and all other injustices di-

15

rected at my people. I have not yielded to sentiment, but have endeavored, by the help of God, to serve aright as He gave me the ability to see the right. And, at the end of twenty-five years, I rejoice in the consolation and satisfaction which follows a successful pursuit in the task undertaken and the principles espoused.

"And now, thank God, the day is coming, yea, the day is almost here, when every land, from orient to occident, from pole to pole, from mountain to shore, and from the shore to the farthest isle of the sounding sea, at last will throw off the yoke of doubt, forget biased conceptions of human rights, and join in glad acclaim by helping to usher in the glad era of an enlightened civilization and the universal acknowledgement of the brotherhood of man."

Yet, except for his family, the man was never deeply loved —not by his two wives, not by his associates, and not by the public! This was perhaps the great tragedy in an otherwise fruitful and unselfish life. And yet he was capable of a humility and generosity of spirit which should have inspired love. For example, a fact unknown to his wives, secretary and associates and only revealed in the course of my researches, was that during the depression he responded to an urgent appeal from descendants of the white man who had held his people in slavery. In response, he regularly sent them money —and indeed contributed financially to the schooling of their children. Moreover, he carried his secret to the grave.

The man had achieved greatness.

The Chicago *Defender* was a concrete expression of Robert S. Abbott's personality and philosophy.

So now we turn to reconstruct the life details of this triumphant personality, who unselfishly dedicated himself to his fellows.

Robert S. Abbott was an Island negro who went to Chicago and made his fortune as owner of the newspaper, "CHICAGO DEFENDER." He left the Island with twenty-five cents, and returned with a million dollars.—A Guide Book of St. Simons Island, 1951.

CHAPTER II

The Black Aristocrats

NEAR CHRIST CHURCH, a tall, gleaming shaft of white Quincy granite stands at the entrance to Fort Frederica, situated on St. Simons Island—one of the coastal islands lying six miles off Georgia. The column, neatly enclosed by a grilled iron fence painted black, was erected at a cost of $1,600 by Robert S. Abbott as a monument to a slave he never knew: his father, Thomas Abbott. The site was chosen by the descendants of Tom's master, who buried him in 1869 with Christian ceremony, because he had been a faithful slave belonging to Captain Charles Stevens. Robert's father was a house servant, and as such was interred after the custom of the period in the Stevens burying ground.

This was a distinction in those days given only to respected retainers. Most of the Stevens slaves were buried by their own people in a "Negro burial ground," about a mile distant from the Stevens mansion; the place was actually situated in the next town of Harrington adjacent to "Obligation Pond"—so called because slave converts were baptized in its waters. Had Tom been buried there, in all likelihood Robert would never have found his grave, because his people followed the African custom of not placing name markers on graves; instead, used

17

only personal articles as identification. Today this cemetery is merely a clearing with a few mounds and scattered personal effects to indicate the remains of perhaps a thousand slaves. Not until 1928, when the Stevens descendants replied to Robert's inquiry and pointed out the precise site of Tom's interment, did he know where his parent lay and where to erect the shaft in his memory.*

It was a tenderly strange moment.

He alone made the pilgrimage to Frederica. He alone witnessed the erection, performed by white stonemasons of the Oglethorpe Marble and Granite Company of Savannah.

As a final gesture of commemoration, he reverently placed a wreath at the foot.

Robert afterwards dutifully wrote his mother asking her approbation—and she replied that he had behaved as a good son. But there was a singular detachment about the way she responded that is worth noting well. He perhaps sensed this, and later begged his sister Rebecca to travel to St. Simons Island and report back to his mother what she had seen.

I talked about Robert and his people with the descendants of Captain Stevens—wives of George, Elliott and Forman Stevens—three old ladies who now reside in Harrington. They spoke proudly of their heritage, and were able to buttress their jointly told story with family records. They knew intimately all the complicated relationships involving the Abbotts, and had followed Robert's career with the satisfaction of parents. According to their account, grandfather Captain Charles Stevens had gone abroad as a young man and married a Lady Sarah Dorothy Hall in England, and sometime in the 1840's brought her back to Frederica to live on the plantation his father had established in 1784.

---

* As a sentimental afterthought, apparently, Abbott included the names of his two aunts, Celia Abbott and Mary Abbott Finnick, and had them inscribed on the base of the monument though neither woman had been buried here but actually in Savannah.

The man who was to become Robert's father was the Stevens' butler. He was a black, well-proportioned man, with what was described as presence, and major-domo of the household. He had complete charge of the male servants—waiters, coachmen, gardeners, body servants, handymen and errand boys. Mornings he wore a swallow-tailed coat; and evenings, an embroidered silk jacket, with his shoes highly polished. He was a fine figure of a man, proudly so, and perhaps envied by every slave on the plantation. His manners were always courteous, dignified, sometimes even elegant. He was said to have had a subtle instinct for social status among white people—an instinct repeated in his son. He was, in fact, the most trusted member of the household, but often a tyrant to the black servants.

Service in the Big House, as distinguished from field labor, was a family privilege conferred on Robert's folks, positions descending from father to son, from mother to daughter. Thus, his uncle Randolph was the body servant of Captain Stevens and was held accountable for his master's safety, whether he was hunting, fishing, gambling, or involved in drinking bouts; his uncle George was the coachman and doubled as gardener; his aunt Celia was Mrs. Stevens' personal maid; his aunt Mary was the nurse; and his youngest aunt, Charlotte, intriguing to men as she was disturbing to women, was capriciously banished to the fields. Even so, as trusted servants, the Abbotts took pride in the Stevens establishment, often rejoicing when guests praised the service or appearance of the Big House.

Except for Charlotte, Robert's folks were pampered and spoiled, albeit slaves—indeed, it is unlikely that their condition was as desperate as Fanny Kemble, noted English actress who married Pierce Butler and came to live on his plantation, described in her *Journal of Residence on a Georgia Plantation*. Her neighbor, Captain Stevens, a rational and light-hearted man, perhaps had observed early that mild indulgences, such as permitting them to attend church services and to learn to read and write, was the only method for dealing with slaves—especially those with Robert's folk's sort of background.

The Abbotts evidently were of Ibo stock. Newspaper advertisements of slave auctions indicate that the slave cargoes arriving at St. Simons Island came mainly from the West Africa areas, and contained mostly people of the Ibo country (now part of Nigeria), who were noted in Africa for their independence, initiative, political sense and love of travel—characteristics Robert displayed. St. Simons lore abounds with tales about them. One concerns their first arrival at Dunbar Creek, near the center of the island. The slave trade had been legally abolished by the Federal government in 1808, but gangs like the Blackbirders imported Negroes from Africa, secretly landed on the isolated island, and eventually smuggled them into the Savannah slave markets. As one shipload neared land, rather than be sold into slavery, the Ibo captives jumped overboard singing and were drowned. Today on moonlight nights—so the legend goes—their bodies may be seen tossing in the waters there, and their chants may be heard whispering through the moss-fringed trees.

No one on St. Simons Island ever forgot the telegraphic dispatch of Friday evening, April 12, 1861, which announced that the Charleston batteries had opened fire on Fort Sumter. By morning, citizens and slaves alike had been alerted by the alarming news. Not long afterwards Captain Stevens, now middle-aged and somewhat infirm, impetuously joined the Confederate Army. Like all affluent Southerners, he took along his body servant, Robert's uncle Randolph, to wash his clothes, polish swords and boots, cut his hair, oil guns and groom his horse. Between these chores, Randolph even had a fling at the fighting.

When the news reached one old slaveholder, he wrote to his own son thus: "I hear you are likely to have a big battle soon, and I write to tell you not to let Sam go into the fighting with you. Keep him in the rear, for that nigger is worth a thousand dollars." Randolph survived, but Captain Stevens was captured early and died of pneumonia in a Union prison camp somewhere in Virginia. Randolph, now left to his own devices, enlisted in the Confederate Army and served for the duration as a private in Company F, First Regiment of the Georgia Reserves, commanded by Colonel William R. Symons. When Randolph was mustered out, he was entitled to $50 back pay which he never received, but he afterwards qualified to receive a Federal government pension as a Confederate veteran.

Sherman soon swept into the little community, carrying the triumphant word of Lincoln's Emancipation Proclamation. The Stevens folk escaped to the safety of kinfolk on the mainland, and in the confusion left the slaves unsupervised. There was little time for reflection, but Tom, aware of his inherited responsibilities and loyalties, lost no time in bulldozing the house servants into carrying on their daily routines. They cared for the Big House with all its valuables and sentimental contents. When Tom heard the Yankees were approaching, he folded the Stevens silver in a dark cloth, carefully tied it into a bundle, and dropped the package into a well for safekeeping. Then he dug holes in isolated parts of the plantation and buried the family's Willow China, heirlooms which Lady Sarah had brought from England; and he afterwards had the valuable pieces of furniture moved to the slave quarters where they might escape the eyes of the Union troops.

When the Stevens people returned—so their descendants report—they found everything intact, even to every piece of polished silver. The bond between master and slave was often second only to that of husband and wife or parent and child. But Tom undoubtedly was held in contempt by his fellow slaves, particularly the field hands. Even so, this unusual conduct, which provided the Abbotts with a reputation for honesty and faithfulness, and found reflection in the behavior and dealings of Robert, persists in the locality to this day.

Robert's father soon shed the plantation like a loose garment. Now between forty and fifty years old, he nevertheless felt urgently compelled to leave the island, if only for a few days or weeks, so he might feel he was actually a free person. He was unmarried and had neither chick nor child. He assumed his full name, Thomas Abbott, though he was not vain enough to decorate it with a high-sounding middle name or initial after the fashion of ex-slaves, and joined the pellmell rush to Savannah. Upon arrival, he headed for the grogshops and fleshpots. Freedom, as an emotion, was indeed a fact, and movingly felt, but freedom as a complex of duties, responsibilities and restraints was yet far in the future. Liberty had simply meant license to the ex-slave.

Tom could have established himself in St. Simons, because each Abbott was provided with a cabin and land to start a new life. Robert's uncle Randolph, who had seen much of the country as a soldier, was content to marry, settle in Frederica, and raise a family. He had three sons—Joseph, Thomas and Bristol. His grandson Randolph, a bachelor, today operates the Blue Island Tavern on the site of his inheritance; and his grandson Malcolm Lee Abbott, a carpenter and chef who also inherited land, today lives with his wife and eleven children in a wooden frame house, where James Edward Oglethorpe, founder and first governor of Georgia, established his home in 1786. Robert's aunt Charlotte, who by now had two daughters, Anna and Charlotte, ignored the bequest, married and went to live in Savannah. Mary joined his aunt Celia, a spinster and oldest of the Abbotts, who somehow had purchased her own freedom sometime in 1853 and settled in Savannah. She now operated a thriving hairdressing parlor on South Broad Street catering to white trade exclusively.

Tom, footloose and fancy free, became something of a playboy. Before long his eyes lighted on Flora Butler, who was to become Robert's mother. She was tall, erect and slender, and wore her black hair in long braids formed into a bun atop her head. Flora worked as a hairdresser at the Savannah Theatre. Tom soon became a familiar figure there as he kept a nightly vigil before the stagedoor. Flora was captivated—after all, as a house servant, Tom had affected the manners of the master class. Besides, bedecked in the hand-me-downs of the late Captain Stevens, his appearance was superior to the average Negro's.

A whirlwind courtship was followed by marriage in 1867. Tom secured employment to support his wife, if only briefly, helping to survey the first streetcar line along Broughton and Whitaker Streets. His master had taught him the rudiments of surveying, but there was little such work for a Negro in Savannah. Tom took his newly-won bride back to St. Simons Island. So small were their possessions when they left that they were able to cram them all into one box. They set up housekeeping in Tom's cabin in Frederica, and to earn a livelihood, opened a grocery store catering to ex-slaves.

This was the place where Robert was born.

It was situated about fifty feet from the dusty Frederica Road, within the shadows of century-old massive oak trees dripping with gray moss. The house was rude, actually a wooden dwelling with dirt floors and a tabby chimney that rose at one end, a type still familiar among old cabins of St. Simons Island. It was so badly constructed as to provide little protection against inclement weather. The furniture consisted of a few stools, a table, and a mattress made of straw. The front door faced a spacious yard, actually a clearing, where the washing, cooking and gossiping was done, and where Flora played with her first man child. Robert described the place as "comfortable." If, with the perspective of wealth, he was able to return and view the house as such, so much the better was it for his peace of mind.

Flora gave birth to a girl and delighted her husband. Two

23

months later the infant died. But Tom often left his young wife to operate the store by herself while, under the pretext of procuring stocks, he skipped off to the dissipations of the big city. What little money they were able to eke out, he splashed up in Savannah. He who was destined to become the founder and publisher of the Chicago *Defender,* gave his first wail in his father's absence, Thanksgiving Day, November 28, 1868.* Flora was attended by no physician or midwife at his birth, and no Abbott in the neighborhood offered assistance. She went through the convulsions of labor alone, and cut the umbilical cord herself. What she thought of Tom in these moments was hidden in her woman's breast. For not even her devoted son ever became privy to her feelings.

The marriage had shocked the Abbotts, for they undoubtedly believed Robert's mother to be a field hand and consequently far below them in social status. Celia was outraged. Mary considered the union an affront. Charlotte fumed. The Abbotts, as house servants whose ancestry dated back to 1784 and beyond, drew the line against field hands. Not only did the distinction of domestic work give them a feeling of superiority over field Negroes, but it even made them feel superior to poor whites. And now they had up-graded themselves socially in the free society, though they had brought along their slave attitudes. Moreover, a budding ambition in the family for better things was shown in Randolph's volunteer service in the Confederate Army, and Celia's entrance into a business of her own; and more important, her decisive role in helping to found the first Negro Episcopal Church in Savannah, St. Stephens. By now they had developed the contours of a clan, and were listed as a group in the Parish Register of St. Stephens Episcopal Church as the "Ab-

---

* Robert S. Abbott believed he was born November 24, 1870, but the Parish Register (1868–1900) of St. Stephens Episcopal Church (now St. Matthews), Savannah, where he was baptized, records his birth as the above date.

bott Family"—husbands notwithstanding. They soon became openly hostile to Tom's wife.

Robert's mother was born a slave in Savannah, December 4, 1847, with a not too prepossessing background—at least, in the eyes of the Abbotts. Her parents, Jacob and Harriet Butler, were born in Portuguese West Africa and brought to this country in their teens. Jacob was a slave belonging to the undistinguished Butler people who operated a paint supply shop. Harriet, a slave of the Falligants, had six children— Flora, Priscilla, Jacob Jr., Abram, Levester and Harriet—who were brought up in a cabin adjacent to the Falligant house, where she served as a Mammy. Her responsibilities were great, so too her labors in supervising the complex task of running two households. Nevertheless, beyond rearing the Falligant children, she managed to raise her own brood decently. When about twelve years old, Flora was handed over to young John G. Falligant, whose plantation occupied the swampy site of what is now Savannah State College (for Negroes), and became a nursemaid to his children—Fannie, Isabelle and Electa. A warm personal relationship developed between Flora and the family which survived until her death.

Flora's father, Jacob, worked with his hands, and this, in the social context of the period, had relatively little prestige. He was a painter and decorator and thus a skilled craftsman. His master had encouraged Jacob's development, because he brought income through wages. He was usually hired out for from $200 to $400 a year. His master kept the wages, but gave Jacob a weekly allowance. Jacob's skills enabled him to enjoy a remarkable amount of freedom and even permitted him to do extra work on his own. He eventually saved sufficient money to buy his freedom, and subsequently the freedom of his wife and children.

Priscilla, who had been sold to the Bullineaue family and worked as a nursemaid, was the exception. She chose to remain loyal to her promise and signature. For she had signed a document at the dying request of her mistress to remain with the family and raise her infant children. Priscilla afterwards bore five children. Three lived: Willie, Walter and Harriet. The two boys were known as Bullineaue, but Harriet, who incidentally became the principal of Parker High School in Birmingham, Alabama, rejected the connection and adopted her mother's maiden name. With emancipation, however, Priscilla married a man named Hammond.

If the background of Robert's mother differed markedly from the Abbotts', it was a difference in degree, not in kind. Whereas Tom, along with his brothers and sisters, was taught to read and write by his master, and was given special privileges as a slave and a stake to start life as a free person, Flora, according to her son Robert's account, had to shift for herself. She had, by painstaking personal effort, tried learning to write by placing tissue paper over the name-plates on people's doors and tracing the letters in pencil. As a free person, she had briefly attended a secret school for slaves, conducted by a Mrs. Dellamorter. Flora left home at five o'clock in the morning, and always carried a bucket of some sort to make it appear she was working or attending an errand; for the slightest suspicion that she was receiving schooling would have been cause enough to return her to slavery. The school was such that she received only the rudiments of reading and writing, but she did pick up a speaking knowledge of German from the German shopkeepers for whom she frequently worked. When Tom met Flora, she was living with her mother and earning a respectable living.

Robert's father, who lived as though each day were the last one, died suddenly on one of his many trips to Savannah, a victim of "creeping consumption." His passing left Robert's strong-minded aunt Celia as head of the Abbott clan. And she, observing custom faithfully, sent Tom's remains back to his birthplace to be buried. Flora, who was pretty much excluded from the funeral arrangements, bundled up her four-month-old infant, and returned to her mother's home in Savannah. The hostility the Abbotts bore her came to a head when they sought possession of Tom's son. They argued that Robert was an Abbott and should be brought up by his father's kin. When Flora flatly refused, and displayed a stubbornness that afterwards was to characterize Robert, they started legal proceedings to have the child handed over to them, charging Flora was an unfit mother.

One John H. H. Sengstacke, a German newly arrived in Savannah, who was to have a profound influence both on Flora and her son, came to her defense. He retained a white lawyer at his own expense, a W. W. Paine, who succeeded in securing a restraining court order, and Flora was able to keep her son in peace and rear him in the manner she thought best. But Sengstacke, who so casually helped a distressed mother, could little have dreamed that this child would one day take a notable place in the history of the Negro in the United States.

I give, devise and bequeath unto my children so soon as they shall arrive at and attain to the age of twenty-one years, my Negro slaves Rose and Ansel, with the future issue and increase of the said Rose to have and to hold the same to them, as slaves, and to their heirs and assigns forever.—HERMAN SENGSTACKE, *Last Will and Testament,* 1860.

CHAPTER III

Childhood in Savannah

THE YOUNG GERMAN, John Hermann Henry Sengstacke, who was to become Robert's stepfather and shape his thinking in such a way that he would be dissatisfied with little reforms, already had started paying court to Flora Abbott, whose speaking knowledge of German had delighted him. To all appearances he was a white person, having light brown eyes, fair, almost white skin, an aquiline nose, black hair of Caucasian texture, and a firm thin mouth decorated with a mustache trimmed in the Teutonic style. He was, in fact, the son of a well-to-do white merchant, Herman Sengstacke, whose personal history bears brief telling for the light it sheds on the nuances of Robert's background and behavior.

The senior Sengstacke was born January 6, 1815, in a small village called Fagenbacke near Bremen, in what was shortly to become the Kingdom of Hanover, and as a young man had gone to sea. Savannah was one of the places he had seen in his travels, and he settled there sometime in the 1840's and opened a general store. One evening he idly stopped to watch a slave auction along the waterfront. He stood under the lamp-lit shed and listened to the auctioneer's cries and the slaves' wails. Among the slaves being sold were girls between the ages of fifteen and twenty. The prospective buyers, while appraising them for physical attractiveness, were carefully examining their teeth, eyes, arms and legs to determine age and health. The girls wore only rude one-piece gowns fastened at the neck with draw cords. Buyers were free to loosen these garments for a closer detailed inspection. The handling was so callous that the newly-arrived Herman Sengstacke, unaccustomed to slavery's businesslike methods, was touched by the tearful shyness of one particular black girl named Tama, and impetuously bid and bought her. He later escorted her to Charleston, S. C., where marriage between the races was lawful and formally married her in 1847. They returned to Savannah and began housekeeping in the modest rooms above his store situated at the corner of Farm and Mill Streets.

The relationship was not too unusual, for white men lived openly with Negro women with little injury to their social prestige. Tama bore him two children: she gave birth to Robert's stepfather, John Hermann Henry, January 27, 1848, and died the next year in giving birth to Mary Elizabeth. And thus a white man founded the Negro Sengstacke family which Robert was to embrace as his own. Children were compelled by law to follow the state and condition of the mother for life, which in fact was the meaning of chattel slavery. But Sengstacke, who had never formally provided for Tama's freedom, was reluctant to have his own mulatto offspring reared as slaves. He booked passage and took them to Germany to be brought up by a sister, Mrs. Conrad Schmidt, who lived with her husband in a village near Bremen called Marechal, and afterwards regularly remitted money to her for their education and upkeep.

Herman Sengstacke prospered as a Savannah merchant and became known as "Mr. Harmon" or "Mr. Harman," because of the difficulty in pronouncing his surname. He never re-married, perhaps in memory of Tama. Years later, his Negro granddaughter Rebecca was driven away when she went to place flowers on his grave in the white section of Savannah's Laurel Grove Cemetery. Before he died in 1862 he made a will. For safekeeping he lodged it in Savannah's Chatham County Court House, and a copy in the Central Railroad Bank. He appointed two white men, Dr. Richard D. Arnold and David R. Dillon, as executors and left his entire estate to his two Negro children.

Accordingly, his property was to be liquidated and the money realized sent to Conrad and Martin Schmidt who, as the children's guardians, were to establish a trust fund and act as trustees of the estate. From the trust fund's earn-ings, they were to provide for the support and education of John Hermann and Mary Elizabeth until they reached their twenty-first birthday. Then the estate was to be equally di-vided between them. Two Negro slaves he owned, Rose and Ansel, were also bequeathed to his children for their "joint use," and arrangements were expressly made to have them immediately transported to Germany. No money ever reached the German trustees, and when John Hermann became of age he decided to come to Savannah and investigate.

Robert's stepfather arrived early in 1869, and took lodg-ings with a Mr. Samuel Bolden, paying six dollars monthly rent. When he met Flora, he was in the process of trying to settle the estate and return to Germany. He never was to see the place of his rearing again, though he often talked nostalgically about Germany in Robert's presence and urged him to one day see the country himself. Not only did the estate become involved in litigation, but he fell in love with Flora.

His position meantime was difficult. He was making little

progress in settling the estate, and he was in need of money. The young man perhaps was foolhardy to have pressed the white executors for an accounting, for a Negro had few rights a white Georgian was bound to respect. His behavior might have been construed as insolence, but the German-reared Negro was not as yet racially inhibited. Thus he learned that an appraisal had been filed by the executors in 1862 which, after deductions, showed the estate had a total value of roughly $10,000.

Liquidation of the property (which included valuable North Oglethorpe land, Joachim Street houses, unsold merchandise, bank deposits, and railroad and bank stocks) should have brought something like $50,000. The old man's careful provisions for his children's upkeep and education, plus his plans for division of the trust fund, certainly suggests he bequeathed a considerable sum. But when the executors reappeared in court, the property had mysteriously dwindled away. Maybe the estate had been wiped away by the plunder and destruction of the Civil War, plus the emancipation of Rose and Ansel, who as slaves had been valued in the inventory at $600 each, but the executors offered no explanation as to why the estate had practically vanished.

The matter was never settled to Sengstacke's satisfaction.

The bulk of the remaining estate was finally sold at auction in 1870 to a Joseph P. Daily, a white man whom Robert worked for as a boy. But Sengstacke managed to salvage only a few pieces of real estate, several thousand dollars (which he presumably shared with his sister Mary Elizabeth), and the now rundown store his father had operated in the area popularly known as Yamacraw.

Robert spent his earliest childhood in Yamacraw, a Negro settlement which takes its name from the town established nearly two hundred years ago by Indian Chief Tomochichi. It is located on the Savannah River bluff in the western part of the city, and so close to the river that the small wooden shanties used to rattle when the winds roared across the water. Before the Civil War, free Negroes moved in and established the area as a Negro community. The educated and progressive, plus the social élite, resided here in comparative comfort. The fact is, a curious development had occurred: free Negroes, forming about ten per cent of Savannah's Negro population, formally separated from the white church. For one thing, they wished to escape the spectacle of masters bringing their slaves, manacled and chained, to church services—which was the custom in white churches. Thus Yamacraw gained distinction when the first Negro Baptist Church in America was established (1779) and Methodism made a start.

When the Yamacraw property was handed over to Robert's stepfather, the tree-dotted area was undoubtedly a pleasant place to live. Next door to the store was a frame dwelling he had also inherited, in which Flora lived with her mother and infant son. This fact, perhaps, influenced his decision to become a merchant himself and eventually remain in Savannah. In any case, he refurbished the building, moved into the rooms above the store, and restocked the place with brushes, ties, socks, shirts, suspenders, tooth brushes, undershirts and cotton pants. Then, as if to underscore his decision to stay, he paid for a policy with the Germania Life Insurance Company of New York.

He now had daily contact with Flora, and, stirred by her yearning for knowledge, he volunteered to teach her. Not long afterwards he persuaded her to give up her nursemaid job and help him run the shop. Yet, busy as he was, he found time to be attentive and attend church with her regularly. When Robert was baptized in 1872, Sengstacke, along with two white persons, a Mr. Joseph Mindledorff and a lady named De Loche, stood as the child's godparents. The ceremony was performed at Flora's house, a fact that suggests

Robert was ill and there was some urgency about making him a Christian.

The shop did not prosper.

Josephine Young, who has lived in Savannah since her birth 101 years ago, distinctly remembers it being sold to a Greek merchant. Sengstacke soon afterwards went to work as a translator for the Savannah *Morning News,* a position of sufficient distinction to be noted in Herringshaw's *American Encyclopedia of Biographies.* But he lost his job when his employers discovered he was a Negro. Sengstacke was shocked, understandably so—after all, he spoke five languages fluently, including English, and was an educated man, with considerable culture and refinement. Back in Germany he had attended the Latin Academy and was a graduate of the Friederichsdorf Institute. He had studied music, and played the piano and organ well. He had traveled on the Continent. He had a taste for literature and art, a taste developed by opportunities he had had of seeing the best sculpture, painting, architecture and drama, and of hearing music in Europe in his impressionable years. But he was a Negro, and this fact made it nearly impossible for him to secure employment congenial with his abilities.

Robert's stepfather finally secured a part-time position teaching German to the daughter of a prominent white citizen. He soon overheard the mother being scolded for having a "nigger" in her house. "The words of the man," Sengstacke wrote sadly, "made little impression on me, for in Germany I have been taught to respect an honest man, not his color." Actually he was deeply wounded. And he later reported the existence of "one-horse nigger cars," meaning segregated public carriers; and by now he was in the mood to observe somewhat bitterly, "Some citizens pay first class railroad fare and are ordered into second class coaches; pay tax on city property and are not allowed to drink soda water at the drug stores." He concluded with a sigh, "The United States is a strange place!"

Strange indeed.

He had arrived in Savannah identified as a German citizen. Beyond this he had had no racial label, and people naturally assumed the young foreigner who spoke German to be a white person—that is, until Savannah learned the details of his parentage and observed his associations, and they made him indelibly aware of the fact that he was a Negro, a thing without dignity and humanity. His feelings were mangled in the process. Now, whenever he and Flora walked the streets, they were victims of obscene jibes from white hoodlums. He was, to be sure, utterly bewildered by this twist in status. He could have escaped the racial designation, plus the social and economic meanings of being a Negro, had he simply returned to Germany—but he chose to stay, and for valid reasons, once he had identified himself with the Negro race.

Even more startling was the discovery that sharp racial distinctions existed among the Negroes themselves. This fact came to a head in a church crisis and had violent overtones in Savannah's Negro community. Back in Germany he had been reared as a Lutheran, but to attend such a church in Savannah would have required his sitting in pews marked "B.M.," meaning black members; or, if he chose any other white church, in allowing himself to be banished to the hard-benched galleries provided for Negro use exclusively. He objected to these racial customs as un-Christian, and observed acidly: "I saw an evangelist preaching and inviting sinners to the altar. But the Negro sinners up in the gallery were afraid to come down for fear of offending white sinners!" With his comparative sophistication, he could not embrace the Negro Baptists, because they were perhaps too noisily exuberant in their religious expression and the clergy were as yet mostly ignorant men. He probably gravitated to the

Episcopal Church because its ritual was somewhat reminiscent in form and content of the ritual he had known as a Lutheran. Soon he and Flora joined St. Stephen's Episcopal Church, though Robert's difficult aunt Celia was one of the founders and thus a pillar of the church.

St. Stephens, first called the Savannah River Mission, was organized by free Negroes in 1854 with the assistance of white people belonging to St. Johns and Christ churches. But by now, the congregation was made up of ex-slaves and those who had been born free people. The majority were fair-complexioned Negroes. In this group, possession of "white blood" gave social distinction. Thus the Scarboroughs, Scotts, Spauldings, Toomers, De Veaux and Desverneys, who operated a number of profitable business enterprises, held almost undisputed sway as leaders of Negro society. They inclined toward an affectation of aristocratic graces, traditions, and manners, and some were indeed the educated sons of white fathers who had thoughtfully made provisions for them. A few were mulattoes who had migrated from nearby Charleston, S. C., where a "Blue Vein" society was coming into being. They consequently felt and thought differently from the ignorant, brutalized blacks who had worked in the fields before emancipation. The fair-complexioned Negroes were "naturally clannish" and thus constituted a colored aristocracy that had little in common with the blacks.

When the Reverend J. Robert Love, a robust black man hailing from the West Indies, came to Savannah to serve as rector of St. Stephens, the ticklish color question arose. From the time he arrived, he firmly declared that the black worshippers should enjoy the same rights and privileges in the church as mulattoes. His position seemed just, but he afterwards was regarded with suspicion. But no eyebrows were arched when he married Chang Hin Lee, a Chinese, to Mary Thomas, a mulatto girl, in the church rectory and a white Italian, D. S. Pacetti, witnessed the ceremony. However, open conflict came in 1872, when his near-white vestrymen sought to exclude all black people and convert the congregation into an all-white one—that is to say, only Negroes whose complexions approximated that of Caucasians would be eligible for membership. Rev. Love thundered brimstone sermons, but was unable to persuade them of the righteousness of his position.

He was finally forced to resign and led the black members in the formation of the St. Augustine Mission, which afterwards was situated at the corner of Bolton and West Broad Streets. Thereafter, blacks joined and attended St. Augustine; and mulattoes joined and attended St. Stephens. There was some overlapping for special cases, but the church which did not admit blacks certainly did not welcome nameless mulatto nobodies. However, the rule against blacks did not apply to the Abbotts, who remained staunchly loyal to color-struck St. Stephens. They afterwards were called "the black mulattoes."

Beginning in 1934, St. Stephens did a bit of proselytizing of blacks to remove the onus of color prejudice. "But the belief persisted," says the present rector, Rev. Gustave H. Caution, "that a color line was drawn, because light people tended to gravitate toward light people." Not until 1943, when these two Episcopal churches were merged and renamed St. Matthews, was the color question finally resolved.

The mulatto John H. H. Sengstacke joined Rev. Love in the protest and formal withdrawal—for, not only was he outraged, but he deeply resented the implied insult to the black woman to whom he was engaged; and indeed to the black woman who gave him birth. He thus chose to identify himself with the underdog. He and his fiancee joined the St. Augustine Mission, and before long he was documenting his color inclinations by marching to the altar. He married Flora on July 26, 1874, when Robert was five years old. The rector, Rev. Love, performed the ceremony with the congregation present. The Abbotts were conspicuously absent, a fact perhaps of little concern to the bride.

Flora moved into her husband's place, where they were to live for the next two years. Sengstacke's sister, Mary Elizabeth, who inherited her mother Tama's negroid features and frizzly hair, had meantime married a blond, pure-blooded German, Friedrich Bödeker, and settled in St. Magnus, near Bremen. They had three children: Hennie, Fritz and Georg, who, in the next century were to become intimately acquainted with cousin Robert, and were to lean on him as head of the family. Flora, attended by Dr. B. S. Pure, a white man, bore seven children: John Jr., Alexander, Mary, Rebecca, Eliza, Susan and Johnnah; only Susan and John Jr. did not survive and grow to maturity. With the marriage, Robert became known as "Sengstacke's boy," and afterwards carried the name Robert Sengstacke.

This fact complicated matters when his aunt Celia died of "consumption," leaving no will and an estate of $5,000, which she had accumulated as a popular hairdresser. The fact is, this was considerable money for a Negro to accumulate in those days. The Atlanta *Constitution*, curious about the progress of Negroes in the twenty-five years since emancipation, made an investigation (1890) into the financial status of Atlanta's wealthiest Negroes. The paper discovered that, on the average, they possessed amounts ranging from $3,000 to $10,000. Much of this was not liquid, and only ten Negroes paid taxes on property worth more than $10,000. Savannah, in this respect, was little different from Atlanta.

Flora petitioned the court for a share in Robert's behalf. When the Abbotts also petitioned for shares, the estate was thrown into litigation. Celia's property included land in Yamacraw and Frederica, a bank account, furniture, equipment, and stocks of hair, which the court-appointed administrator, John T. Rowan, had to sell quickly because it was "perishable." When Celia's personal debts were paid (including burial in the Colored Cemetery), legal fees deducted, and division finally made among four heirs, Robert received only $127.09, less twenty-five dollars legal fees; and because of the complications in his name, Flora had to petition the court to allow her to spend the money as a temporary guardian. The request was granted on her offer to post an indemnity bond of $200, secured by her attorney, W. W. Paine. This was the last contact direct or indirect the Sengstackes were to have with the Abbotts until Robert reached manhood.

It is not difficult to picture the life which Robert's parents lived during the years of his early childhood. It was a pinched existence, though not desperate. Before Sengstacke's marriage to Flora, the ground had all but crumbled beneath his feet when he was caught in the depression following the panic of 1873. He recouped, but after his marriage he unwisely became involved in a dubious transaction. He joined and soon was elected to office in the Ancient, Free and Accepted Order of Masons of Georgia, a Negro group which was planning the erection of a fraternal building. Sengstacke put up a piece of property as collateral to enable his lodge brothers to procure a loan. When they failed to meet the obligation, his property was sold at auction to satisfy the loan. He was thus forced to borrow $500 from a Joseph Scarborough and secure his Yamacraw holdings. He repaid the loan, but he had to find employment as a school teacher, which, along with preaching, was practically the only white-collar occupation open to a Negro.

The struggle for survival was hidden from Robert during his early days, and there is no question that life in Savannah was enjoyable for him. He grew up, at first a slender, wiry stripling, and bit by bit became a chubby, square-shouldered boy. He happily joined playmates who loved to hunt and fish. Beyond a few simple pleasures, there was little for his parents to do. "The conspicuous lack of diversified social activities," he recalled, "is among the vivid recollections of my days in Savannah. Other than the social life connected with the church, there was little else. The people, however, did gather on some notable occasion such as a birthday or wedding and hold 'shouts'. To stage a 'shout', the parlor of the home in which it was to be held had to be cleared of all the furnishings. The guests then gathered in a ring around the room with a leader in the center to lead the songs. With clapping hands and stamping feet, the guests marched around the room while the leader sang out:

> *"Let's set the song, boys*
> *Let's set the song!*
> *Let's set the song, boys*
> *Let's set the song!*
>
> *"I want my bass, boys*
> *I want my bass!*
> *I want my bass, boys*
> *I want my bass!"*

Then, "All the men singing bass would enter the center of the circle and repeat the chorus of whatever song was then being sung. The leader would then, in the same manner, summon each group—baritone, tenor, contralto and soprano. After all the groups had appeared, the leader would sing out again: 'Let's set the song, boys!' And as he repeated the lines the guests would march, clap hands and sing gleefully. Such simple entertainments, along with ice cream socials, and prayer meetings were the extent of the social life of the townspeople at that time."

Now that Robert's stepfather had embraced the Negro race, he developed the passions of the newly converted. What transpired in this impressionable period of his stepson's childhood and youth is revealed in a collection of letters, papers, documents, and a diary which Sengstacke kept during his lifetime—indeed, he was so methodical a man that he even kept rent receipts dating back to the day of his arrival in Savannah. The collection spans the important transitional period in which the Negro was making adjustment to freedom. Sengstacke's diary, in particular, sets the period in quite a new light, and gives ample views of his mind and doings, and indeed the doings of Robert. The most singular fact about his diary is the persecution complex he reveals, a belief in the malice of others, a belief that the world was against the Sengstackes. This persecution complex, persecution by individuals or society, is so persistent as almost to bring its own Nemesis. Though he obviously had no blood kinship to his stepfather, Robert nevertheless distinctly showed this trait, which he perhaps got by proximity and indoctrination.

Negroes in Savannah now formed more than fifty per cent of the population, and their multiple problems were acute. No one was more distressed than Robert's stepfather. He converted one room of his living quarters into a classroom where he taught both children and adults, because he was driven by the fact that "the people are ignorant and must be taught." He received ten cents a week for each pupil. He had meanwhile paid visits to Scarborough's place in Woodville, a suburb of Savannah to which he had to travel by horse and buggy, and discovered an even more desperate situation among the rural Negroes. He promptly wrote an open letter to the superintendent of Public Education in Savannah urging the opening of a Negro school in Woodville. When no response appeared to be forthcoming, he impatiently appealed to the American Missionary Association, the philanthropic arm of the Congregational Church. The association's magazine had already commented editorially on the need to train "a race of young [colored] ministers," because in "any attempt to educate the old [colored] ministers of the South—their age, the necessity of toil, their prejudices—are all in the way."

When the young and educated Sengstacke, who was now casting about for a career, approached the association he was promptly labeled as first-rate ministerial material. The association did not open a school, but Sengstacke, following a two-year novitiate, was ordained a minister by the Congregational Council in 1876 and installed as a missionary in Woodville's Pilgrim Congregational Church. Subsequently, Savannah's public school superintendent appointed him a teacher at a salary of thirty dollars monthly. And thus for the next quarter century, Robert's stepfather preached and taught, labors which involved great personal sacrifice, for the purpose of uplifting his race. The passion he developed in the course of his work infected his family.

Robert carried it into the Chicago *Defender*.

My father taught the people [Negroes] not only how to live in fellowship of God, but how to live comfortably and intellectually under handicaps.—ROBERT S. ABBOTT, Chicago *Defender,* 1940.

CHAPTER IV

Missionary Boyhood

THE ROLLING ACREAGE and luxuriant green foliage of Woodville, a suburb three miles from Savannah and reached only by bicycle or horse-and-buggy, was the first home Robert S. Abbott really remembered, though in the summers he would make frequent trips to the city. He was eight years old when his stepfather, the Rev. John H. H. Sengstacke, assumed his duties as a Congregational missionary and permanently moved his family to this rural area.

Woodville was a pleasant place in which to grow up.

The house in which they lived was the parsonage. When finally completed, it was a modest two-story frame dwelling containing eight rooms and a porch, surrounded by a picket fence enclosing a vegetable garden. The place, built piece by piece by Rev. Sengstacke with the aid of paid helpers, was situated where Alvin Road now crosses Augusta Road, and located in a splendid grove of trees a short distance from the banks of the Savannah River. Above the entrance he nailed a sign which read: "Overcome Evil With Good." Beyond, "so as to be safe in case of fire," there was a wagon shed and a stable.

Nearby, only a few steps away, was the rude edifice of the

Pilgrim congregation, where Robert first worshipped his God and his stepfather labored for the next twenty-five years. It was a white frame structure, seating about two hundred people, and was erected with money provided by the American Missionary Association. The building had a steeple, with a belfry containing a clock and later a bell which tolled the beginning and end of church services. A stairway led to the church entrance. The association apparently made no provisions for furnishings. Consequently, hand-me-down carpets, for example, lined the aisles; and for pews there were wooden plank benches. A stained glass window formed a backdrop for the pulpit, upon which sat an imposingly large Bible, a gift of a Mrs. William B. Wheeler, a white woman of Dubuque, Iowa. Light in the evenings was provided by a huge chandelier, which hung from the ceiling in the center of the church; but during benedictions, wax tapers were lighted, perhaps to give the primitive surroundings grandeur and solemnity.

Sundays were days apart.

When Robert was small, the Sengstacke family, as well as their neighbors, observed the Sabbath with great scrupulousness, always reminded by the head of the household of the emptiness of all earthly pleasures. Beyond attending morning and evening services and Sunday school, the day was spent quietly indoors, ordinary pursuits being abandoned. Robert's recollections of the day were far from somber and depressing. He and his brother and sisters were delighted to see the table loaded with chicken and ham, and all kinds of nice pies and cakes. But come weekdays, Robert and his younger kin were free to romp and play, and in consequence he had the usual number of stone bruises and stubbed toes and the average number of nails in his foot that fell to country boys. He loved horses, but before his stepfather would buy him one, he had to agree to care for the animal faithfully. He soon learned to harness a horse in the dark, and balance a sack of corn on a horse's back. But Robert's days were not all play, for he had to hustle out of bed to feed the horses and get ready to drop corn or potatoes by the time the sun was up.

"My summers," he wrote, "were spent in the city and made it possible for me to hold odd jobs as soon as I was big enough to run errands. First I worked as an errand boy in a grocery store." His wages were fifteen cents a week, and his mother, as a method of training, made him pay ten cents weekly for room, board and laundry. "When I became larger," he recalled, "I got a job on one of the oldest newspapers in Savannah, *The Echo*"—and thus did Robert S. Abbott make his first contact with a newspaper.

The experience ended disastrously.

"I worked there," he said, "until a misunderstanding with the foreman made it imperative that I 'hot foot' it home to my mother. My ambition one day overpowered me and I set out to perform a more complicated assignment than was my duty. As a result I scratched up the imposing stone on which the printer made up types, and dug holes in it with an awl. The foreman started after me, when he saw my handiwork, intending to 'give me the works,' but I beat it and took the nearest exit and the shortest cut home."

It was the custom of Robert's family to assemble evenings, particularly in winter, around the dining room table after dinner. Heat was obtained from a pot-bellied stove, and light came from the old-fashioned kerosene lamps. His mother would sit sewing for her family and listening to the conversation of her youngsters or to the reading of her husband, whom she had now given the pet name "Shinney." But Rev. Sengstacke's fixed habit of evening Bible reading was not nearly so much fun as the group singing in which the family frequently indulged.

His children, who called him "Papa," respected and admired him—indeed, they came to idolize him. And he was loved by his wife. He neither smoked nor drank, and was a fond father and devoted husband, but he was not a demonstrative man—a Sengstacke trait which Robert adopted. Not one entry of warmth or affection towards his wife or children appears in his diary. He showed so little emotion, that perhaps only by subtle implications, or maybe a woman's intuition, did his wife know the depths of his feeling. When away on a trip, he would merely write her husbandly notes like this one: "Dear Wife: — I may be home Sunday night. Have a good supper and some Irish potatoes and stew and brown bread with butter. Also some good coffee or tea. Hope all are well. Papa." His distant manner, perhaps a result of his stern German rearing, made him a difficult person for Robert to reach and to know deeply.

Evenings, this strong and silent, even lonely man, would abruptly leave the house and take long walks by himself in the woods nearby to wrestle with his problems. He was not an arbitrary man, though firm with his family. His plans and thoughts were ever concerned with his wife and children—indeed, his plans included the purchase of a plot of land for each child, and he carefully kept up life insurance, paying nine-dollar yearly premiums. He diligently worked his vegetable garden, in which he raised tomatoes, beans, corn, peas and potatoes to provide food for his family. He sold the surplus to augment his income, often shipping crates of produce as far as New York.

Rev. Sengstacke regularly went to the city to pay his bills, (the entries in his records noting "payment in full" always had a nice flourish to the penmanship), and afterwards he might walk to the Laurel Grove Cemetery to view his father's grave. Savannah's *Colored Tribune* frequently published the names of tax delinquents, but his never appeared among them. Sometimes his wife would complain of neglect, and he would appease her by devoting a whole day to what he described as "manual labor"—that is, he would help "clean the house, and fix the sidewalk and fence."

If Robert's stepfather was sometimes moody, perhaps often unhappy, he had enough worries to keep him constantly upset. He enjoyed vigorous health, for he frequently walked the entire distance from town to city, but he was unaccustomed to well water, which was the only type available in swampy, undeveloped Woodville, so he had distilled water delivered to his home for the use of his family and himself, and yet he often contracted fever. He also suffered from raging toothaches, and had to travel in pain to Savannah to find a dentist, but the only relief he received came from his wife's applications of poultices made of home-grown flaxseed.

His worries multiplied with Flora's pregnancies, especially when her physician submitted bills for sixty-six dollars for obstetrical services. The situation occasionally was aggravated by his wife's wayward family. He once wrote this irritable-sounding note to Dr. B. S. Purse: "I send by Robert one dollar also a half on my wife's mother's bill. It is the best I can do just now. I shall continue to send a little now and then, as it pains me to have this just debt unpaid. If the husband and son, who live in the city, will not pay; I shall do what I can with God's help." No wonder he kept careful records of "home expenses," even duly recording thirty cents given Robert to celebrate Jasper's Festival.

He did, in fact, place considerable emphasis upon the careful management of money, yet his records show eighteen people owed him money he had lent them. Despite his many cares, he found the time and money to take his children on outings like the military celebration of the Fifteenth Amendment, and to witness the fireworks' display in Savannah's new park.

The man was haunted by the fear he would not be able to provide his children with a college education, but he was content to lean upon the Lord. He had a deep and abiding respect for learning, a characteristic afterwards reflected in Robert. He consequently never neglected the schooling of his children—indeed, he tried to do more than educate them: because he believed that intelligence was necessary for Christian salvation, he attempted to inculcate the idea that teaching the Negro race was a Sengstacke mission, and thus infuse them with missionary zeal. He maintained a library of considerable size and variety. His books provided Robert and his brother and sisters with their earliest reading. Judging by his records, they included such hardly digestible volumes as Watts' *Improvement of the Mind,* Tanner's *The Negro's Origin,* Kerney's *Compendium of History, The Schoolmaster,* and *The Life of John Wesley.* His few books of poetry included a work by Frances E. Watkins, the only Negro author in his collection.

Beyond formal schooling, he insisted that his children learn German. Nights, at the dinner table, they had to ask for things in German and speak the language in observing the social amenities, especially when visitors like his old sailor friend, Herman Kropp, arrived from Bremen. But only Robert's brother, Alexander, seemingly became fluent enough to understand his father's German-script letters while he was away at college. Robert himself had no facility with foreign languages and was to spend considerable money later in life trying to learn French and having his German correspondence translated.

However, Rev. Sengstacke successfully taught his children music, for which Robert had a real feeling, and tried to acquaint them with art. He allowed himself the luxury of buying two reproductions of masterpieces to instruct his youngsters in art appreciation and to decorate the living room. He made a down payment of fifty cents on the purchase, and promised to pay twenty-five cents weekly until the full amount of six dollars was paid. He never neglected his own self-improvement, nor abandoned his love of art, music and theater. He often admitted that the reason he loved his work was because it gave him "time for self-improvement."

He belonged to a literary society which met regularly in Savannah, and for having completed a correspondence course of study in the Bryant Class he was awarded a diploma by the Chautauqua Literary and Scientific Circle of Plainfield, N. J. He subscribed to several publications including two Negro newspapers, the Savannah *Colored American* and *The Negro American,* published in Boston by Thomas T. Simmons. He often hitched up his horse and buggy and drove to the city alone to attend either a concert or the theater, where by the logic of things racial he was compelled to pass as a white person or not have any cultural outlets at all. He might have had a happier life had he not believed in the moral necessity of improving himself every moment of his time.

Robert, now fourteen years old, was the eldest boy. He soon became his stepfather's constant companion and often accompanied him on his missionary errands, except during the months when, in preparation for college, he was attending Beach Institute in Savannah. When he was a small boy, old Woodville residents say it was a common sight to see the clergyman striding along the roads with his stepson happily perched astride his shoulders. When time allowed, as Robert grew older, Rev. Sengstacke would journey to nearby Hinesville with his stepson in tow and sit in on the court sessions to watch justice being meted out to Negro defendants by judges who were determined "to keep the Negro in his place." If permitted, he often intervened in behalf of an inarticulate man.

These trips made an indelible impression on young Robert. For example, he was with his parent when the Reverend became involved in a dispute at a post office in Savannah—for he protested the attempt by white clerks to serve white persons before Negroes, even though Negroes had reached the windows first. The Pilgrim congregation's pastor, who was a life-long Republican and paid his poll tax assessments of $8.45 regularly, often carried his stepson along when he went to the polls to cast his ballot. When a fire broke out near the Wade Collins property, Robert, along with his stepfather and neighbors, helped to extinguish the flames and he afterwards received his parent's blessing.

Robert's stepfather frequently took him to the Scarborough farm, situated at the Five Mile Hill two miles from his place. It was the well-to-do and bewhiskered Joseph Scarborough who supplied his family with distilled water and twice had loaned his father money. The minister often went there to transact business or gossip with the man who had become one of his few real friends in the area. But Robert's eyes fell upon his mulatto daughter, Catherine—a sight he never forgot. And there, too, he met her brother Joseph, a youngster about his own age, and developed his first lasting friendship. In those days there was no mail delivery in Woodville, so he was to see Joseph and Catherine often, because the Sengstacke mail was delivered to the Scarborough town house at the corner of Pine and Ann Streets in Savannah, and there it was picked up once a week by Robert. Later, when he worked as a printer's devil on a daily paper owned by Jonathan Stern and Company, a position he was to hold until he left for college, he would see much of his buddy Joseph.

Until now, Robert's stepfather had conducted Woodville's only school in the parsonage. The community's problem of education could have become acute had not the American Missionary Association come to his aid. Savannah's Board of Education had refused to erect a school and denied what support it had been giving, though Rev. Sengstacke was not stricken from the Board's payroll. The Association appropriated $150 for the purpose of lifting the church and building a low-ceilinged basement underneath, which afterwards was divided into school rooms and used for church socials, prayer meetings and suppers. The pupils paid ten cents a month tuition. The rooms were of the plainest type, primitive, in fact, but Robert and two generations of Sengstackes were to receive their early education there. The only equipment was a few rows of backless wooden benches and two tables. Undaunted, Rev. Sengstacke kept school open three months a year, teaching children in the day and adults at night, until he was able to increase the school year to five months.

He wrote the A.M.A. complaining that a five-month school year, three hours a day, was not a good plan, because the "children cannot make good improvement in such a short time." He asked an extension to eight months, and later even appealed for the erection of a college. He taught grammar, arithmetic, geography, history and English composition, but he never had more than fifty pupils in regular attendance. "We labor under great disadvantages," he wrote a friend. "We have no fire in the grammar room; and when it is cold we are compelled to crowd all the children in one room, the seating being very uncomfortable." He needed a stove, school books, slates, pencils, pens and a blackboard.

Truancy was the bane of his existence. And in addition, he found Robert's classmates "very hard to govern," though he believed that "with patience, firmness and mildness, I shall accomplish my task." In a moment of discouragement, the clergyman confessed to his diary: "I would rather run two churches than an overcrowded school and one church. I might organize a mission in Savannah and give up the school work." Instead, he enlisted the help of Deacon Jordan Loyd, a Savannah resident, and asked the A.M.A. to appoint him as his assistant.

The arrangement was finally concluded, and Deacon Loyd became the assistant, teaching the primary grades at twenty dollars monthly, to which Rev. Sengstacke contributed five dollars. He himself only received thirty dollars a month from the A.M.A. up to 1891; thereafter, forty. Presumably his congregation was expected to supplement his wages, but the people themselves were abysmally poor. For example, one month he was given as little as forty-three cents, and in 1882 the congregation could only pay one dollar towards his whole year's salary. And yet he frequently asked the A.M.A. to deduct five dollars from his salary and apply it to the missionary fund, because "This Woodville work must be pushed."

Woodville was a little settlement containing about four hundred Negro families and a handful of white shopkeepers, isolated by distance and indifference from Savannah. A few of the residents had been settled here by white people, but the majority were ex-slaves who had belonged to two plantations that before the Civil War were the area's showplaces— The White Hall and The Hermitage.* An immigrant Scotsman named Henry McAlpin started The Hermitage in 1814 and when the war came had 227 able-bodied slaves. The White Hall had a similar number. When their masters abandoned these white-columned mansions after destruction by Sherman's troops, Negroes were left in the area to shift for themselves. When Rev. Sengstacke arrived in Woodville, they were living mostly in wooden shanties in the old slave quarters where Robert would play with their ragged children.

Underneath these tumble-down shanties, the land had been sold to the inhabitants in half-acre lots at seventy-five dollars apiece by a Charles J. Hull who, the local people say, was a carpetbagger hailing from Chicago. He somehow had acquired great stretches of Woodville real estate, subdivided the land into small lots, and sold them on the installment plan. He afterwards willed them to a Helen Culver who in turn continued the squeeze. Negroes were unable to meet the

---

* The remains of The Hermitage were purchased by Henry Ford in 1935 and moved twelve miles away to erect a Negro school in a town called Ways, whose first Negro mayor was named Legree.

installments and were deeply in debt, for poverty had spread like plague. Illiteracy, hunger and disease were their only wages. Rice fields had reverted to swamp lands. Corn ground was covered with thick stands of splash pine and undergrowth. The whole face of Woodville county was distorted with pain and unemployment.

When Rev. Sengstacke, a pioneer as well as a missionary, first stood on his porch, gazing over the landscape to the undeveloped hills in the hazy distance, as he was frequently to do, it was not to yield himself to beauty but to ponder how to make his barefoot people self-sufficient and end their dismal ignorance. The land, rugged and pinched as it was, was to yield him and his family food and an income. He was unable to persuade his flock to do likewise. His sermons often dwelt on the money to be earned by selling fruits and vegetables in the city. He himself had set the example, even to the extent of participating in the programs of the State Agricultural Association.

The city markets, needing produce of any sort, joined the Negro missionary's campaign to stimulate industry on the Woodville farms by offering prizes. The first quart of English peas brought to Savannah was given ten dollars, a munificent sum in those days. The first strawberries and cucumbers also brought high premiums. Before long, farmers were competing for these prizes, and in the process began to eke out a living. When Rev. Sengstacke was able to say his people were "creeping towards self-support," he established The Society of the Sengstacke Band of Hope of Pilgrim Congregational Church, a sickness and death benefit organization.

The Negro missionary discovered, perhaps in bewilderment, that many old slave inhibitions stubbornly lingered among these people, but while he dealt with them positively, his stepson was absorbing these very folkways. The inhibitions which pulled at daily behavior like an undertow were the social realities of his day. For example, Negroes had to make new and profound adjustments in their relations with the white people, some undoubtedly under compulsion. They adopted such placating terms as "Boss" and "Mam," in place of "Marsa" and "Missus," to assert their freedom and yet avoid causing hostility by familiarity. (It was, in fact, in this era the "Uncle Tom" approach began among Negroes as a tactic for survival.)

But Robert's stepfather was faced with teaching his people the actual rudiments of civilization. For they had to learn to eat meals at regular hours, use tablecloths and napkins, and to sleep in beds with sheets. He had particular difficulty in teaching them the use of toothbrushes and nightgowns, and the importance of bathing regularly. And they had to be taught to comb their hair mornings, keep hands and faces clean, keep buttons on clothes, patch torn places, and remove grease spots. Six who pooled their resources and bought one toothbrush were undoubtedly perplexed by his explanation that its use by six persons was not hygenic. With admiration, Robert recalled how his stepfather, in time, persuaded the people with big families to abandon their small one-room, dirt-floored cabins, actually rural tenements, and build healthful dwellings of four and five rooms.

Rev. Sengstacke's leadership was felt by nearly everyone in Woodville, particularly since a preacher was a highly important figure in that day. Thus, "When the earthquake hit Savannah in 1887," Robert reported, "the members of my father's church had been expecting it for a week or more, for the slight tremors which had been occurring intermittently were dealt with at great length in the daily papers.

"My father had explained to the people of his congregation the nature and cause of an earthquake, so that they would be prepared to go through this experience without much emotional disturbance. As a result they were considerably more calm than the uninformed folk of the community when the quake did come. Those who were not expecting it, and to whom this singular phenomenon was beyond comprehension, felt certain their doom had come. Some screamed, prayed, others ran out crazily in the fields shooting their rifles in the air creating thereby greater confusion and fright. But the resolute calmness of others was an inspiring evidence of my father's influence in the community."

The Rev. Sengstacke was what his stepson described as a "book preacher." The reason he was so dubbed was that he endeavored to educate, inform and lift his people. He often described to them the big world beyond the isolated confines of Woodville, for many had not even seen nearby Savannah. It was not unusual for him to read the newspapers at prayer meetings. "The people soon were educated to appreciate such services," Robert reported, "and prayer meetings became a forum at which world events were discussed." He achieved, in time, considerable stature as a clergyman among his educated colleagues, both white and Negro, and frequently delivered sermons in the Episcopal and Presbyterian churches. He soon was able to say "even the German Lutheran minister treats me with kindness and respect whenever I call on him in Savannah."

Formal recognition came with his election as secretary of the Georgia Ministers Union Alliance, and he afterwards was persuaded to preach in Macon and Atlanta, Beaufort and Charleston, S. C. He was awarded the degree of Doctor of Divinity by Bethany College, and was invited to deliver the commencement address at Alabama's Talladega College, but he declined the honor because of the pressure of work. He became a member of the American Academy of Political and Social Science, and published a theological dissertation entitled, "Was Christ a Baptist?" He contributed articles to magazines, primarily translations from German, dealing with religious history and social developments abroad. His correspondence with white people in various parts of the country was considerable, and perhaps accounted for the many contributions to his missionary work.

The day-to-day chores of Pilgrim Church, which he described as "an ornament to our growing suburb," were his main concerns. Robert's stepfather maintained a schedule that would have made a less dedicated man quail. Besides teaching and preaching, he kept up his pastoral duties—christenings, baptisms, visiting the sick, and what he described as "funeralizing" the dead. And his diary reports his frequent attendance at social and political meetings "in the interest of colored people." Whenever Deacon Loyd fell ill, he cheerfully picked up the slack. After twenty-five years of missionary labors, he was able to count only ninety-four people (men, women and children) as members of his church—a fact he reported to the Georgia Congregational Association with no evidence of embarrassment. Even though there had been a large increase in Woodville's population, not more than thirty or forty worshippers attended regularly, and, he complained, when Deacon Jackson failed to ring the bell no one appeared.

This restless man had in fact utilized much of his energies in securing the bell, which seemingly was an urgent matter to him. He perhaps thought it might increase attendance and he had appealed to white friends, including people in Germany, for money to make the purchase. "We are at a great loss for something to call us together," he explained. "We have no certain timepieces to go by, as all our clocks differ." He lifted the need to the proportions of a community project, and the young people even gave a benefit festival and raised twenty-five dollars. He methodically procured six estimates, and found a four-hundred pound bell costing a hundred dollars. He finally accumulated sufficient money, but its erection was delayed when the authorities declared the edifice unsafe for occupancy following a great storm. The bell was finally installed in the belfry and tolled its first notes one Sunday morning, but it produced no appreciable increase in church attendance.

Robert's stepfather was essentially a fundamentalist who had found his spiritual home in the ranks of the Congregationalists. He strongly opposed whiskey drinking, membership in fraternal organizations, and the singing of spirituals. When he organized The Society of the Sengstacke Band of Hope, he made every applicant pledge never to drink or smoke. He believed that the Congregational Church had the best form of worship, though he was liberal enough to observe that "Christ is the only true way, and not some particular sect." He fanatically opposed all worship that displayed ecstasy or hysterics. He heartily approved when Mayor Schwartz closed the noisy Second African Baptist Church as "a public nuisance." While he could preach sermons like "Why Does Christ Love the Sinner," he could expel a backslider for the slightest infraction. His records constantly refer to expulsions for whiskey drinking, adultery, selling liquor and membership in secret societies. "I honestly believe," he wrote a friend, "that all good and intelligent people will help us build up Pilgrim as soon as they find out that her doctrine is pure."

In justice to him, it must be said his problems in Woodville were not all of his own making. Perhaps, as Nietzsche said of the Germans, he had no feeling for nuances. The community already was divided into two hostile factions, representing the two plantations—The White Hall and The Hermitage. Each adopted the vendetta that had existed between their masters during slavery days, and this was further complicated by the fact that each swore loyalty to a different Baptist church. Rev. Sengstacke, in introducing the Congregational Church, stood squarely in the middle. But the nub of his difficulties stemmed from the fact that he had chosen to do missionary work in "Baptist country."

There were three competing Baptist churches whose ministers vigorously protested against his proselytizing. Tempers soon flared and the conflict reached the point of violence. One evening he emerged from prayer meeting to discover someone had killed his horse. (He bought another one, which his children remember was called "Fanny," and insured her for a hundred dollars.) When a girl attending his school decided during her course of studies to join his church, her father flogged her so severely that she was absent from school for more than a week. Thus, in his eyes, the Baptists were his implacable "enemies," and he afterwards cried, "We have suffered and have been misrepresented."

Robert's immigrant stepfather, ignorant of Negro folkways and prejudices actually had been placed in an almost untenable position as a Congregationalist missionary. For, as he reported to the A.M.A., anyone who joined the Congregationalists were denounced with, "Shame on you to go down so low! We Baptists are independent people," meaning their church was not connected with or controlled by white people. The Negro missionary was regarded as an agent of white people, and as such was not to be trusted because the motives of white Congregationalists were suspect. Negroes who had had plantation experiences as slaves warned him that the A.M.A. would turn against him, "as all white people usually do."

Eventually, he did come into conflict with the association, when the A.M.A. started litigation to recover certain properties in Woodville which it claimed were owned by the association and which the Sengstacke family occupied. But until this turn of events, he stood staunchly by his mission and brooked no criticism of the Congregationalists. He was a solitary man fighting a community on what he believed to be moral principles. If he had not been utterly lacking in a sense of humor, he might not have been so sensitive. For instance, when a Woodville preacher, not otherwise identified, was haled into court for stealing a pair of shoes, he promptly complained to the newspaper which reported the incident. He declared the culprit should have been clearly identified as a "Baptist preacher," so people would know that a "Congregationalist clergyman" was not involved!

The role white people were to play in lifting up the Negro was a burning question in Rev. Sengstacke's day, but due to the latter's lack of racial experience and historical knowledge, much that transpired was beyond his grasp. The ex-slave, Frederick Douglass, acknowledged leader of the Negro people, had framed a formal "Declaration of Independence" from the "swarms of white beggars that sweep the country in the name of the colored race." He declared, "We have been more injured than benefited by the efforts of the so-called benevolent societies." He called on Negroes to "repudiate" all such groups, including religious organizations doing philanthropic work.

The A.M.A. was startled by his position and opposed him. It held that Negroes needed the help of white people before they could take their place in society, a position Rev. Sengstacke endorsed, thus standing with Booker T. Washington, the Tuskegee educator. But Douglass replied in a devastating public letter: "We need justice, and the protection of the law, more than alms. I demand education for my race through all the channels open to other people, and allow [Negroes] to work out thereafter their own destiny." Douglass had clearly taken a position against white philanthropy, and he was supported by rank and file opinion among Negroes.

The Negro leader was dealing with a philosophical question in the national arena, but Robert's stepfather, intimately acquainted with the desperate condition of Woodville Negroes, was grappling with the social realities on the local level. For example, he reported to the A.M.A. that "Intemperance is strong in this community; professors of religion openly drink at the bar, even preachers drink." Then, he asked for a definition of policy regarding membership in fraternal organizations. He observed that "All the churches here admit members of secret societies to membership. So far as I know, we are the only people here who oppose them." He declared that persons whom he rejected became the church's "worst enemies and help to build up other churches."

"Equally important," he said, "was opposing dreams and visions [meaning superstition], and spiritual fathers and mothers," meaning illegitimacy. To illustrate the ignorance prevalent among the Baptists, he told of Deacon Jackson becoming involved in a heated discussion with a Baptist minister as to whether or not "John the Baptist, after he was beheaded, was put in a boat which drifted to the island of Patmos." The intelligent people, he argued, "agree with us regarding ignorance, sectarianism, intemperance and immorality, but on the secret society question, we stand alone."

He waited four months for a reply. Then he took action on his own initiative by submitting the question to his congregation, and after an affirmative vote, it became firm church policy that "It is the duty of all truly converted men to give all their time, not devoted to family, business, or needful recreation, to the church of God, instead of dividing a part of it with secret organizations."

This decision was contrary to every inclination of Negroes —indeed, Rev. Sengstacke had not fully grasped the realities of the community in which he had to function and was trying to beat back the social tide. His own disastrous membership in the Masons might have prejudiced him. To begin with, there was little in the way of organized recreation for the people living in Woodville. Their pleasures came from the rather simple experiences of visiting, singing, or attending meetings of organizations to which they belonged. There was considerable companionable drinking, but not as much as Rev. Sengstacke thought. They enjoyed the parades and dances and socials given by the fraternal groups. Actually, the development was a manifestation of the Negro's struggle to become socially self-sufficient, and explains why there was a remarkable growth of fraternal orders among Negroes. Undoubtedly, the secret rituals and the wearing of colorful uniforms were attractions, and organizations like the Masons, the Knights of Pythias and Odd Fellows flourished.

Belatedly, Rev. Sengstacke changed his tactics, though he never retreated from his position. But even his efforts at rapprochement were failures. One night he invited a Savannah Baptist minister and his deacons to take part in Pilgrim Church's services, but one deacon walked out when he invited the congregation to unite in celebrating the Holy Feast—"And yet," he afterwards observed bitterly, "this same man can be found often in a barroom and in such company as frequent such places." By now, a tone of bitterness and invective is more and more evident in his communings with his diary. But he was optimistic to the last and was soon rejoicing because "the leading people are opening their eyes, that it is Christ they need, not John the Baptist." How wrong he was is indicated by the fact that more than half of the Negro population belongs to the Baptist Church today.

Toward the close of his life, perhaps weary with the endless bickerings over dogma, he observed in his diary, "There is but one church, and all who are born of God are members of it. God made a church, man made denominations. God gave us a Holy Bible, disputing men made different kinds of disciples." And in a sort of farewell entry, the tired old man remarked, "Both the white and colored are improving slowly; the first is getting more friendly and the second is growing more intelligent." Even so, the backwash of his raging controversies swept over the members of his family, was reflected in their day-to-day relations with the people of Woodville, and conditioned their thinking profoundly, and perhaps explains Robert's life-long search for a spiritual anchor.

*My son Robert is anxious to attend your school this
year. He is willing to work all day and study at night.
He is willing to do any kind of work, but prefers the
printer's trade.*—REV. SENGSTACKE, Letter to General
Armstrong, Hampton Institute, Sept. 16, 1887.

CHAPTER V

Love, Learning and Law

BY THE FALL of 1886, Rev. John H. H. Sengstacke
had determined that his stepson Robert should have the ad-
vantages of a college education, though his first problem was
securing for him an essentially sound secondary schooling.
Few such schools existed for Negroes. He finally decided upon
Beach Institute, a small Congregationalist institution located
at Price and Harris Streets in Savannah, about four miles
from Woodville. The school, taught by white missionaries
and supported by funds contributed by the American Missionary Association, was named after Alfred E. Beach, editor
of the *Scientific American* of New York, who originally purchased the land for the association. The Freedman's Bureau
had started the school, but the A.M.A. formally assumed support in 1868 as the first public school for Negroes in Savannah.

By the time Robert entered, the association had recruited
and trained a few Negro teachers and now had a mixed faculty. Had Robert's stepfather grasped the profound nature of
color distinctions among Negroes, he never would have sent
Robert to Beach. Perhaps the nuances of color prejudice es-

caped him, but Robert nevertheless felt the heavy hand of this color-conscious environment. It is a period he omits completely in his *Defender* autobiographical series, but this very omission suggests that he wished to forget the episode.

The student body was composed primarily of the fair-skinned offspring of Savannah's first families who had already documented their color inclinations by membership in St. Stephens Episcopal Church. The youngsters, aping their elders, were cruelly unkind to the black boy from Woodville. His only friends at school were Joseph and Catherine Scarborough. He probably was particularly pleased by daily sight of the mulatto girl whom he was beginning to look at with love in his eyes, but her presence was not enough to mitigate his racial lot. Not more than two or three black children were lucky enough to be admitted in a semester, and, according to dark-skinned Mae Perrin who attended Beach twenty years later, these black children were denied the opportunity of being selected valedictorians of graduating classes.

Whatever the quality of education offered, and it was apparently of a rudimentary nature, Robert suffered deeply—though he never confided this fact to his parents, nor to anyone else. There is not a glimpse in Rev. Sengstacke's diary that he had any inkling of what was happening to his youngster. Perhaps one clue to Robert's reactions is the fact that he insisted upon leaving Savannah and going away to school before he had finished Beach with, as he himself later confessed, "no definite purpose in life save that of laying a foundation of a good education for whatever my field was to be." His stepfather consented to his choice of Claflin University at Orangeburg, S. C., about one hundred miles from Savannah, though he felt Robert was by no means ready. He confided his misgivings in correspondence with the university's white president, Dr. L. M. Dunton: "I wanted him to stay home until next year and prepare himself financially and intellectually for school, but he wants to 'go now'." The decision put a heavy financial burden on Rev. Sengstacke, and to a Mrs. S. N. Millard, a Christian white woman who made contributions for Robert's education, he wrote bemoaning the cross he bore. He sent an identical note to a Mr. I. Hudson of Kalamazoo, Michigan, who had contributed fifteen dollars. His stepson entered Claflin on October 6, 1887, registered as "Robert Sengstacke."

Claflin University, Methodist sponsored and founded one year before Robert's arrival, offered an education equivalent to elementary schooling. Like most Negro institutions of the period, it provided students with work to enable them to help pay room, board and tuition, but the burden of Robert's education was his stepfather's. One month after his matriculation he received this note: "Robert. Send your school bill for this month. What is due? How much did you pay on it in work? How much is due now?" Robert, with his rural background, had been assigned to the farm conducted by the school, and thus made a contribution to his expenses.

He apparently did his work cheerfully, and seemingly made a quick adjustment to his new environment. Upon arrival, he reported expansively, "I had the rare privilege of being allowed in the Senior cottage where I gathered a great deal of information which I could not have obtained had I not been a great favorite of the upperclassmen." It is more likely that Robert, who now was nineteen years old, had been assigned a place with the older students because of his age. At any rate, the newly admitted freshman was permitted to join the glee club, but we can only smile at his belief that they liked him because of his "operatic tenor voice." No records of his grades exist, but his classmates remember him as an average, although talkative, student.

The new world was a revelation to him, and his curiosity was daily sharpened by his experiences—one experience in particular he was to profit by and long remember. Two young men, he recalled, "unbeknowing to them, influenced my decision to learn a trade. They were trying to work their way through school by selling books, because they felt that menial labor was unbecoming their station [as college men]. Their circumstances were tragic. They would come into the cottages looking like tramps and only through the kindness of their schoolmates were they able to get suitable attire to attend classes. Their lot discouraged me, for I learned that these two men had not been trained to work with their hands. I was determined that I should not fall into that category."

If the Rev. Sengstacke sent his stepson to Orangeburg in the hopes of raising up a Congregationalist missionary, his money was wasted. After six months at Claflin, Robert returned with his visions considerably expanded, and determined to learn a trade. He wrote to Hampton Institute on June 6, 1888, asking admission and offering to work his way through. While awaiting a reply, he resumed his apprenticeship at the Savannah *Echo*. His decision perhaps coincided with his stepfather's plan to publish a newspaper, which Robert's sister Rebecca regards as the original founding of the *Defender*. The urge to publish a paper may have been inspired by the fact that Woodville doings were ignored by the local publications. He then tried contributing a column, "Woodville Dots," to the Savannah *Tribune*, a Negro newspaper, but the editor often killed his copy without explanation.

Seeking a remedy, Robert's stepfather wrote a Philadelphia firm inquiring into the price of printing presses, type and paper, and offering to pay on the installment plan. He soon abandoned this plan as too expensive and chose a Savannah printer. Next, a newspaper advertisement offering typewriters for sale attracted his attention, and he wrote explaining that he "would like to try one, but fear I cannot make it work, and there is no one to show me how in this city." No Negroes apparently could operate a typewriter, few white persons would teach a Negro, and the typewriter manufacturer had no suggestion to offer. He finally had to prepare his copy longhand.

The paper was nearly six months in preparation.

The first issue appeared in November, 1889, as the Woodville *Times*. The masthead carried the Rev. John H. H. Sengstacke as editor, and Deacon Jordan Loyd as business manager. Though his stepson's name did not appear on the masthead, we can assume he performed as general handyman and was no little assistance to his stepfather with the printing details. Robert S. Abbott thus had his first active contact with the technical processes of makeup, editing and printing a newspaper. Three generations of Sengstackes were to work at publishing a paper in Woodville. Robert's brother Alexander assumed the editorship with Rev. Sengstacke's death and renamed the paper the West End *Post*. Later he was assisted by his son John, who today is the editor and publisher of the Chicago *Defender*.

The Woodville *Times* was a four-column, four-page sheet and sold for five cents a copy. The most singular fact about this organ was that it published nothing concerning the desperate social and political condition of Negroes, and what little news appeared contained no "racial angle" whatsoever. The third issue is the earliest extant, and is fairly typical of every subsequent edition in existence. The paper, cleanly edited, was essentially small town in character, but ambitiously attempted to cover topics of educational value. For example, the front page carried long articles like Thomas Edison's "A Great Inventor's Mind," reprinted from the New York *Times*. Not until one reached page two, where the "Editor's Notebook" appeared did the distinctive personality of the paper shine through. This was a long column supposedly detailing newsy items about happenings in the city, but Rev. Sengstacke used it to lash out against the Baptist Church. Under a sub-head, "News from Savannah," he carried this report: "The colored Baptists had another row yesterday morning. This time it was at the First Bryan Baptist Church. Rev. Griffin is beated over the head with a communion pitcher; all sorts of weapons drawn, and several people injured in the melee. Sister Ryals had her head split open with a communion pitcher. The police quelled the row, and nine arrests were made."

Then Rev. Sengstacke slyly tried to take the curse off his propagandizing by adding an editorial note immediately following the story which read: "From the [Savannah] *Morning News*." Beyond this bit of hatchet work, page two was filled with advertising and a column labeled "Woodville," with folksy items about the local people. Page three contained a long story, "Snow Is Not White," purporting to be a scientific explanation for the color of snow. Page four, used as a catchall, carried fillers like "Street Scenes in Lima," and advertising of such products as "Beecham's Pills," "Seaweed Tonic for Dyspepsia," and "Hood's Sarsaparilla for Rheumatism." Dr. B. M. Woolley of Atlanta, Ga., bought a special ad and under the caption, "Opium and Whiskey," solemnly declared he could cure both habits "at home without pain."

While the paper was being launched, Robert had marked time until he could enter Hampton Institute. Before he entered Claflin, his stepfather had written to Hampton's white principal, General Samuel Chapman Armstrong, to secure his entrance, but was informed that the school was overcrowded. Soon after Robert's return to Woodville, his pal Joseph Scarborough decided to attend Atlanta University where a "classical" education was offered those who wanted to become teachers and preachers. Robert, waywardly forgetting his resolve to become a printer, tried to persuade his stepfather to allow him to join Joe. Rev. Sengstacke turned a deaf ear to his plea and shipped him off to Hampton specifically to learn the printing trade. He entered Hampton

November 30, 1889, exactly six days after his twenty-first birthday. He gave his name as "Robert A. Sengstacke," using the "Abbott" as a middle initial, and, significantly, gave 66 New Street, Savannah, Ga., as his home address, when his family still resided in Woodville. But by now, he had developed a thin skin about being labeled a "country boy" and, to avoid the jibes expected of his classmates, said he came from Savannah.

Hampton Institute, staffed by white missionaries and supported by Northern philanthropy, was founded at Fortress Monroe by the Congregationalists (A.M.A.). General Armstrong, a Union officer in the Civil War, afterwards established the school in the town of Hampton in the tidewater region of Virginia, as a trade and agricultural school. He wanted to see continued the skilled artisan tradition that had existed among Negroes before the war. When Robert arrived, the green, sweeping campus contained several ivy-covered buildings shaded by century-old oak trees—one towering timber came to be known as "Freedom Oak"—a sequestered spot where legend says General Armstrong disbanded his troops. Today's wide, smooth streets and well-kept lawns give no indication of the hardships, setbacks and financial woes of the institute during her pioneer days. The school was co-educational and included Indian boys and girls (wards of the Federal government), as well as a handful of white students, children of faculty members.

Hampton was mainly an institution for Negroes. The general's most famous pupil was Booker T. Washington, but he could hardly have imagined that Robert S. Abbott would become the school's second most distinguished alumnus. The Negro educator, founder of Tuskegee Institute, became the apostle of industrial education for Negroes. There is no doubt —quite apart from the pedagogical merits of this type of education—his message was extremely timely in salvaging any kind of schooling for Negroes in the hostile atmosphere of the South. But Hampton, and similar industrial institutions, were criticized by the Negro intellectuals as merely producing a better servant and laborer, one taught not to rise out of his "place."

General Armstrong, who believed "doing what can't be done is the glory of living," had little direct contact with the student body, yet knew and handled their problems almost before they themselves were aware of their difficulties. He spoke humorously about Hampton graduates as "cats that he threw out of the window when they finished," and always landed on their feet. "Look at Booker T. Washington," he would say—"when I looked for him I found him at Tuskegee, teaching, just like I said."

Robert was pathetically anxious to make a good impression, but, perhaps to cover up his rustic background, he became pushy and aggressive and thereby created troubles for himself. "As soon as he arrived," says Charles H. Thornton, his senior classman in the print shop, "he refused to serve his 'devilship,' which lasted about six months and was Hampton's form of hazing. The boys soon resented his attitude, especially since his printing ability didn't measure up to the school's standards. He also got into difficulties in the classroom, from which a Georgia buddy, Phillip Chipp, often tried to extricate him. Chipp would tug his coat in class to prevent him from making a fool of himself, for he would talk on any subject that came up, always making up a story describing how he did the same thing the teacher related. I guess from the beginning I looked upon him like a younger brother, maybe because everyone always picked on him."

His classmates soon discovered that he was sensitive to remarks about his color, and his Nemesis became Isaac Peake who was fair complexioned and had the distinction of being the scion of a Negro family which had helped found the school. One day he invited Robert to visit his home in nearby Newport News, and when they arrived before Peake's door he ordered Robert to "Set outside, 'cause you're too black to come in here!" It was a painful experience even though meant in jest, and Robert was crushed. His social life was equally frustrating, especially when he approached girls. "He liked the gals," Thornton reports, "but they wouldn't give him a tumble, and Peake would always kid him and say not to bother those girls [in the nearby town], because he was too black to associate with fair women!" Thornton, known affectionately as "Bung," would always bandage his wounds. They afterwards became fast friends and Robert repaid him in later years with permanent employment on the *Defender.* He now is a pensioner.

There he was, a young and eager boy, not wholly obtuse, pursuing his ambition, having to learn little by little to live with men. He often spent sleepless nights wondering how he would fit into a world "where prejudice and discrimination dogged every step a black man took." One evening as he sat on his bed alone in Stone Hall, downcast and discouraged, someone suddenly tapped lightly on his door. When he opened it, there stood Hampton's chaplain, Dr. Hollis Burke Frissell, who was to become one of Robert's staunchest friends. He was a white New Englander who had dedicated his life to Negro education and was regarded by the students as "our Beloved Father." Next to General Armstrong, he really was the strong man on the faculty. He was next in seniority, and eventually became the head of the school. His missionary spirit guided the formulation of institutional policy, and he brought to his work qualities of sympathy and considerate attention that won for him the student's respect and love.

It was a surprising visit, but Robert invited him in, and when the amenities were laid aside, Dr. Frissell got down to brass tacks. "I shall never forget that moment," Robert said afterwards.

Listen to his account of what transpired:

"He told me that for a week he had been observing my work and behavior. He had come to the conclusion that in spite of my popularity, I appeared somewhat bewildered and unhappy. He could assign but one reason for it, that I was meditating too frequently on the fact of my color and the handicaps that usually accompany men and women placed in the same racial category. . . . His friendliness was such as to extract from me all the inner thoughts and impulses to which heretofore I had given scant expression. I told him, among other things, that I could not understand why there should be so much prejudice. . . . His last argument was in effect that I should so prepare myself for the struggle ahead that in whatever field I should decide to dedicate my services, I should be able to point the light not only to my own people but to white people as well."

The white man eventually taught Robert to value knowledge above words, mistrust mere formula, learn accomodation to realities, and observe rather than judge; more important, he taught him a method of functioning smoothly in a hostile world.

"From the moment of that talk until I left Hampton," Robert recalled, "I was able to show a much more jovial spirit than I had thought possible. I did my school work and participated in extracurricular activities with zest and pep that finally earned me the title 'Happy Bob.'"

In his own eyes his most worthwhile achievement was becoming a member of the Hampton quartet which toured the country to stimulate financial interest in the school. To be a member of the quartet was like being a member of a varsity football team today. "The first night I arrived at Hampton," he recalled, "I was sitting in chapel with a group of boys from my home town; they started singing a song that I used to sing at Beach Institute and at Claflin. I joined them and soon an inquiry was going around about who the boy with the tenor voice was. I saw General Armstrong call the music teacher, Professor Rathbone, aside. As a result, I was asked to remain after chapel and was made a member of the choir. From then on I sang in the choir and later in the famous Hampton Quartet."

Thornton, who loved Robert like a brother, relates quite a different version of why he was chosen a member of the quartet: "One day they needed a boy for the Hampton quartet and Abbott got the job, because his color was right for traveling around the country trying to raise money for a Negro school. In those days white people resented seeing light complexioned boys in the group, and wondered out loud whether Hampton was really a school for Negroes. So the teachers always preferred very dark Negroes for the quartet. The effect was more pronounced if the singers were black, because, after all, they came from a Negro institution and there should be no mistaking that."

If mulatto boys were denied the privilege of being members of the quartet, so too were the Indian students. Hampton's officials perhaps recognized the emotional appeal four black boys forlornly singing spirituals might have on white audiences, particularly moving them sufficiently to reach into their pockets and support the school's program. The group's rendition of "Were You There When They Crucified My Lord?" often brought sobs. Robert, for once, enjoyed the luxury of being black, though he hardly was aware of his curious role in the fund-raising campaign.

He afterwards became a campus hero, for not only had he been selected to represent the school as a singer, but he had the distinction of being the first freshman in the history of Hampton to be made a member of the quartet—which besides Robert, included John H. Wainwright, William H. Daggs and David Jones. So elated were the "Georgia boys," those coming from his home state, that their leader, Aaron Grant, actually carried him on his shoulders as the group headed for a celebration at the Holly Tree Inn, where the students usually assembled to swap stories, conduct "bull sessions," and review recently written chapters on campus love life.

The quartet toured the country at intervals, always with a tutor along, singing to white audiences from Columbus, Ohio, to Bar Harbor, Maine. The group often had difficulty finding adequate accommodations and Dr. Frissell, who frequently traveled with the quartet, often had to share a bed with Robert. When they reached New York during one tour, the four boys performed for Walter Damrosch, the famous conductor and musician. He afterwards offered Robert a scholarship to study music at Julliard. His mentor, he reported, "discouraged my acceptance, saying that the time was not ripe. I was not otherwise prepared to earn a living, and if after years of sacrifice and study preparing for music, the field was closed to me because of my racial identity, I should be hopelessly lost."

Beyond the camaraderie with his fellow singers and intimate associations with Dr. Frissell, his experiences with the quartet were a significant part of his development at Hampton. He spent the next seven years at this institution, leaving only during vacations and tours. He became a campus celebrity and naturally expanded with the applause his new status won him, and he became a member of the debating society and lyceum. With this new state of mind, his relations with the faculty improved. He afterwards said, "The paternal interest manifested by the teachers, and the moral and intellectual discipline that was inspired by the faculty of cultured men and women—all these things conspired to create the impression of being in a large family in a big, spacious room."

Now he boldly took the lead in forming a secret society, The Black Cats, whose rituals involved the hazing of freshmen, and whose name suggests he had made some conquest of his color inhibitions. He also was the founder of the Georgia Boys Association, a group that hailed from the "Empire State of the South" and banded together for social and fraternal relationships. He established friendships with teachers that persisted beyond his graduation, particularly with his "campus mother," Miss Flora Loew, and Miss M. F. Sherman of Brookfield, Mass., whom he corresponded with even after her retirement in 1925.

By now, he was paying strict attention to his studies and was forever experimenting in the print shop, so that "none of the minute details of the trade might escape my observation." The course involved practical work, such as setting type and printing *The Home Bulletin* of the Kecoughtan Veterans Hospital nearby. Thornton recalls how Robert, when a freshman, begged to be allowed to work on this paper. But with all his application, Robert's grades were not spectacular. The first semester, when he was morbidly resigned to defeat, he had a below "C" average; but in his triumphant final year, he received a "B" plus average in all his subjects. He finished his training as a printer in 1893, and remained to complete his academic work in 1896. He did not forget to send Catherine Scarborough's parents a photograph of the graduating class, and wrote his mother asking her to let him know what they had to say about it.

Robert S. Abbott afterwards held the deepest affection for Hampton, an affection lasting to the end of his days. Soon after his success as a publisher, he was elected president of the Hampton Alumni Association and became a sturdy supporter of the institution—indeed, he considered support of his alma mater a "moral duty," particularly with the decline in philanthropic contributions. For, he declared, the school had given him the "inspiration and preparation for accomplishment."

He asked in a letter to the alumni as late as 1937, "Are we, who have profited by the sacrifices [of General Armstrong], to allow it to be said that we forget so easily, that we are so unappreciative?" Besides making the usual alumni contributions, he gave Hampton the first $1,000 for the erection of the athletic plant, Armstrong Field. He became an advocate of trade school training for Negroes, even sending his nephew and heir, John H. H. Sengstacke, to Hampton in preparation for his eventual assumption of the editorship of the *Defender*, and vigorously endorsed Booker T. Washington's theory of industrial education.

In 1940, with the perspective of age and experience, Abbott reflected on the value of the schooling offered by Hampton and declared: "The basic foundation should be laid before engaging in the upbuilding of a superstructure. The Negro came out of slavery with nothing on which to maintain his freedom. He was poor, property-less and illiterate. To talk about college degrees at that stage of his career was tantamount to putting the cart before the horse. The stressing of industrial training for a race that had just emerged from slavery was, to my mind, a very important and necessary step, and Hampton wisely pursued this policy with relentless vigor."

Now twenty-eight years old, Robert still was undecided about what career to pursue. Three years before his graduation, while in Chicago singing with the Hampton quartet at the World's Columbian Exposition (1893), he had written his mother: "Tell father if he will back me, I will come home and run a paper. If not, I will stay out here in the west and try to make a fortune. Let me know his intentions before I begin to make up my mind as to what steps to take." He undoubtedly had been impressed by the display Negroes made of their progress in Chicago, but he was especially heartened by speeches delivered by Frederick Douglass and Ida B. Wells, who had been driven from Memphis, Tennessee, where she had a newspaper, *Free Speech*.

At any rate, he returned to Woodville and secured part-time employment as a printer, helped his stepfather publish the Woodville *Times*, and taught school on the Givens plantation. Up to now, women had been no part of his life—not even a casual flirtation with a Jezebel—but with his frequent trips to Savannah, he had more and more contact with Catherine Scarborough, and his affection for her blossomed into love. Immediately complications entered his life, which touched him profoundly and perhaps gave him direction finally.

The mulatto Scarboroughs bore a distinguished name—one of the wealthiest old slaveholding families of Savannah was popularly believed to be distantly related to them by some "left-handed marital" connection. Catherine's father, Joseph A. Scarborough, had inherited a good deal of property and was one of the richest Negroes in Savannah. When Robert started paying court to his daughter, the Scarboroughs, according to L. B. Toomer, president of Savannah's Carver Savings Bank, "were unquestionably one of the first families."

Miss Cathy, as Robert respectfully referred to her, might have been mistaken for a white person. She was one of the town's belles, and had already made her debut into Negro society. She stood about five feet three inches in height, had big, liquid black eyes, braids of curly black hair, and possessed the poised, self-confident manner of the wellborn. Her family belonged to fashionable St. Stephens Episcopal Church, and this fact made courtship difficult for Robert, in a period when the church was the center of Negro social life and people of his color were unwelcome.

Robert followed the dictates of his heart, and his love deepened and developed into a passion. When Catherine accepted a gift of a watch which bore his picture on the inside, he boldly asked her to marry him. Her father was outraged—after all, his daughter, who, in comparison with the average Negro girl, met more nearly Caucasian standards of beauty, possessed an enviable position in the Negro community and had been expected to make a good marriage—at least, a marriage with one of her own kind.

As a boy, in his love of horses, Robert often had happily leaped into Scarborough's horse-drawn dray, only to be driven away in annoyance. Robert, though, was not aware of this gentleman's hostile attitude toward him—but it was carefully observed and reported by Rebecca, Robert's half-sister. Scarborough, though a personal friend of Robert's stepfather, flatly drew the color line.

Robert was not only black, but he was indeed penniless. Catherine, behaving like the well-brought-up young lady she was, bowed to her parent's decision. Robert was desolate but confided in no one, not even his family. Nor was he consoled when her handsome brother Joe later married a decidedly black girl, a Negroid type akin to himself—for, after all, Robert's rejection was a deeply personal injury, but he somehow came to the conclusion that if he possessed money, maybe his blackness would be forgiven.

Trivial and inconsequential as color distinctions among Negroes may seem, they were the realities with which Robert had to deal. He now was baffled by the choice of a vocation. He pondered the three lines that could possibly lead to status and maybe money in the Negro community—teaching, preaching and the professions—and not one had appeal for him. Soon afterwards he left home and headed for Chicago, determined to make something of himself, though he hardly knew that he would never again live in Woodville. Upon arrival, he sought employment as a printer but faced racial obstacles and, for a time, could only secure work one day a week. His difficulties, plus his yearning for money and status, made him ponder the merits of the legal profession and perhaps persuaded him to turn to law as a career, though he had little forensic ability.

He enrolled at the Kent College of Law, now Chicago-Kent, in the fall of 1897. He gave his address as "Savannah, Ga.," though he lodged at 353 West 33rd Street—a fact suggesting his own view of the temporary nature of his stay in Chicago. He registered, unaccountably, as "Robert Seng-stacke Abbott," and thus assumed his surname for the first time in his life. His stepfather wept when he received the news. Abbott attended classes evenings and worked during the day, and in spite of the problems he faced in his trade, he managed to pay his yearly tuition of seventy-five dollars and maintain himself decently.

In retrospect, though, Robert, with his inclination for exaggeration and self-dramatization, described his purported "starvation" and "hunger" during this period. It was a very close fit, to be sure, and he wrote to his Hampton friends, "I tell you this is an uphill fight, but one I enjoy very much, on the whole."

While he was adjusting to the city, he was much perturbed that his family failed to write him and his stepfather had not acknowledged receipt of the German newspapers he had sent him. He nevertheless plodded forward, using his spare moments constructively. With his abundant energy he found time, according to a report in the Chicago *Herald,* to form a drill corps of the boys living in his neighborhood, "so they would spend less time on the streets" and thus combat juvenile delinquency. He often dissipated his energies in this manner, and consequently was only an average student at Kent, though curiously he achieved a grade of one hundred per cent in medical jurisprudence. He graduated in ceremonies held at the La Salle Street Association's Auditorium, May 20, 1899, the lone Negro, with no well-wishers, in a class of seventy, and was awarded a Bachelor of Laws degree.

Robert S. Abbott never was admitted to the Illinois bar.

His legal dream, if he held one, quickly evaporated. Anxious for counsel as to the most acceptable city in which to take his initial step, he could hardly have gone to a more competent person than Edward H. Morris, a prominent Negro attorney who had white clients mainly. But this fair-skinned gentleman told him, Abbott reported, that he was "a little

too dark to make any impression on the courts in Chicago."
He bundled up his belongings and went to Gary, Indiana.
Robert's unfamiliarity with this city and his unobtrusive appearance militated against his employment as counsel. Petty
suits dealing with debts, wills, mortgages, foreclosures and
divorces were yet far in the future for most Negroes, and,
though he struggled and searched, fees, even small ones, were
not to be found.

He soon headed for Topeka, where he talked with Nick
Chiles, politician and editor of the *Plaindealer*, who in effect
said he would starve to death as a Kansas attorney. He returned to Chicago discouraged, but with him brought a contract to handle the local distribution of the *Plaindealer*. This
project proved none too lucrative, so he did a little job printing like the convention report of the National Negro Business
League when it met in the Windy City. Through the intercession of Louis B. Anderson, a powerful Negro politician, he
was given a job in a Loop printing house that did the city's
work. Anderson threatened to use his influence to halt the
city giving any further business to the plant unless Abbott
was hired. Under this direct political pressure, the company
relaxed the rules against Negro hirings, but gave Abbott the
tedious work of setting type for railroad time tables, with
the proviso that what mistakes he made had to be corrected
on his own time without pay.

Yet he was able to exult in a letter to his mother, "Things
are beginning now to look bright for me," because he figured
he could now earn about twenty dollars weekly as a printer.
His imagination suddenly began to soar and he wrote to his
old teacher, Miss M. F. Sherman, asking her to send him the
story of Toussaint L'Ouverture, leader of the Haitian Rebellion and founder of the Black Republic. But the death of his
stepfather, June 23, 1904, of nephritis was to sharply alter his
plans. Rev. John H. H. Sengstacke, fifty-six years old when
he died, was buried in the colored section of Laurel Grove

Cemetery. He had traveled a long and flinty road. The inventory of his estate reveals that he left a house, barn, buggy, a horse and several pieces of Woodville property, insurance and a newspaper. The estate was worth about $5,000, but not liquid. He had done his work to the best of his ability, never submitting himself to the dictates of the crowd and not making his own intelligence subservient to the ignorance of the multitude. If he had not become a beloved figure, he had made the resolve, taken the responsibility, and bequeathed a legacy of service to his people.

Robert S. Abbott had lost his greatest source of intelligent advice and strength. His letters, and indeed his frequent public statements, bear abundant testimony to the love and veneration which he felt for the old man, and to the influence the latter had exerted over him. Robert, deeply saddened, attended the funeral but had to borrow fifty dollars from his cousin, Thomas Abbott, for the return trip to Chicago. His next step was to try to memorialize his stepfather's name and work, and he wrote to Dr. Frissell, now principal of Hampton, "I have accomplished my work here in this city at law and have now decided to return back to the South and enter my life's work doing what I can to help my people both from an educational standpoint and in the way of giving them legal advice." He added that he was soliciting funds for a school he planned to start in Woodville, and asked his old teacher to put him in touch with any influential white people he knew.

The Pilgrim Academy had disintegrated with Rev. Sengstacke's long illness. Robert's brother Alexander, who had attended Atlanta and Talladega universities and become an ordained minister, had recently resigned his post in the public school system as a teacher in protest against the introduction of dancing, dramatics, games and story-telling for children, and now was ministering to his father's flock at Pilgrim Church. So Robert decided to carry on his stepfather's educational work. With himself as president, and his sister

SENGSTACKE MEMORIAL

Military and Mechanical Academy.

FOUNDED 1901.

Term Opens Thursday, Sept. 15, Woodville, Savannah, Ga.

R. S. ABBOTT, L.L.B., . . . **President.**
REBECCA SENGSTACKE, . . **Principal.**

This school is situated three miles West of Savannah and about a quarter of a mile from the termination of the West End Car, which makes it convenient for city children to attend. Arrangements are being made with the managers of the West End Co for fares and all children living in the city may come at reduced rates. All students are required to wear uniforms, girls as well as boys; in this way it saves money to the parents of the child and gives to the school a better appearance than it would otherwise have. The school prepares its students for college, for the United States Army and Navy; also to enter immediately upon their trade at Hampton. Special instructions for Civil Examination, Short-hand, Typewriting and Music, both instrumental and vocal.

Be it remembered that the scope of the courses is such that no limitation are set upon the students ambition. All the young men are expected to drill.

TERMS.

Academic Course, $10.00 per year. | Grammar Course, $5.00 per year
Scholarship (will educate a boy or girl for a year) $25.00

All students are required on entering the Academy to pay a part of the years tuition. Those in the Academic Classes must deposit with the Principal $5.00; those in the Grammar Classes $3.00. And in January after the Christmas Holidays the rest of the tuition must be paid. All students failing to meet these requirements will be dropped from the roll. No reduction for students entering the school late in the term.

Address Mail to **R. S. ABBOTT, L.L.B., 3159 State St., Chicago, Ill.,**
Or to **MISS REBECCA SENGSTACKE, Gen. Del., Savannah, Ga.**

Announcement of the Proposed Academy in Woodville

Rebecca as principal, he established the Sengstacke Memorial Military and Mechanical Academy in the old quarters of the Pilgrim Academy, and ambitiously offered courses for boys and girls preparing for college, plus shorthand, typing and music, both vocal and instrumental.

But in the midst of these preparations from distant Chicago, he decided once and for all that he should own a newspaper and that the place to launch it was the big city. Though history would confirm the choice as a happy one, his selection disappointed the Sengstacke family. Luckily for him, his personal revolt found itself aligned with the forces driving Negroes along new paths, so that his refusal to accept the pleas of his mother, brother, sisters and neighbors to return to Woodville spelled success instead of martyrdom.

80

I wanted to create an organ that would mirror the needs, opinions and the aspirations of my race.—
ROBERT S. ABBOTT, Chicago *Defender*, 1930.

CHAPTER VI

Notebook to Newspaper

WHEN HE CONCEIVED the idea of publishing the Chicago *Defender* there were nearly 40,000 Negroes living in the city—indeed, a Negro, Jean Baptiste Pointe de Saible, was the first permanent settler sometime in 1790. Yet a European historian and traveler, arriving in the city in 1891, remarked that "the severity of the climate repels the Africans." But when Abbott trudged into the metropolis, buoyed up only by ambition to accomplish something noteworthy, not only was a Negro community well established, but the area was rapidly developing the characteristics of a colored corral. This section, a hodgepodge of frame and brick houses, was sandwiched between a well-to-do white neighborhood and a so-called "shanty Irish" fringe, and was ultimately to become Chicago's "Black Belt."

A few Negroes had managed to attain some prominence and wealth, and a handful possessed well-established businesses catering to a white clientele. John Jones, first Negro to hold public office in Chicago, was prospering as a tailor in a building of his own in the heart of the city. Charles H. Smiley, a caterer whose son, J. Hockley, was to become Abbott's first paid employee, was laying up a small fortune staging Gold Coast affairs. No one had forgotten the spectacular achievements of Dr. Daniel Hale Williams, who founded Provident as the first Negro hospital in Chicago and afterwards became the first American surgeon to operate successfully on the human heart (1893).

The atmosphere of success and progress perhaps dazzled the young migrant and caused him to report somewhat inaccurately to Hampton's magazine, the *Southern Workman*, that he was practicing law and was employed as a printer on the Chicago *Daily News*, when in fact he was doing piecework for job printers. Albert G. Barnett, now the *Defender's* editorial coordinator, remembers Abbott in his unemployed hours setting type to perfect his technique in the print shop of his father, Ferdinand L. Barnett, who edited and published a newspaper, the Chicago *Conservator*.

By now, Abbott had joined the Choral Study Club, and thus was becoming a part of an evolving community life, erected upon the narrow economic base of domestic and personal service work. This life centered mainly around twenty churches, a dozen or so lodges, and a few social, sports and cultural clubs. But Abbott was excluded from the emerging social élite, made up of a few business and professional men, politicians and the dignified domestics of the white rich. The paternal interest of such prominent men as George Pullman, P. D. Armour, Gustavus Swift and Potter Palmer, traditional up to 1900, was now coming to an end, and Negroes were beginning to develop a "racial self-reliance." Under the impact of new aspirations, Negroes started a drive for wider employment opportunities, and indeed were vocal in assailing discriminatory bars; and they started, too, the quest for political power. What apprehensions Negroes may have had centered primarily around the influx of foreigners, whom they feared might take their jobs as butlers and maids, janitors and waiters. Even so, Abbott, along with the other Negroes, was caught up in the rapid growth of the city and could see green pastures ahead.

The Georgia migrant had lived among these people nine years now, and had become a familiar figure along State Street. "He talked to any and everybody, and seemingly had the touch of the common man," one oldtimer recalls. "Whenever anyone wanted to find him, he merely had to walk along this stretch, and he was sure to run into him." People quickly recognized him by the clothes he wore almost with the regularity of a uniform: a black derby hat, white shirt, white tie and a blue suit, threadbare and turning green. In winter he added a skimpy overcoat lined with paper. If his shoes were run over at the heels and he often had to fill holes in the soles with cardboard, he nevertheless gave the appearance of neatness.

He afterwards wrote somewhat painfully, "It was not often I found work. I would go hungry and probably would have starved to death but for the generosity of some folk who would loan me a dime now and then. Even when I did work, I did not earn enough money to pay back rent, repay loans and eat three meals, too. Consequently I was always broke. Such was my experience during the early days of struggle in Chicago."

Abbott lodged with a Mrs. Henrietta P. Lee, a motherly widow with three children, who regarded him with the affection of a son. She was to become his most dependable friend and, perhaps, in the process helped to keep his newspaper alive. He now had lived in her second-floor, gas-lit apartment more than five years and occupied a small, rear room with a brass bed, a chair and an oak chiffonier. The flat was situated in a red-brick, three-story building with white stone trim, at 3159 State Street. Below was a music shop, and next door a white club devoted to crap-shooting; and nearby was Hugh Hoskins' saloon which was to become the hangout of the *Defender's* staff, though Abbott himself never frequented the place. From in front of Mrs. Lee's door, he would take the horse-drawn streetcar daily to hunt work, and punctually return evenings to take his meals, especially when she had prepared boiled dinners.

Now thirty-seven years old, his character and habits seemed clearly defined to people who knew him then. They say he was sedate and dignified, lived quietly, almost ascetically, and was somewhat introverted. He did not drink, smoke, play cards or gamble. Nor did he ever swear. He rarely laughed, and only infrequently smiled, though he was capable of a droll humor. He was a friendly person, but not the kind to find a brother in every man. He often found himself confined to the loneliness of his room, and in those moments he felt the separation from his family keenly. He never entered the saloons, poolrooms or night clubs that abounded in the area until he became a publisher, and then only for business purposes.

He avoided the camaraderie of drinking and carousing companions. Nor did he take part in sports of any sort, but he sometimes attended the dances at the Lakeside Hall, frequented by the respectable people. Oliver A. Clark, whom Abbott called "Georgia boy," says his inclinations were such that "He never mingled with low class people. He always sought to be with the top people." His tidy moral ways soon created an aura of piety and spirituality about him though he was not a religious man. But he distinctly impressed people as a man with a mission. Henry D. Middleton, a post office employee who was friendly with him, nails down this mission as "a burning, consuming ambition to establish a newspaper to express his views on the race question."

What few people knew then, and he only revealed when he became a success, was that he had repeatedly received rude jolts to remind him he was black—repetitions of his experiences in the South that caused him to recognize the limitations for a black man even in a northern Negro community. For example, he had boldly sought a place in the choir of Grace Presbyterian Church which he had joined in 1898. The congregation was largely made up of "Old Settlers," a term meaning Negroes mostly born in Chicago and fair complexioned, who placed a premium on refinement and gentility. These people were far from enthusiastic about the arrival of southern Negroes, even though they eventually would profit by the expanding Negro market and the black electorate. They declared that these "uncultured elements" had made conditions worse for Negroes in Chicago and had disturbed the nice balance between the white and Negro communities.

Actually, the southern Negro's ebullient presence profoundly altered the relationship between Negro and white residents of the city, and indeed changed the basic economic and social structure of the Negro community. Consequently, when Abbott sought admission to Grace Church's choir, his application was rejected, not only because he was dark-skinned but mainly because he was southern-reared and a migrant of recent vintage. Class prejudice was operating more so than color prejudice, but Abbott declared that he was barred because he was black. Though, years later, he was to sing in the choir and become an esteemed church member in the eyes of the pastor, Dr. Moses H. Jackson, his early belief that the congregation drew the color line gave impetus to his need to achieve and gain respect. It was indeed in no sense an ignoble passion, and his ambition never caused him to swerve from his principles.

Robert S. Abbott soon recognized that he would not prosper as a printer, nor did he consider printing an occupation that would bring him money and status. He himself explained that he was not interested in the trade as such. He already had confided his ambition to his Hampton classmate "Bung" Thornton, "I want to run a newspaper someday!" Thus, one evening early in 1905, he confided his plans to publish a newspaper to a few friends, including Mrs. Lee, Henry Middleton and James A. Scott, a lawyer. He had been talking about a paper for more than five years and bent anyone's ear who would listen. Soon after his graduation from law school, he had tried to persuade a group to join him in launching such a project, and even had sent word to his old Hampton classmates that he was about to start a big print shop and newspaper, and held out the prospect of jobs for them as printers. When this failed, he took a flyer on his own with a daily newspaper that collapsed after two or three issues. The papers apparently were consigned to the trash can as no copies exist today.

When he announced the new venture many people laughed, even ridiculed the idea. As yet, no one had recognized his imagination as talent, nor his aptness for gathering rumor and hearsay and weaving them into stories, which he often did to the delight of his friends. They only saw the obvious: that Abbott was no master of the King's English; that when he spoke he split verbs, fumbled his tenses, and dropped his final consonants. Clark's sympathetic estimate was seemingly the popular one: "Mr. Abbott was fairly intelligent, above average, but his English was poor, sounding much like a southern dialect." His friends frankly said that his future as an editor was none too encouraging.

As a final crusher, they pointed to the three already existing Chicago newspapers—Julius C. Taylor's *Broad Ax*, S. B. "Sandbag" Turner's *Illinois Idea,* and Ferdinand L. Barnett's *Conservator*—which had achieved little monetary success, and were primarily vehicles for the editors to expound their views, punish opponents, and advance their personal political ambitions. Besides, there were two well-established and well-edited organs published elsewhere and read in Chicago—the Indianapolis *Freeman,* edited by George L. Knox, and the New York *Age,* edited by T. Thomas Fortune—which exerted considerable influence in the Negro community and seemed to have the field covered between them.

Journalism was a distinctly unprofitable venture.

Richard W. Thompson wrote rather sadly in 1902: "It's a stinging indictment of our much-lauded 'race pride' that the greater proportion of our Negro journalists are compelled to depend for a living upon teaching, preaching, law, medicine, office-holding, or upon some outside business investment."

Even though the prospects of success were dim, Abbott declared he would still publish his own paper, and confessed to his friends that he was so far along with his plans that the only obstacle now was an attractive name. His oft-repeated pledge that his paper would be a defender of his race made Scott suggest "The Defender"—and thus, with Abbott adding the word "Chicago," the paper acquired the name that was to become a torch to thousands.

Between stints as a job printer, he furiously made plans for publication. He called on a Harry Robinson, who operated a flat press in a small shop at 3436 State Street, and made arrangements for printing the paper. When Abbott pleaded poverty, Robinson reluctantly agreed to payment after sale of the papers, but cautioned that failure to meet the obligation meant disaster. Abbott then rented desk space from George W. Faulkner, who had real estate and insurance offices on the second floor of a loft at 2935 State Street, with the promise he would take Abbott's messages. The future publisher moved in equipment consisting of a folding card table and a borrowed kitchen chair. His total capital was twenty-five cents, which he used to buy notebooks and pencils; and his total manpower was himself, though Mrs. Lee's teen-age daughter Genevieve offered to help after school.

Soon he was hurrying to the Institutional A.M.E. Church, where the weekly rehearsals of the Choral Study Club were being held. The group, led by Professor Pedro T. Tinsley, formed a choir of 150 voices in which Abbott sang tenor. Between numbers, he announced his plans to publish the *De-*

fender, as he never lost an opportunity to test public opinion, even in the most casual contacts. The group liked Abbott as a man but had little confidence in him as an editor and publisher, and they loudly disparaged the idea. Beyond earshot some called him a "crazy fool," but Abbott had shrewdly sized them up as future readers and news sources, and promptly whipped out his notebook and proceeded to pump them for information and gossip. He returned to his office late that night and wrote up his gleanings.

The first weekly issue of the Chicago *Defender* appeared on the streets May 5, 1905, an appropriately balmy spring day on which the thermometer reached 68° Fahrenheit. The initial printing was three hundred copies and cost $13.75. The first paper does not exist, though the *Defender* was to be published continuously without missing an issue for the next fifty years. The earliest one extant is dated September 16, 1905, and only pages one and four are readable. This paper, actually handbill size, was a six-column, four-page sheet (sixteen by twenty inches), undoubtedly a replica of every preceding issue. The format and style closely resembled old Rev. Sengstacke's Woodville *Times,* and the masthead of subsequent editions carried the legend: R. S. Abbott, LL.B., founder and editor.

The paper contained a balanced typographical makeup, which gave the impression of symmetry and order. With an eye on his competitors, Abbott ran a streamer boastfully announcing the *Defender* as "The Only Two-Cent Weekly In the City." The front-page contained no banner headlines, but carried the two big stories of the week with two-column heads supported by four decks. The lead story, with sub-heads and pictures of Dr. George Cleveland Hall and Dr. George C. Williams, was two columns long and jumped to page two. The heads, which pretty much summarize the whole story, ran thus:

CHICAGO PHYSICIANS HAD
ONLY TWO REPRESENTATIVES

AT THE RICHMOND CONVENTION, DRS. GEORGE
C. HALL AND WILBERFORCE A.
WILLIAMS

CHICAGO'S PROGRESSIVE MEN

The Public Will Do Well to Keep Their Eyes on
Men Who Will Spend Their Money For Deeper
Research and Newer Information.

The West Virginia Advocate Gave a Most Glowing Account of
the Meetings and the Wonders of Our Own George C.
Hall—Dr. Kenney, a Hampton Man, and Head Physician at Tuskegee Institute, Won Praise

The second big story, of identical length, type and sub-
heads, balanced the page with:

AFRICA, THE LAND
OF MILK AND HONEY

A TRUE HISTORY OF OUR FATHERLAND—MR.
SIDNEY H. ARNETT, OF ROYSVILLE,
LIBERIA, AFRICA.

INTERVIEWED BY A CHICAGO DEFENDER'S
REPORTER

He Gives Below Full Details of That Great
Country and How the White Man Is
Fighting Over That Land.

Africans Have a Watchword, "Africa for Africans," Which Is
Being Interpreted in All Tribal Languages—Mr. Arnett
Gives The Defender Great Praise and Says He Will
Get It in Every Home in Liberia from
the President Down.

Little in this *Defender* gave promise of the ebullient organ it was to become, an organ that would revolutionize the Negro press of the country. He packed the paper with names, for he already recognized that "names make news." The items used were undoubtedly newsworthy in the small Negro settlement of that day. Unlike its competitors, the *Defender* gave the impression of being a paper of impersonal journalism. Not one story carried a byline, and there were no columnists. The emphasis seemingly was placed on the paper's service to the community and Negro achievement, though the story about the doctors' meeting was a transparent plug for his friends, Dr. Hall, who was Booker T. Washington's personal representative in Chicago and consequently wielded considerable influence; and Dr. Williams, who later conducted the paper's popular health column.

If Negroes had problems of a social or racial character, they were not apparent in the *Defender;* nor were there any accounts of accidents, suicides, murders, trials or incidents of racial discrimination, lynching or conflict—sensational news which was eventually to distinguish Abbott's journalism. Political news and editorials were ignored. What stories he published were filled with clumsy diction and heavy sentence structure, a vice of the era. Except for the two articles above, all stories were of a local nature with label heads, but in volume they represented considerable legwork for one man.

This, then, was the content of the infant *Defender:*

Under the crossline head, DR. AUTER OF PROVIDENT, a paragraph complimented a young physician who had been a Loop doorman and now had passed the State Board examinations. A NOTICE TO THE PUBLIC announced that John Irwin was no longer connected with the Southern Upholstery Company, and anyone doing business with him "does it at their peril." Willis Tyler, THE MAN WHOM ROOSEVELT HONORED, was visiting Chicago and the paper remarked that the Harvard graduate had been labeled by Theodore

Roosevelt "as the coming light of the 'Nation,' mark you, not the race, but the nation." Mrs. Rosa Richardson, "wife of our scientific dentist," was weighed and found that THE TRIP DID HER GOOD. Next to this was an obituary in verse, and a report of Miss Frances I. Bonner's ten-day visit with Miss O. Rankin in which THEY DID THINGS UP BROWN.

Abbott's landlord, Mr. Faulkner, addressed the Colored Businessmen's League, and this was duly reported under the caption, ST. MARKS LITERARY. He naturally found space for a nice paragraph about THE CHORAL STUDY CLUB, but the prominently displayed story of Mrs. Emma Pilgrim, "Only Woman of Race In Successful Grocery Business in Chicago," bore her picture and the strong scent of advertising. Abbott neatly interpolated a little promotion into the story, MRS. J. H. CARR RETURNS FROM MEEKER, COL., when he reported her as "an ardent reader of the *Defender* [who] says she looks for her little paper just as eagerly as she does for a letter from her best friend."

The edition was not without humor of sorts. Under the head, POLLY TOOK HER VACATION, Abbott reported on the front-page: "On last Monday while Mrs. Staten, 2700 Armour Avenue, was busy cleaning her house her parrot stood on its perch complaining of the heat. 'Say, Mamie, take me out of this kitchen! Say, give me a fan, woman! It's too devilish hot in here for me!' With this expression Polly left her perch, jumped to the window, and did not stop flying until she reached Mrs. Simpson, at 2451 Wabash Avenue, where she stayed until last Saturday when the *Defender's* reporter located her. When Polly returned home, she cried, 'Say, Mamie, how is the temperature?'"

The bulk of the paper's humor was allocated to a back-page department called OUR BUDGET OF FUN, illustrated with cartoons which carried "Jokes and Jokelets that Are Old, Curious and Laughable." This is a sample reprinted from the Cleveland *Leader:* "'Your money or your life,' growled the footpad. 'Take my life,' responded the Irishman, 'I'm saving me money for me old age.'"

Page four carried nearly eighty per cent advertising. The space rate, according to Abbott himself, was "as much or as little as an advertiser wanted, at his own price." There were thirty-seven ads, essentially services rather than commodities, averaging one-column in width and one-inch in depth. Together, they perhaps served as a useful directory of Negro business. Beyond the variety of Negro occupations shown, the ads also reflected the urban character of living among migrant Negroes. The ads ranged from "nicely furnished rooms to rent with toilet, gas and bath," to "Imperial sachet powders," and included a butcher, lawyer, undertaker, physician, two tailors and a moving man, as well as a dancing academy, dance band, cornet instructions, three hotels, bath rooms, two barbershops, three night clubs, a confectionery store, a restaurant and a shoe shine parlor.

Accompanying these, were offers of "easy payment" plans.

Mr. R. W. Johnson, wearing a fuzzy mustache, a checkered coat with black velvet lapels and a high stiff collar with a big jeweled stickpin in a flowered tie, looked out from his oval-shaped picture and asked the world to "Chew Yalu Cream De Mint Gum" which he manufactured. The news columns were tied in with the advertising page in two apparent instances. For example, Mrs. Mamie Staten, whose parrot rated a front-page story, carried advertising of furnished rooms for rent, and the Southern Upholstery Company, which had a public notice on the front-page, bought a deep, two-column ad. The big advertiser was Charles Ford, whose display ad occupied considerable space down in the corner of the page and announced a "Wonderful Discovery." He sweepingly claimed that his "elegantly perfumed" product, FORD'S ORIGINAL OZONIZED OX MARROW, was "the only safe preparation in the world that makes kinky or curly hair straight, soft and beautiful." The ad carried a before-and-after illustration as proof.

The *Defender's* printing and folding did not end Abbott's labors for the week, for he had no established arteries of distribution and no newsboys as yet. His first regular newsstand sales did not begin until 1912, when a Mrs. E. E. Claytor, organist of the Choral Study Club who had a newsstand at 35th Street under the elevated railway, approached him with a proposition: she offered to sell forty copies of the paper if he would carry a report of her aunt's death. He seized the opportunity of selling that many papers in one swoop, and published a fulsomely written obituary. Mrs. Claytor exceeded her promise by ten, and was afterwards persuaded to carry the paper regularly. She thus became the *Defender's* first newsstand agent with a quota of ten papers a week.

Until then, Abbott was his own newsboy.

His first customers were the members of the Choral Study Club, and every week he carried a bundle of papers to sell at rehearsal. Rain or snow, slush or mud, he carried a load the length and breadth of the community ringing doorbells and peddling the paper. Nights he visited every south side barbershop, poolroom, night club, saloon, drugstore and church, indeed anywhere Negroes assembled, selling papers and gathering news and advertising. He often was made the butt of coarse jokes, but he merely turned his head aside. Yet he had a voracious appetite for knowing and understanding these people well, and thus, in the process of hustling about the city and rubbing elbows with these people, he learned a good deal about the Negro community, and was able as well to keep his fingers on the pulse of the mass man.

Even so, the paper only limped along and in a few months was about to collapse. Harry Robinson threatened to stop printing the paper unless Abbott paid up his indebtedness. The publisher quickly recognized that he would have to cut his overhead to keep the paper afloat. He already had made every personal sacrifice—he spent no money on entertainment, allowed himself not even the luxury of a new suit, and every day he lunched on fish sandwiches and bottles of pop. Unable to meet the printer's bill and pay rent to Mr. Faulkner, he accepted Mrs. Lee's offer to use her dining room as an office. The address of the *Defender* now changed to 3159 State Street and remained so for the next fifteen years. From the day Abbott moved, the paper seemingly prospered. This may be the reason he always referred to the location as the home of the *Defender,* and held the site with much sentimental affection, even to representing it as the original birthplace in official versions of the paper's founding. When he eventually expanded, rather than move he rented the second and third floors of the building. He frequently said 3159 State Street had been "lucky," a superstition that embraced the woman who had taken him and his little newspaper to her bosom.

A word about Mrs. Henrietta Plumer Lee. According to Henry B. Middleton who knew her well, "she was unschooled and a caterer, but she recognized in Abbott someone who shared her ideals for the race. Abbott sold her on the need for a newspaper to champion the cause of Negroes, and she afterwards did everything to help him succeed. She expected nothing in return. She had reward enough in the fact that Abbott allowed her to participate in the project." Had Mrs. Lee not taken the *Defender* into her home in all likelihood the paper would have folded. For she not only underwrote office space, but she actually fed Abbott, frequently supplied him with carfare, often patched his shabby clothes, and gave him encouragement. The year before the *Defender's* launching, he had an attack of double pneumonia which the doctors thought might prove fatal, and she had nursed him back to health by wrapping him in red flannels and feeding him onion stews. For the next four years he made only token payments toward his rent and food. The telephone, which she made available to him free, remained in her name for many years after the paper was established.

The *Defender* became a family concern: Mrs. Lee's daughter, Genevieve, took Abbott's messages and performed such chores as running to the printer with copy and later became a regular staff member; her son, Benote, often loaned Abbott five or ten dollars from his post office earnings to help pay the printer. Mrs. Lee herself even permitted Abbott to paint a sign on the transom of the front door designating the place as: THE CHICAGO DEFENDER. He himself said she would always "set a pot aside to allow me to work in the kitchen." Abbott was deeply grateful—so much so that when he started to make money his first thought was of her: he bought an eight-room, brick dwelling at 3112 Vernon Avenue at a cost of between $3,000 and $4,000 and presented her the deed as a gift in 1918, perhaps the first such gift he gave anyone; and he made her son a stockholder in the Robert S. Abbott Publishing Company.

He himself followed her to the new house as a lodger.

The *Defender* was still largely a one-man operation, with Abbott tediously learning by rule-of-thumb. But in 1906 his sister Rebecca, demonstrating a family loyalty that characterized the Sengstackes, left her work as a Woodville school teacher and arrived in the city to help her struggling brother. She assumed the job of proof reading and running errands, and lifted many of the routine duties from his shoulders. Though he assured "Georgia boy" Clark, "I'm going to make it," he actually was so uncertain about the project's future that when Rebecca's school principal wrote and offered her a permanent position, Abbott urged her to accept the sure thing and she returned to Woodville. And he attempted to solve his monetary problems as his journalistic colleagues had, by seeking a political appointment.*

Before long, Abbott published a two-column picture of Republican Governor Charles S. Deneen on the front page and praised him, along with Sheriff Nellis, for having "successfully averted another lynching in Cairo, Ill." and for having supported the Illinois anti-lynching bill. He unabashedly reminded his readers that they "should not forget them at voting time." How serious he was about a political appointment, is suggested by a letter he wrote his mother: "I am doing all in my power to make a man of myself," he said. "I am trying to get an appointment as Assistant Register of the U. S. Treasury. Don't mention this to anyone for it may hurt my chances. I have friends working for me." He presumably meant Governor Deneen and Booker T. Washington (through Dr. George Cleveland Hall), who was head of the Republican administration's "Kitchen Cabinet" and consequently dictated all Negro federal appointments. Abbott predicted that he would be so well fixed that his mother "would be able to see all of this great country before you lay me down to sleep."

His toadying never paid off, and Abbott learned a profound lesson about practical politics. He abandoned the political arena for the time being, except to urge the election of a Negro alderman in Chicago. Negroes had no representation in the city council, and Abbott ran articles that demonstrated a common sense approach, albeit racial, urging the man-in-the-street to exercise his right to vote. In these pieces he often struck the high note of patriotism that afterwards characterized his every utterance. For example, under the head, DO YOU WANT A COLORED ALDERMAN?, he wrote: "Don't think because you are working in that lunch

---

* Ferdinand L. Barnett (*Conservator*) already had been appointed assistant state attorney; S. B. Turner (*Idea*) was a state senator; and Julius C. Taylor (*Broad Ax*) had been on and off the public payroll for years.

counter downtown, or that hotel over there, or running on the road, that you are exempt from the effects of whatever laws may be passed. You have got to live under them and abide by them the same as anyone else, whether you like it or not. Then wake up and take hold of your privilege as a citizen of this great country and have a voice in what is done either for or against you."

With his press run now a thousand copies weekly, he shifted his editorial direction, and now had adopted the slogan: "If You See It in the Defender, It's So!" Imperceptibly, the slant of the paper turned toward uplifting and educating his readers, though he never omitted writing up small items like the ragman's having bought new tires for his cart. Even the fillers published were calculated to broaden and inform, and consequently he carried such non-racial items as a report about the Paris floods, Chicago's high cost of living, elections in England, and one about "Prince Henry of Germany superintending the preparations of an arctic exploring party." But not until he launched his first muck-raking crusade did his paper actually begin to catch on with the public, and eventually outstrip his competitors.

Chicago had the reputation of being a "wide-open" town whose citizens were undisturbed by graft in the city government and by alliances between politicians and the underworld. Following two great Chicago fires, the city's Red Light district took refuge in the Negro neighborhood, which was largely untouched by the fires. When the city was rebuilt, the Red Light district remained among Negroes and expanded with the area's growth. William T. Stead, an English journalist, had already published an explosive book, *If Christ Came to Chicago,* giving names and addresses of places where prostitution was carried on—it started a controversy which lasted for the next seventeen years.

The exposé created a sensation in the white community, but started a battle in the Negro neighborhood between those who believed in a legal Red Light district and those who believed it should be abolished. The struggle, in which Abbott was to join those opposed to prostitution, involved the entire Negro community, as many Negroes made a living directly or indirectly from a wide-open town. The Chicago Vice Commission reported in 1909 that the growing Negro population had never managed to outrun the continuously expanding Red Light district. It also revealed that the great majority of the employees in the "resorts" catering to white clientele were Negro men, women and children. The commission held that the most exclusive "houses" were situated in the Negro neighborhood, and the reformers exhorted Negroes to clean house.

Robert S. Abbott responded by launching his own campaign. One story will illustrate the manner in which the *Defender* performed. The paper carried this sensational head:

MOTHER TAKES INNOCENT DAUGHTERS TO HOUSES OF ILL FAME

The story, which contained the anti-climactic sub-head, "To Play Piano," luridly reported that girls between fourteen and nineteen years old were actually put to work in "the red light district of Chicago." The paper then asked: "Are our women societies like Phyllis Wheatley Club, going to sit idly by and let womanhood be trampled under foot, or are they going to join hands in the holy war of the protection of the 'unknown' black slaves." Abbott discovered a racial angle which he could exploit. "The police department," said the *Defender*, "through the pull of white men of means, removed all the colored men piano players because the white girls in these places thought too well of them; therefore the colored girls were used as piano players and turned into prostitutes."

The puritanism of the missionary-reared editor had found, if only temporarily, a spiritual home; and found, too, a crusade he could happily strike against sin. Consequently, week after week the *Defender* in editorialized stories demanded an end to the Red Light district. The conservative Negro leaders accepted the assignment, but the more militant ones refused to admit complete blame for vice in the Negro community— indeed, according to Cayton and Drake in *Black Metropolis,* one prominent Negro minister declared himself a "firm believer in the segregation of vice," but accused a prominent white pastor of trying to widen the boundaries of the Red Light district at the expense of the Negro community. The white minister was charged with a desire to push "the boundary lines of vice beyond his own bailiwick" in order to prevent "a large exodus of his parishioners to a locality less honeycombed with dance halls, brothels and saloons. The Negro, like the whites, does not care for his wife and daughter to elbow the Red Light denizens."

When Booker T. Washington publicly urged Negroes to wipe out vice, a Negro civic leader retorted: "A good deal of the vice in the 'colored belt,' is the white man's vice, thrust there by the authorities against the protest of the colored people." Not until 1912 were the reform forces able to abolish the Red Light district. Prostitution went underground and the Negro community never was able to live down the stigma. But this campaign led Abbott directly into his racial crusades, for he had learned many profitable lessons during the campaign. A significant one, perhaps, was that Negroes respond to a rousing fight, especially if underscored by a racially high-minded purpose. More important, however, was his discovery that with the close of the Red Light district the *Defender* suddenly had no first-rate issue to exploit.

Abbott afterwards handed down the dictim: "Never choose a campaign you can win!"

Many people helped Mr. Abbott because they felt they were somehow helping their race.—FRANK "FAY" YOUNG, Chicago *Defender* sports editor emeritus.

CHAPTER VII

The Recruits: Porters, Waiters, Barbers and Hoofers

THE MAN had a remarkable appeal for many different sorts of people, and this fact drew them to his side during the infancy of the *Defender*—people ranging from Jesse Binga, a huckster who became president of a bank, to saloonkeepers and intellectuals. It may be they recognized Robert S. Abbott as a man of incorruptible racial idealism. Whatever the reason, Henry "Teenan" Jones, a Negro saloonkeeper, was one of those who firmly attached himself to the publisher. He himself had been born black and a slave in Alabama, and perhaps felt an affinity for the black "Georgia boy." He was brought to a small town in Illinois when he was eighteen months old. At the age of sixteen he came to Chicago, which meant trying to make a living against the great odds of inexperience and racial prejudice.

He learned quickly, and in 1895 he was well established with a saloon and gambling place in Hyde Park, where he ran games of dice, roulette, draw and stud poker. Everything went well until in 1910, when he was driven out by the Hyde Park Protective Association, which sought to make the area an exclusively white residential section. He then opened the Elite Cafe in the Negro settlement, four blocks from the *Defender* office, and again flourished. "Teenan" Jones was a patron of Negro theatricals and athletic contests. He soon embraced the *Defender*, and afterwards the cafe's cash box always had ten dollars if Abbott needed all or any part of it to help pay the printer. He often engaged the busy publisher in long conversations, while a meal was being prepared, to force him to eat. For "Teenan" Jones, touched by Abbott's ambition, also respected the racial purposes of his black landsman's enterprise.

By now, Abbott had left Harry Robinson's small shop and contracted with the Chicago Newspaper Union, a white publishing house, for a four-page "boiler plate" sheet, for which he had only to supply the news. This scheme produced a sharp reduction in his overhead. The company tendered a bill October 3, 1908—to illustrate—itemized thus: composition, $6.04; makeup, $2.40; 1,000 copies, $4.50; and time on mailing list, 15 cents, which came to a total of $13.09. Even so, the paper was not earning enough for Abbott to pay himself a salary. The masthead listed the staff—actually unpaid helpers—as R. F. Spriggs, assistant editor; L. N. Hogatt, cartoonist; and H. H. Byron, theatrical editor. But the *Defender* was still a one-man show, and Abbott had to seek assistance from a variety of people.

For example, he turned to his lawyer friend, Louis B. Anderson, who had done some reporting and had been a publicity man in connection with the World's Columbian Exposition of 1893. He often helped him with the editing and preparation of articles; Henry D. Middleton, between his post office chores covered commencements, political meetings and socials. Julius Nelthrop Avendorph, a Fisk University graduate and president of the Columbia Baseball Club, reported sports. Eventually young men and women who shared Abbott's racial idealism and needed an outlet for self-expression joined the *Defender* and contributed their services free. They were compensated sufficiently merely by being identified with the paper, for each in his way perhaps felt he was performing a race duty.

Middleton says, "Never once did Mr. Abbott give me carfare or even a cigar, or reimburse me for stamps, paper and etc., in the course of my work for him." Perhaps, in the beginning, Abbott took the help offered for granted—after all, he was a product of a missionary background. In any case, Abbott was not wanting for helpers. For instance, Noah Thompson, a Negro who worked in the morgue of the Los Angeles *Express,* sent Abbott anything he could lay his hands on concerning the Negro in his part of the country. Howard Drew, a Negro intercollegiate sprint champion at the University of California, was making headlines in the daily newspapers, and Thompson would clip the coast stories and send them to the *Defender* publisher. Fon Holly and Langston Mitchell, a young artist competent enough to hold a position at the Chicago *Evening American,* both contributed cartoons gratis, simply because it gave them an opportunity to comment on racial subjects.

Alfred "Alf" Anderson, crippled and hunchbacked, took time from his duties as superintendent of Provident Hospital, to write the blistering editorials. W. Allison Sweeney, a free lance writer and former editor with a vitriolic pen, produced the tirades against the anti-Negro politicians and in the process developed a considerable following. Frank P. George, a New York Central dining car waiter, supplied the bulk of the newspapers from which the staff culled out-of-town news pertaining to Negroes. At the end of each run, he brought to the office bundles of papers and magazines he had picked up during his regular trip from Boston to Chicago. He often enlisted the help of the Pullman and railroad porters, who gathered up the newspapers and periodicals left behind by passengers. So that the *Defender* would not be without a weekly supply,

George persuaded a crony, Alexander O. Taylor, a parlor car attendant, to bring in papers when he was at the Boston end of his trip.

To understand this collective behavior, we must try to grasp the meanings of the Negro press; and grasp as well the social factors operating in the background. To begin with, the Negro press was already a firmly established institution in the U.S. when the Chicago *Defender* stepped upon the stage in 1905. The fact is, Negro newspapers have been a vital though largely unseen force since 1827—when the first one, *Freedom's Journal*, edited by Samuel Cornish and John B. Russworm, made its appearance in New York City.

It was a four-page weekly which served, as the editors expressed it, "to hook together, by one solid chain, the whole [Negro] population so as to make it think, and feel, and act, as one solid body." The *Journal* was of necessity an organ of propaganda. Only "strange necessity," said the publishers, compelled them to emphasize the racial aspects of the Negro's problems. The editors, to be sure, were impatient to end human bondage at a moment when high-minded people were gathering for a mighty assault on slavery. Yet they shocked the country by reprinting the pamphlet of David Walker, a Bostonian who called upon the slaves to rise in revolt against their masters.

The paper died in 1830, but twenty-four Negro periodicals appeared before the Civil War. Many were published so seldom or irregularly that they can scarcely be described as anything but pamphlets or handbills. A few titles will suggest the temper of the times: *Mirror of Liberty*, the *Alienated American*, the *Colored American*, the *Elevator*, and the *Rights of All*. The most famous was the *North Star*, edited by Frederick Douglass. These publications found themselves without a cause toward the close of the conflict, and the end of the

Negro press was clearly in sight. But the assassination of Lincoln alerted them to the new problems ahead.

The post-war assumption of political power by the anti-Negro "poor whites" of the South demanded a vigorous voice in public affairs. Meantime, the white Northern leaders, who had so ably championed the cause of Negroes before the war, now turned their attentions to the rush for dollars, and left Negroes to work out their own destiny. As Negroes sized up the situation, a Negro press was an urgent necessity to combat the rapidly mounting anti-Negro sentiment and to unify the black population for aggressive counter action. At the close of the century, when the status of the Negro as a citizen was steadily declining, Negro newspapers had not only become numerous but they had become a formidable entity, and Irving Garland Penn, a Negro editor, wrote their history in a book called *The Afro-American Press*.

By 1910, according to the Atlanta University Negro Conference, there were two hundred and eighty-eight Negro periodicals in the U.S., with at least one in every city with a considerable Negro population. These papers had a combined circulation of roughly a half million. The actual number of readers was undoubtedly far in excess of this figure. Every literate Negro read at least one Negro publication. The millions living in poverty, rural isolation and illiteracy in the South, often had one person read a paper aloud in places like barbershops and churches and followed this with group discussions. Papers frequently were passed from hand to hand. The spectacular decrease in illiteracy among Negroes was a natural boon to the Negro press: the percentage dropped to 44.5 in 1900, and to 30.4 in 1910, with a coincident increase in economic competence.

Tradition decreed that the Negro press should be biased to the Negro's cause. Consequently, rare was the paper that made a pretense at objectivity—perhaps the logic of its very existence compelled the Negro press to be such an instrument. At any rate, Negro newspapers wielded an influence in American life far beyond the imagination of most white people. The modern newspaper, ushered in with the founding of the *Defender,* soon rivaled the Negro church in influence, and today has pretty much stolen the show, unencumbered as it is (and was) by religious dogma; or, for that matter, by rigid party lines.

Even so, the Negro press leaned toward the Republican Party, and generally followed the conciliatory course of Booker T. Washington. Until the advent of the *Defender,* Negro newspapers were vehicles for personal journalism, as illustrated by the papers conducted by Abbott's early contemporaries: Nick Chiles' Topeka *Plaindealer,* T. Thomas Fortune's New York *Age,* William Monroe Trotter's Boston *Guardian,* George L. Knox's Indianapolis *Freeman,* and William Calvin Chase's Washington *Bee.* But they prepared the stage for Abbott by cleaving close to the line of race rights and originating the idea of "race loyalty."

Not until the *Defender* assumed its inherited role as an organ of racial propaganda, did it leap into prominence. This development followed the hiring of J. Hockley Smiley in 1910. He performed the work that today approximates that of a managing editor, though he held no such title. Smiley, a slender, brownskin dandy troubled with hacking coughs, was a gifted newspaperman with perhaps a touch of genius. He was born in Chicago, graduated from high school, and had had little previous newspaper experience, but he tackled the problems of the *Defender* with imagination and skill. Before his arrival, the paper had operated on a hit-or-miss basis. Middleton, who was present at the paper's birth, believes "Abbott was so enthused with his mission that he formulated no definite plan or policy for his paper. But imbued as he was with a passion for the rights of Negroes, a passion amounting to fanaticism, he was able to transmit this passion to his associates."

Smiley, who wore a handle-bar mustache, proved a perfect foil and helped Abbott transform the paper from a "boiler plate" sheet to a standard weekly. Utilizing Abbott's ideas, he began by frankly copying the front-page styles of the Chicago daily newspapers, especially introducing something of Hearst's techniques of yellow journalism. Then the publisher had him change the format; second, adopt banner headlines; third, treat the news sensationally; and fourth, lay emphasis on the concerns, fears and aspirations of the rank-and-file, which were dear to his heart. Abbott's competitors frowned at this new departure in Negro journalism, but the *Defender's* use of sensational headlines printed in red ink, for which it has since been remarkable, made circulation jump with leaps and bounds.

A few headlines will illustrate the new presentation of the news:

100 NEGROES MURDERED WEEKLY IN UNITED STATES BY WHITE AMERICANS

NEGROES MARRIED TO OCTOROONS MUST LEAVE LOUISIANA

JIM CROW CARS RUNNING OUT OF CHICAGO DEPOT

LYNCHING—A NATIONAL DISGRACE

WHITE GENTLEMAN RAPES COLORED GIRL

GOOD WHITE PEOPLE OF GEORGIA? DASTARDLY LYNCHING THIS WEEK SAMPLE OF BOASTED INTEREST

WHITE MAN TURNS BLACK IN ST. LOUIS

There perhaps was provocation enough for such headlines.

Negroes had hardly forgotten the summer of 1908, when they were shocked by a two-day race riot in Springfield—capitol of Illinois and home of Lincoln. The wife of a street-car conductor loudly claimed she had been dragged from her bed and raped by a Negro whom she identified as George Richardson. Before a special grand jury the woman changed her story: she admitted she had been beaten by a white man whose name she refused to disclose and confessed that the Negro had no connection whatsoever with the incident. Nevertheless, white men ran amuck. Frustrated by Richardson's protective removal from the local jail to a nearby town, white mobs surged through the city killing, burning and pillaging. One Negro, eighty-four years old and married to a white woman thirty years, was hanged from a tree within the shadow of the town hall. Before order could be restored by 5,000 troops, scores of Negroes had been killed and wounded, many driven from Springfield. Nearly two hundred arrests were made, but not one white man was convicted even of disturbing the peace.

The refugees turned up in Chicago.

But let us look again at Smiley.

He was a drinker of prodigious proportions and a newspaperman in the classic mold of the period. "From his vivid imagination," Middleton reports, "came lynchings, rapes, assaults, mayhems and sundry 'crimes' against innocent Negroes in the hinterlands of the South, often in towns not to be found on any map extant. If there was a dull week in the quality and quantity of news, he would fortify himself with jiggers of gin and simply manufacture stories"—so inflammatory in fact that galley proofs often came back from the printer with the notation: "Our women proof readers refuse to handle this copy!" He was not above perpetrating a hoax now and again. For example, one day Roscoe Conkling Simmons, a famed Republican orator, but often a wayward character, borrowed money from Abbott to pay his railroad fare to a speaking engagement in St. Louis, Missouri. Simmons promised to return a day or so later to repay the loan. Middleton recalls that "One week, two weeks, three weeks went by and no Simmons and no money, and Abbott casually complained to Smiley." The next edition of the paper carried the following streamer across the front-page: COL. ROSCOE CONKLING SIMMONS DIED SUDDENLY IN ST. LOUIS—adding in small type below, "other papers please copy." It was a "scoop" for the *Defender* and every Negro newspaper reprinted the story. When Simmons read his obituary he hurried back to Chicago somewhat chastened and promised repayment. Abbott, with a twinkle in his eye, reprimanded Smiley for his sly wit.

Yet with all his flamboyance, Smiley could give a human touch to mundane stories. He once tantalizingly reported this item of progress on the front page: "Mr. Mose Samuels has installed an electric telephone in his home." Then he quoted Mr. Samuels as saying that he was tired of standing up to talk at the telephone, "so he had a desk phone put in with an extension at his bed, so when he is resting he will lay down and talk to the boys when they call up." The story closed with, "He is planning to put in a fireless cooker for the summer."

WHAT'S THE MATTER WITH SAMBO, a racially irreverent headline asked. The story, written on Abbott's specific instructions, ran as follows: "Rev. Chas. Nelson Granderson, [Negro] who lectured at Bethel Church on Monday evening to a fair audience, would have made a great hit if he were in the South, but in Chicago, where at all colored gatherings there is always a sprinkling of white, that kind of lecture won't do. The reverend gentleman should have been told this fact. Quite a number of these colored churches are saved from the auction block by white people and we cannot afford to have such affront hurled at them as was done on Monday evening."

Smiley, in the language of today, was essentially an "idea

man" with, as Middleton observed, "an enthusiasm for his work that was unsurpassed by Abbott himself." Not long after his arrival, Abbott had him departmentalize the loosely organized paper, creating theater, sports, editorial and society departments, a structure until then unknown to the Negro press. For example, Julius Nelthrop Avendorph, a prominent figure in Negro society who had been writing sports, was made the *Defender's* first society editor and a sort of black Ward McAllister, a position he was to hold until his death in 1923.

Not long after his famous hoax, Smiley was scanning the front-page of the Chicago *Tribune* as Abbott walked into the office. He greeted him with: "Look, chief, the 'world's greatest weekly.'" Now, in those days the *Tribune's* reporting of stories involving Negroes was irritating to the community, but Abbott decided at once that the *Defender* would henceforth be described as "The World's Greatest Weekly" —and the slogan was afterwards incorporated into the masthead of the paper.

Among his innovations, Smiley discarded the terms "Negro" and "Afro-American" to describe the race in the *Defender*. These terms were used universally by the Negro press, and Abott had complained that they were meaningless. What to call themselves has plagued Negroes to this very day. Early in its career, the Negro press attempted to settle this knotty problem—that is, should the race be referred to as "Negro," "Colored," "Afro-American," "Aframerican," "African," or plain "Black." If white people often were in doubt as to the acceptable form, so too were the Negro writers and public speakers. Absence of color made one *white*, obviously; so for nearly two centuries American Negroes called themselves merely "people of color." The Dutch, Spanish and English settlers leaned towards "black"—hence the term "Negro," which means black. Jupiter Hammon, a slave on Long Island, New York, and the first Negro poet in America, addressed himself to "Negroes" in 1786, but this term did not have real currency until the years before the Civil War. Sometimes "African" was used by Negroes but was discarded when schemes were advanced to colonize Negroes in Africa.

T. Thomas Fortune, editor of the New York *Age*, excluded "Negro" from his vocabulary because of the disagreeable connection with the word "nigger"—which perhaps is the clue to this tempest in a teapot. He is credited with being the originator of the term "Afro-American," which was adopted by the Baltimore *Afro-American* newspaper. But Smiley, to satisfy Abbott's dislike of the word "Negro," established a style sheet that excluded "Negro," "Afro-American" and "Black" altogether, and instead used "Race"—thus "Negro business" became "Race business," "Negro men" were "Race men," "Negro achievement" was dubbed "Race achievement," and the group was labeled "The Race." Sometimes Smiley used "Colored," which, of all the terms, had the nice sound of respectability and refinement. Today the adjective "colored" and the generic designations "Negroes" and "Negro," used currently by the *Defender*, are considered acceptable terms, but the use of "negress," and "negro" in lower case—and of course "nigger"—is unforgivable.

Perhaps Abbott was indulging a peculiarity, but with his unfailing instinct for that which was deep in the hearts and minds of Negroes, he struck a chord that caused sympathetic echoes. He afterwards explained the use of the term "Race" this way: "We use that as a bridge, as you might say, which we intend to blow up pretty soon. We are leading the people away from the word 'Negro,' especially in our paper. And in cases where white men are well known in the country we never put 'white' after their names. We never put 'colored' after a colored man's name in this city."

Negroes had few popular heroes in those days, but Smiley made the most of Jack Johnson, Negro heavyweight cham-

pion of the world. When he was scheduled to meet Jim Jeffries, a former champion, at Reno, Nevada, July 4, 1910,
Smiley exploited the coming battle to the hilt. The Negro
with the golden smile was good copy, but more important to
the Negro editor was the fact that the fight caused considerable excitement and had stirred emotions among Negroes.

Jack Johnson had come into prominence by winning the
title from Tommy Burns in 1908, and almost immediately a
frantic search began for a "white hope" to dethrone him.
Jeffries, then past thirty-five, was goaded into coming out of
a well-deserved and prosperous retirement to meet the Negro. A large section of the white press had whipped up the
sentiment that the security of "white civilization" and "white
supremacy" depended upon the Negro's defeat.

Smiley, with about the same amount of restraint, told his
readers, "If J.J. wins his battle, it can be said that he is really
the best man on earth." When Johnson was arrested for speed-
ing, he commented acidly: "Why not arrest the man who
built the auto for speed violation instead of the innocent pur-
chaser. Then Jack would go free." And when Johnson had
legal difficulties because his dog bit a man named Pinder, the
Defender saw an attempt to "persecute" the champion.

Feeling ran high among Negroes, for they knew the crack-
ling hostility Negro prize-fighters met. Consequently, Smiley
ran a three-column-wide cartoon on the front-page, clearly
calculated to exploit this feeling. It was an excellently drawn
cartoon by L. N. Hogatt and carried this boxed head: HE
WILL HAVE THEM ALL TO BEAT. Jack Johnson, mus-
cles rippling, was shown standing in a prize ring shaking
hands with his white opponent, Jim Jeffries. The legend below declared: "The future welfare of his [Johnson's] people
forms a part of the stake." The cartoon had men seated at
the ringside bearing signs inscribed with "Jim Crow Dele-
gates." A bearded white man, with the face of a devil and
resembling Uncle Sam, stood directly behind Jeffries. He was

represented as "Public Sentiment," and was saying to the white fighter, "We're with you this time—go ahead." Alongside Jeffries, as opponents of the Negro, stood three ghostly gladiators called "Race Hatred," "Prejudice," and "Negro Persecution."

The Texas-born champion was not an attractive character, if measured by conventional standards. He was, though, a product of a boisterous and rowdy era, and as such, one of its gaudy expressions. He drove about recklessly in big high-powered automobiles, wore flashy clothes, spent money lavishly, and generally led a fast life. Trevor C. Wignall, the famous English sports writer who looked at Johnson more dispassionately than Americans, found him to be no better and no worse than other boxers. But Johnson's behavior offended many people, both white and Negro. Perhaps it was his sense of humor that carried him over many of the rough spots in his rather stormy career. Yet his conduct brought him disfavor, even persecution, and increased prejudice towards his race. His marriages to white women were not helpful—virtually identical bills against inter-racial marriages were introduced in Wisconsin, Iowa, Kansas, Minnesota, New Jersey, Michigan and New York. Similar bills were introduced in Congress, with penalties varying from imprisonment to enforced castration. Yet Smiley, indulging in a bit of black chauvinism, declared: "If more of our men were as considerate of our women as Jack Johnson is, what a great race of people we would be!"

When the two men finally squared off in Reno, the *Defender* reported that Negroes were "all agog"—indeed they were agog and present in large numbers at Chicago's Coliseum where "illuminated electrical figures nine feet high re-enacted every move and blow on an electrical board." No *Defender* reporter covered the fight, simply because there was no money for railroad fare, but Smiley announced on the front-page that the paper would receive reports via "special private wires from the ringside"—a statement that was sheer fiction. (Actually, he planned to quiz Negroes who saw the fight and rewrite the reports of the dailies and give them a racial twist.) Then the paper commented: "If he [Johnson] is forced to fight Jim Crow Delegations, race prejudice and insane public sentiment—and if he wins in the face of all this, he is truly entitled to a Carnegie Hero Medal." The *Defender* finally assured Negroes that "When the smoke of the battle clears away, and when the din of mingled cheers and groans have died away in the atmosphere, there will be deep mourning throughout the domains of Uncle Sam over Jeffries' inability to return the pugilistic scepter to the Caucasian race."

The Negro won handily, but the rejoicing was short-lived as Negroes were attacked by white mobs in various parts of the country. Mob passions reached such a point of violence and destruction that Congress, to forestall further incidents, passed a law prohibiting the interstate shipment of moving pictures of prize-fights.

J. Hockley Smiley was paid ten dollars weekly as a salary, but he rarely drew more than five dollars, and frequently he received no pay at all—indeed, paydays were always a deathless agony for Abbott. What Smiley collected was often dissipated in Hugh Hoskins' saloon nearby the office. Yet his drinking seemingly interfered in no way with his efficiency as an editor. His needs were modest: as a single man, he paid one dollar a week for a furnished room, and whenever he was broke and hungry the saloon's free lunch counter satisfied his appetite. He eventually developed the habit of pocketing monies paid the *Defender,* and of afterwards heading for Hugh Hoskins' bar to splash it up in drinks. Abbott patiently admonished him about this practice and, failing to remedy the situation, was forced to hire a cashier. It was thus he employed his second paid worker—Bessie Boykin Rayford, a trained nurse, who became the bookkeeper, telephone opera-

113

tor, information clerk and secretary as well as watchdog of the paper's finances; evenings she sometimes worked as a social reporter.

Momentarily infuriated by what he considered Smiley's faults, Abbott failed to acknowledge his value in a tangible way when his editor became gravely ill of pneumonia. He thus became involved in his first open conflict with a rival paper. Before Smiley died in 1915, "Sandbag" Turner, who edited the Illinois *Idea*, belabored Abbott editorially for being miserly and ungrateful. Abbott ignored the charge in the columns of the *Defender*, but Turner had a field day until Abbott finally came to Smiley's aid. Incidentally, this incident started the legend of Abbott being a penurious person. But a few years later, the *Defender* ran a front-page, two-column picture of Smiley described as "In Memoriam," acknowledging his contribution to the paper's growth. In Abbott's words, "He was a man who never watched the clock."

Frank Withers succeeded Smiley. He in turn was followed by Carey B. Lewis, who had learned the fundamentals of newspaper work under Colonel Henry Watterson, editor of the Louisville *Courier*. But Abbott, doing leg-work daily, stood firmly at the helm. He never relinquished the leadership or title of editor, though he afterwards was to often express his personality through his associates. He was sufficiently secure in his position to give the imagination of his editorial employees full play, and consequently attracted many talented people. Frank "Fay" Young, who worked for the paper for nearly forty years and became the dean of Negro sports writers, was one of these. He asked to join the staff in 1912, and Smiley had explained there was no money to pay a salary, but any contributions would be gladly accepted. Fay Young, now sports editor emeritus, had had some experience writing for the Indianapolis *Recorder*, and Smiley put him to work writing sports.

He meantime was regularly employed as a dining car waiter on the Chicago & Northwestern Railroad, and had a schedule that allowed him to give a good deal of time to the paper. "Five days a week," says Young, "I reported at the railway station at six o'clock in the evening. The train left for Minneapolis at 6:30 P.M. on my regular run. The diner was cut off at Milwaukee, thus giving the crew a good night's sleep. We left Milwaukee the following morning early and arrived in Chicago at 9:00 A.M. That gave me five days all day at the *Defender* office, plus the days and nights I was off. I received no salary. I expected none. I paid car fares to cover assignments out of my own pocket, sometimes even paying Mr. Abbott's. Not until 1914 did I receive any money, and then much to my surprise Mr. Abbott handed me three one-dollar bills to show his appreciation."

Wherever Fay Young went, while traveling as a dining car waiter, he would clip the newspapers and mail them back to Abbott. Sometimes he sent them directly to Smiley. Whenever the work piled up and the staff had difficulty meeting deadlines, Young would volunteer to help. As the paper expanded and picked up circulation, the *Defender's* personnel needs increased and by 1915 Abbott found himself seeking help. The loose, mostly unpaid organization was not dependable. He asked Fay Young to resign from his railroad job and work for the paper, but Young was reluctant because Abbott offered him only fifteen dollars a week, less than he earned as a dining car waiter; moreover, joining the *Defender* meant a reduction in social status, as railroad men were among the sought-after figures in Negro society, and newspapermen were considered merely hustlers. Negroes employed by the railroads had the big paying jobs of that day, and Abbott's standard of pay was set by the salaries Negroes earned as post office employees. Even so, the staff regarded themselves as adequately paid, as no one then thought of Negro journalism as professional work.

Young, who now conducts the sports column "Fay Says," was finally persuaded by his ambition to be a newspaperman. The manner in which he solved his financial problems was afterwards typical of those who joined the *Defender*. "When ends didn't meet," says Young, "I did extra work. There was the post office during the Christmas holidays and extra work week-ends as a waiter at the Palmer House and Edgewater Beach Hotel, thanks to headwaiters John Webb and Albert G. Barnett." His decline in income soon caused him to fall behind in the payments on a typewriter he had purchased on the installment plan. He offered the machine to his boss on condition that he pay off the balance. Until now, all copy was written in longhand, so Abbott quickly agreed, and thus did the *Defender* come into possession of its first typewriter. Before long Young's salary was upped to eighteen dollars weekly, and he became the editor of the first sports page in Negro journalism.

One morning early in the spring of 1916, by some freak accident, a letter addressed to *Overton's Monthly Magazine*, a Negro publication, was delivered to the *Defender's* office. Young, presuming it the paper's mail, opened the letter and discovered an application for a job, signed by one Lucius Clinton Harper. He described his abilities as a typist, and added that he owned a typewriter. The twin qualifications made him a good prospect, and Young wrote across the top of the letter in a memorandum to Abbott: "What about this young man?" The office needed a secretary who could type, so the applicant was invited in for an interview.

Harper, a barber by trade, was of fair enough complexion to pass as a white person—so fair in fact that when in later years he attended a reception for President Truman at Chicago's Blackstone Hotel as a *Defender* representative, and a picture was being arranged showing prominent Negroes seated with the President, Harper was gently drawn from the group by a Secret Service agent with the remark, "This is for Negroes only!" His color clinched the *Defender* position for him, as Abbott concluded that he could be used to cover stories in places where those visibly Negro might be barred. He eventually developed into an outstanding figure in Negro journalism, became executive editor and conducted a column, "Dustin' Off The News," which was one of the most widely read features of the Negro press. Like Smiley, he was an idea man and was credited with many significant innovations. Except for a brief period with the Chicago *Whip,* he remained with the paper until his death in 1952.

He was born in 1895 in Augusta, Georgia, son of James S. and Ellen Harper. He was educated at Haines Institute, Atlanta; Fisk University, Nashville, Tenn.; and Oberlin College, Oberlin, Ohio. He began his career as a printer's devil on the *Georgia Baptist,* a religious publication, and later contributed articles to the Indianapolis *Freeman,* New York *Age* and Cleveland *Gazette.* Harper afterwards became an advance man for a minstrel troupe, "Down In Dixie." While working as a bellboy at the Press Club of Chicago, he rubbed elbows with the newspaper greats of his period and there developed the ambition to be a journalist himself.

The mulatto editor was unsurpassed as a teller of tall tales, and his humor was legendary. Harper was also a voracious reader of books and a student of Negro history, and had a phenomenal memory for names, dates and places. He often was described by his associates as "a walking morgue." Possessed of a pixie sense of humor, he delighted in baiting such well-known figures as Westbrook Pegler, and the late Senator Theodore Bilbo, who incidentally once offered a reward of $1,000 to anyone who nabbed him on the soil of Mississippi. One early associate, P. L. Pattis, now executive editor of the Pittsburgh *Courier,* describes him accurately as "the lovable raconteur who despised work."

The description could well serve as his epitaph.

Fortunately for the *Defender,* Abbott still was not satisfied with either the quality or content of the paper, and he consequently continued his search for bright young men in a field distinctly limited. Abbott thus employed Sylvester Russell, who could review theater doings with a critical scorn that outraged stage folk, to contribute articles. And finally, he brought in Phil A. Jones, a youngster whom he regarded with the affection of a father, to work after school as copy boy and handyman. Phil afterwards became route man and finally rose to general manager, a position in which he contributed considerably to the prosperity of the paper.

As a group, these people embraced Abbott and his ideas and, though emerging from varied backgrounds, they seemingly had a talent for the give and take of teamwork. Abbott himself was gifted at teamwork, for he had the necessary self-control. Consequently, the *Defender* developed an atmosphere of camaraderie, in which each one assumed personal responsibility for the progress and success of the paper. Nights when they were correcting galley proofs, they often chipped in ten cents apiece to buy meat and vegetables for supper. Fay Young did the cooking, using Mrs. Lee's gas range, pots and dishes. If Abbott happened to be out while the cooking was in progress, they always prepared enough for him. Bessie Boykin often brewed tea to wash down the vittles. Upon Abbott's return they would all sit down like one family to eat. Afterwards they would gather around the potbellied stove in the parlor and discuss the *Defender*.

The publisher carefully observed the social amenities, but he never allowed them to deflect his concern from the operations of the paper. Nor did this friendly atmosphere become so chummy that he ever lost control of his men. The fact is, they never hurdled his aloof, dignified manner. No matter how provoking a situation, he never angrily upbraided anyone. Fay Young says, "Mr. Abbott often went on the warpath whenever a deadline was missed or the presses were late in starting a run." But he never made a direct criticism, nor did he ever give a direct order. He gave utterance only to suggestions and observations.

His approach to a problem was always indirect. This, perhaps, was a vestige of his rearing in the South, where Negroes rarely can make frontal attacks on a problem; if they do, they do so at the pain of reprisals. In Abbott's case, the indirect approach became habitual and as much a part of his character as being a teetotaler. For example, one night he returned to the office late to discover his staff down on their knees shooting craps. He never said a word of reproof; instead, he scribbled a note on the back of an envelope, which was a characteristic of his, and next morning handed it to his managing editor—in effect, he had gently but firmly announced that there was to be no more crap shooting in the *Defender* office, and that ended gambling on the premises and closed the incident.

Whenever his staff disagreed with the slant of an editorial written by "Alf" Anderson or anyone else, Abbott would slip away for a few hours and return with one written by W. Allison Sweeney or someone else. Bypassing his managing editor, he would send it to the printer himself with "R.S.A. MUST" scribbled across the top. Abbott's "MUST" afterwards became famous as the final word—indeed, an eleventh commandment.

Fay Young recalls that "Nothing that he ever sent to the printer, or notes he ever made on backs of envelopes and read off to you for stories, no names he had jotted down, did he ever forget. Once the paper was off the press, even in his late years, he would sit down and carefully go over the paper, column by column, to see if the news he gave you was there.

"When the *Defender* became a standard-size paper, he found plenty of room on the margins to make notes. Such notations as 'no sense' or 'no first name' or 'no address' would apppear. But the things he made the most of, were those he noted with *Adv.*, followed by a question mark. This meant in Mr. Abbott's mind that someone had been paid for an article." For, by now, the *Defender* was charging for the insertion of special personal items: "Wedding announcements, $1.50; wedding write-up, $5.00 and up; card of thanks, $1.50 and up; in memoriam, $1.50; business announcements, $1.50 and up." And these were payable in advance.

The "old man" was especially a stickler for accuracy, because experience had taught him that every correctly spelled name and every correct fact produced a potential buyer of the *Defender*. Consequently, until the day of his death, he was admonishing the editorial people against loose and inaccurate reporting with, "Don't put that trash in my paper!" But what he actually thought of the young staff he had assembled was contained in a letter to Emmett J. Scott, Special Negro Assistant to the Secretary of War during World War I, asking their deferment under the draft law.

"I have for the past eight years," Abbott wrote, "battled unceasingly for such a group of men as I now have surrounding me. You can easily realize what a trial it is to find competent, reliable and trustworthy newspapermen among our people. My efforts have been rewarded. I say with absolute certainty that they are highly trained newspapermen, have labored long to perfect themselves, and are succeeding beyond all expectations. For these men to be unceremoniously divorced from my service would mean a severe blow to my publication."

With drops of ink, we make millions think!—ROBERT
S. ABBOTT, Chicago *Defender*, 1916.

CHAPTER VIII

The Printed Page, Racial Style

SAID THE *Defender:* WORLD WEEPS FOR
WASHINGTON.

This banner head heralded Robert S. Abbott's first "extra,"
which appeared in 1915 announcing the death of Booker T.
Washington, one of the most influential and widely known
Negroes in the United States. This circumstance coincided
with the launching of a standard-size newspaper, described
extravagantly as "the only eight column, eight page Race paper published in the world." But the noisy fanfare did not
conceal the subtle fact that the death of the Tuskegee educator, whom the publisher admired inordinately, marked the
passing of a period of patience, moderation and conciliation
among Negroes, a development that was to be loudly and
insistently emphasized in the pages of the *Defender*.

No Negro emerged with sufficient prestige to counsel the
race as Washington had done. Nor was the Negro temper
one for conciliation. Black reaction rode hard in the nation.
Negroes had long been the victims of almost daily violence
somewhere in the country. Girls had been flogged for allegedly crowding white folks in streetcars, and boys beaten for
accidentally riding bicycles on sidewalks. Any attempt to use
public parks caused bloodshed, and Negro communities had
been "shot up" by white men on drunken sprees. Before a

Extra **Chicago Defender** Extra

SUNDAY, NOVEMBER 14, 1915

Booker T. Washington

DEAD !

1:23 Sunday Morning at Tuskegee

Full Particulars in Saturday's Paper

The *Defender's* special announcement of the death of
Booker T. Washington.

122

cheering mob a Negro had been publicly burned in Texas; a Negro farmer had been killed for refusing to sell cottonseed at a price fixed by a white man in South Carolina; and nearly three thousand white people had witnessed the burning of "a live Negro" upon the invitation of a newspaper in Tennessee.

To be exact, 1,100 Negroes had been lynched prior to the death of Washington.

The Negro now reached a new turn in his history but was bewildered what direction to take. The *Defender's* publisher was faced with a choice of two distinct methods of meeting the situation, for two main streams of Negro thought were then current on ways and means of solving the Negro's problems. The views of one highly articulate group had been, and continued to be, symbolized by the recently deceased Booker T. Washington. For the second group, equally articulate, the symbol was another Negro of national fame, W. E. B. Du Bois. Beyond the psychological insights revealed, the significance of the position Abbott eventually took lay in the fact that the *Defender* was rapidly becoming the most influential and widely read Negro newspaper in the country. To grasp fully the meanings of his choice, we must recall briefly the significant differences between the two leaders—differences that had their roots in background and education and stirred the entire Negro community in the United States.

Booker T. Washington, principal of Tuskegee Institute, had assumed leadership of the Negro following a memorable speech in 1895 at the opening of the Cotton States Exposition in Atlanta, Georgia. He soon was acclaimed as the economic emancipator of his people—a mighty leap from a slave childhood. The cardinal principle of his philosophy was to make the Negro into an efficient worker. To raise the Negro's economic standards and win the white man's respect, he had encouraged Negroes to become independent by establishing businesses and learning trades. "In all things purely social," said Washington in his famous Atlanta address, "we can be as separate as the five fingers and yet as one as the hand in all things essential to mutual progress."

With this one stroke he succeeded in winning the approval and support of the influential white people, both North and South. He became the leader of not one race, but two—a conciliator between the white and black, between the North and South, and in the process demonstrated extraordinary statesmanship. Eventually he could dictate the rise and fall of Negroes occupying political and private positions controlled by whites, and few Negroes dared criticize him in public or let it be known that they were not in sympathy with his work and philosophy. His leadership of a liaison group, which functioned in an advisory capacity to Federal officials and became known as the "Kitchen Cabinet," cemented his strategic position.

But the Negro press gave him very little personal publicity. Eulogistic articles written by his secretary, Emmett J. Scott, were often turned down and critical comments published instead. Especially vocal in opposing him were Trotter's Boston *Guardian* and Fortune's New York *Age*. The Tuskegee educator made a drive to capture the Negro press. Through the aid given by his well-to-do supporters to financially shaky papers, he gained control of a large section of the press and commanded wide publicity. For example, when he was priming his personal representative in Chicago, Dr. George Cleveland Hall, for an appointment as head of Freedman's Hospital, a government institution, he wrote him thus: "Send me your best photograph and a sketch of your life, and put in the most prominent and successful operations you have performed. I can use this in a way to be of great service." Hall speedily replied, and within a few weeks articles describing his success as a physician appeared in thirty-five papers.

Not until 1903, when W. E. B. Du Bois made a reasoned attack upon Washington's conciliatory philosophy, did his opponents have a figure of national stature around whom to rally. Du Bois, already the author of a distinguished book, *The Souls of Black Folk,* was educated at Fisk, Harvard and Heidelberg. He had spent two years in Berlin and returned to his homeland wearing gloves and carrying a cane. He accepted a teaching position at Wilberforce University, Xenia, Ohio, and later the University of Pennsylvania employed him to make a study of the Negro in Philadelphia. As a professor at Atlanta University, Georgia, he continued his scientific study of the Negro.

His racial philosophy in a nutshell was this:

The Negro would be saved by its exceptional men. This group he described as a "Talented Tenth," or educated élite. "The best and most capable of the youth," he declared, "must be schooled in the colleges and universities of the land. . . . Not too many college-bred men, but enough to leaven the lump, to inspire the masses, to raise the talented tenth to leadership." He labeled Washington's speech in Georgia as the "Atlanta Compromise," because the Southern leader had pursued tactics of accommodation and had distinctly asked Negroes to surrender political rights, civil rights and higher education. When the National Association for the Advancement of Colored People, today the most powerful organization championing the cause of Negroes, was formed in 1909 he was called to edit the group's mouthpiece, the *Crisis,* which he eventually turned into a personal organ. Du Bois, bearded, ornate and scholarly, became a towering figure through sheer force of his ideas and afterwards exercised tremendous influence among Negroes.

Robert S. Abbott stood aloof from the conflict until the *Defender* had solid footing, though Dr. George Cleveland Hall had needled him to take a position in support of Washington. But not so his competitors in Chicago: both Taylor's *Broad Ax* and Barnett's *Conservator,* kept alive mainly by contributions, succumbed to Washington's blandishments. Maybe Abbott was jolted into a position by remarks about his idol like J. K. Vardaman's: "I am just as opposed to Booker T. Washington as a voter, with all his Anglo-Saxon re-enforcements, as I am to the coconut-headed, chocolate-colored, typical little coon Andy Dotson who blacks my shoes every morning. Neither is fit to perform the supreme function of citizenship."

Whatever the reason, Abbott's deep-seated convictions were slow in coming to the surface and taking concrete form. When he finally moved, he arrived somewhere between the two giants of the Negro community. His was essentially a pragmatic position. Thus, while Washington urged Negroes "to cast down your buckets where you are"—meaning remain in the South—Abbott cried: "Come North, where there is more humanity, some justice and fairness!" And while Du Bois sought to create a "talented tenth," or educated élite, to lead the race, Abbott declared himself "for the masses, not the classes!"

He had, in effect, chosen to articulate the aspirations, fears and grievances of the rank and file and oppose the aristocratic tendencies and intellectualism of Du Bois; and oppose, too, the conciliatory and patient course of Washington. He advocated the unity of Negroes. He opposed divisive conflict between Negroes—all so that the race would be able to face the white community with a common front. He ultimately formulated a "platform" which became the *Defender's* "bible." His enumerated policies, which are published below the masthead to this day, were:

1. American race prejudice must be destroyed.
2. The opening up of all trade-unions to blacks as well as whites.
3. Representation in the President's Cabinet.
4. Engineers, firemen and conductors on all American railroads, and all jobs in government.

5. Representation in all departments of the police forces over the entire United States.
6. Government schools open to all American citizens in preference to foreigners.
7. Motormen and conductors on surface, elevated and motor bus lines throughout America.
8. Federal legislation to abolish lynching.
9. Full enfranchisement of all American citizens.

Briefly: his nine-point "platform" meant the end of segregation and complete equality for the Negro in American society—in a word, integration—a position which went beyond that of both Du Bois and Washington. His codified policies gave a rallying point for action. In this sense he led public opinion, and Negroes now turned to Abbott for guidance.

His demands seem tame today, but then people regarded them as radical. Even so, he simply sought to accelerate the evolving society. He had, in fact, a diamond-hard patriotism, for he deeply believed that to be born an American citizen was to be part of a really good thing—like being born into a rich and powerful family. To him, the United States was the fabulous land of rags-to-riches, and in letters to his mother he repeatedly promised he would make enough money for her to travel and see "this great, big beautiful country." But his vigorous racial policy was a measure of Abbott's ability to accurately reflect the mind of the rank and file, and it paid off in rapid growth.

Perhaps he understood Negroes because he was so thoroughly a Negro himself—one might say the Negro saw his image reflected in the *Defender*.

This must be coupled with the background. Feeling among Negroes was negative to the white dailies. They felt those organs could not be trusted to tell the truth about the Negro. They believed that many deliberately placed the race in an

unfavorable light. The Associated Press was particularly excoriated for a policy of discrimination in favor of whites and
against blacks. It was true that in reporting developments in
the South, the stories collected by this syndicate were frequently written by people who belonged to the community
where the news originated, and it perhaps was natural that
such news should reflect the facts as seen by the white people
in that community. Negroes were not so naive as to presume
things would be otherwise; but the slanting of news involving
them frequently approached the point of propaganda.

Apart from the Associated Press, there were specific charges
against local newspapers, both North and South, which in
substance were these: when anything evil was reported, the
race (or nationality) of the culprit was mentioned only when
he happened to be a Negro, and then, indeed, his race was
emphasized. Rarely was anything praiseworthy said about
the Negro; in fact, the race was generally ignored. Abbott, in
his droll manner, often repeated the story Booker T. Washington used to tell with amusement of having spoken to a
large white gathering in a small town and of having picked
up the local paper next morning expecting to see a report of
his speech prominently displayed; instead he found an inch
or so on the back page. He had made a successful address, but
much of the front page was given to a Negro who had made
an *unsuccessful* attempt to snatch a woman's purse.

The principle operated in pronounced form whenever there
were conflicts between whites and blacks, especially race riots.
Consequently Negroes looked more and more to their own
press to fight their news battles, even, indeed, to apologize
and defend their wrongdoing. This may be the reason that
Negro crimes against whites were generally found to have
extenuating circumstances by the Negro press, viewed as
they were against the whole social background. But there
was neither pussyfooting nor ambiguity in the *Defender*

whenever incidents involved crimes against Negroes. For example, in 1916 the Tenth Cavalry Regiment, an all-Negro outfit, was moved to the border in a punitive expedition against Mexican bandits believed to be led by Pancho Villa. They had made bloody forays into Texas that outraged the nation. Major Charles Young, a West Point graduate, was sent along. Young, incidentally, was the brother-in-law of Louis B. Anderson, Abbott's close friend. This was a fortunate fact for the *Defender*. Through this pipeline, Abbott received eyewitness accounts when twenty-two Negroes of the Tenth Cavalry were killed in Mexico. When the regiment returned to its station in Houston, Texas, its members met the open hostility of the civilian population. The *Defender*, sensing trouble, warned that the racial manifestations might blaze into race riots.

These stories proved sensational.

But what caused Abbott's excitement to mount—and this is an interesting psychological sidelight—was the fact that somebody had told him on good authority that Pancho Villa was a *Negro*, and none other than H. O. Flipper, a West Point graduate who had served briefly and was dismissed without cause from the United States Army. He wanted a splash in the *Defender* heralding Pancho Villa, or Flipper, as an example of what Negroes could accomplish when rejected by the American white people, thus proving his thesis of Negro equality. The story in truth would have been a scoop and would perhaps have been picked up by other papers. But his informant's facts were garbled, although Abbott's news sense was acutely sharp. Fay Young says, "Of course we couldn't write such a story, because the country was virtually at war, and Flipper was discovered to be right here in the United States, harmlessly working as a porter."

Abbott was disappointed by the story's denouement. But the next year red hot news came out of Texas, involving Negro troops of the Twenty-fourth Infantry Regiment which had been lately stationed in Houston.

Negroes had run amuck and shot up the town!

The Negro public, unsatisfied by reports in the white dailies, wanted more details from a racial point of view. The *Defender* alone among Negro papers met this need completely, and achieved what was tantamount to a scoop. The editors clipped all the newspapers published in Houston. These, plus the reports of Pullman porters who had recently returned from the area, provided the material for a series of vigorous articles. According to the *Defender*, Negro soldiers had been subject to much goading and insult before the riot, and they were disarmed when it was feared that they would use their weapons in defending themselves. However, they had seized arms and killed seventeen white persons. The *Defender* clearly placed the blame on the white population. Accompanying the initial account was the only picture to appear in the Negro press of the Negro soldiers involved, a reproduction from an engraving loaned by the Chicago *Examiner*. Finally, with only a slight pretense of a trial, thirteen Negroes were hanged for murder and mutiny, forty-one were imprisoned for life, and forty others were held pending further investigation. The *Defender* echoed the popular view: "The Negroes of the entire country will regard the thirteen Negro soldiers of the Twenty-fourth Infantry as executed martyrs!"

The stories, plus the follow-ups, brought a circulation increase of 20,000 as all over the country Negroes clamored for copies of the *Defender*. The paper was well able to hold this jump, and from this point on the circulation climbed steadily. For its strident opposition to lynching was staple copy, and week after week a tireless crusade hammered at racial discrimination and violence, often to the point of being abstract and tedious. Negroes were even counseled to fight back—and they liked that sort of talk. The heads of a page-one story which appeared even before the Houston riot will illustrate:

GOV. SHOULD STOP DAILY LYNCHING

When the Mob Comes And
You Must Die Take
At Least One with You

Green Gibson Shoots Twelve
Before He Dies

The *Defender* fed its public red-ink sensationalism—and when pushed for the reason, Abbott had the identical defense his white colleagues offered: he wanted to reach the largest possible number of readers, in order to use that following as an instrument for improving and advancing the race. In his struggle to increase circulation, sensationalism seemed to him a rational policy.

The battles the paper waged were not always momentous —but in the minds of Negroes they were of critical concern and thus were given loud treatment. For instance, Negroes were frequently humiliated by a feature of most amusement parks throughout the country, called the "African Dodger" game, in which a Negro would be made the target of balls thrown at his head. Barkers would urge the customers on with, "Hit the coon and get a cigar!" A *Defender* reporter approached the management of a local park protesting the game as degrading the race but was told that the sport would not be discontinued because "It's too good an attraction!" The correspondents reported similar experiences in other parts of the country. The *Defender* finally attacked the sport in a story carrying this head:

DRIVE OUT DISGRACEFUL AFRICAN DODGER

AFRICAN DODGER
AT SUMMER PARKS
SHAMEFUL DISGRACE

131

"Does not your very soul ache within you," asked the *Defender* in the story that followed, "when you behold a crowd of white men pelting wooden balls at a Colored man whose head is used as a target for the amusement of these folks? This of course means that his head and his brain combined is not worth more than a cigar." The paper had only scorn for those who performed as targets, and declared: "We would go the barker one better and say: 'Kill the fool and win a prize!' The individual who will someday throw a lucky ball—no, fire the lucky shot that would kill or maim one of these jackasses —would be indeed doing a great favor to the Colored race and to society in general." But when the *Defender* was unable to persuade the amusement parks, it launched a campaign against Negroes who accepted this type of employment, hoping thus to end the sport. It labeled them with heads like this one:

MEN WHO SEEK THIS
WORK ARE CRIMINALS
AGAINST THE RACE

The "African Dodger" game, a curious folkway of the period, is unknown to the present generation—indeed, no such sport is conceivable today. But in his day, Abbott suddenly discovered that the *Defender's* handling of such topics, albeit loudly "race angled," appealed to Negroes everywhere in the country. Fay Young is convinced that this was the turning point of the paper's fortunes.

Consequently, solution of the distribution problems now became urgent. Abbott began by establishing a makeshift circulation department headed by Phil Jones, a jack-of-all-trades who already kept account of the papers sold and returned. Next he sought to develop his local outlets, and launched a newsboys' contest. He offered a prize which the contestants especially coveted. Any boy who disposed of one hundred or more copies in a week was rewarded by having his picture published in the *Defender*. This scheme apparently developed keen rivalry. Thus one week Spencer Wilson's picture appeared, and the following week Napoleon McQueen's. Afterwards a newsboys' basketball team was formed with Al Johnson, now a Los Angeles dentist, as coach. Then, some years later, a newsboys' band was organized under the direction of Major N. Clark Smith. It included the now popular band leader Lionel Hampton. The *Defender* supplied the uniforms, equipment and instruments. By 1920 the paper had 563 newsboys. Together with newsstand sales, the paper was able to eventually push aside all competitors and cover the city's Black Belt like a blanket.

Simultaneously, Abbott had bent his energies toward building the circulation countrywide. Phil Jones was assigned the job of going through the out-of-town weeklies and checking them for the names and addresses of Negro ministers. Then letters were sent asking them to recommend someone in their areas to sell the *Defender*. A remarkable number of people, including many unsolicited, wrote asking to become agent-correspondents. The position, though unpaid beyond the profits from the paper's sale, gave each representative prestige and status in his own community, a fact which enabled Abbott to pick and choose. By 1916 the number of localities represented in the paper had reached seventy-one, and circulation was spiraling. When the *Defender* ran a series of articles applauding the conditions for Negroes in the North as compared with the South, the Chicago Urban League received 940 letters from Negroes who wished to leave the South. When 520 legible letters were examined, the distribution by states was: [*]

[*] Frederick G. Detweiler, *The Negro Press in the United States.* Chicago, 1922.

Louisiana	85
Mississippi	87
Alabama	64
Georgia	102
Florida	79
Scattering	103
	520

To push circulation, a number of lively promotional schemes were employed, such as popularity contests, which the *Defender* introduced to the Negro press. The prize for the first one, conducted in 1913, was a diamond ring given to the winner, a Miss Irene McCoy. Abbott sentimentally chose the first paid subscriber, a Mr. T. F. Dyson, to make the formal presentation—incidentally, this gentleman, according to the paper's account, made "a masterly address" boosting the paper. But Abbott mostly called attention to the "strong and fearless editorial page," and frequently boasted that every issue of the *Defender* "contains up-to-the-minute city news, while the best correspondents obtainable cover the outside points."

Every inch of progress was announced with fanfare. When the standard-size paper was adopted, a boxed story was run on the front page, captioned THE BIGGER DEFENDER, informing the public that "in laboring to produce the World's Greatest Weekly," the paper had spared no efforts "to give its readers all the news, interestingly written and attractively illustrated." Not content with this much, a long article was published on page two spelling out the details. The story carried these promotional heads:

LEAP IN JOURNALISM: EIGHT
PAGES FOR THE DEFENDER

First Weekly Race Paper in Chi-
cago to Carry Eight Pages—
New and Original Matter in its
Columns—Correspondents
Everywhere.

134

ONLY ASKS SUPPORT

Staff Laboring to Give Readers Best Paper
in America—Calls on Business Men to
Advertise in its Columns Solely
Because of Largest Circulation
and Most Influential.

Branch offices were established in New York and in far-away London—to be exact, at 17 Green Street. With the introduction of new features, the paper urged the public to "Let us be your spokesman and defender. In defending you, we defend ourselves. Consult our legal and health editors. Their advice is free. Bring your troubles to us!"

Finally, Roscoe Conkling Simmons, a spellbinding orator with considerable prestige as a Republican politician, was sent on tours of the South as the paper's representative-at-large to stimulate sales. He was the "star" personality of the *Defender*—indeed, he eventually became the highest paid employee in the organization and perhaps in Negro journalism—$125 weekly. Consequently, he was steadily plugged. He conducted a regular column, but nearly every week he appeared on the front page. To boost his audiences, the paper described him as "America's Greatest Orator." One story declared, "With nothing behind him save truth and his amazing genius, this man at 35 years, is the ambassador of 12,000,-000, the wisest champion his Race ever had, and his country's foremost orator." Abbott was no fool: Simmons, a nephew of Booker T. Washington, could in truth attract audiences of several thousand anywhere he spoke, and he often made five or six promotional speeches a week, which enabled the *Defender* to cash in on his popularity. His critics referred to him as "that rascal Roscoe," but Abbott had an undeniable affection for him.

His itinerary South included every town with a Negro population of five hundred or more, where he made a speech on the merits of the *Defender*. His talks often were heavily larded with reminiscences of his colorful and entertaining experiences. He frequently lauded mother love, described the little white fence around the old plantation homestead, and glowingly applauded the sacrifices made in his behalf by "Mammy." If he was not scheduled to speak, he managed to find a place on the platform of planned meetings or church services in progress. He always arrived with the Negro population figures, plus the paper's local circulation, to guide his program. The politician already had a reputation for liquid conviviality, and he used it to good effect in the barbershops and poolrooms. The proprietors, made captives by Simmons' persuasive logic, would readily agree to sell the paper—and, if they already sold it, to increase their quotas. Then he would call upon the leading citizens, such as doctors, lawyers, businessmen, preachers and civic leaders, and repeat his booster spiel. One person would be selected to supply the hometown news, and before leaving Simmons would collect photographs of the town's most popular girls, cheesecake preferably, and send them back for front-page publication.

This pattern of promotion was followed for many years and produced considerable results. When the *Defender* reached its peak circulation there were 2,359 agent-correspondents representing the paper throughout the United States. But the Pullman porters, dining car waiters and the stage people in road shows are chiefly responsible for giving the paper national circulation. It began by word-of-mouth, and it was J. Hockley Smiley who first enlisted this footloose army to hurdle the thorny problems of distribution. Chicago was a principal railroad terminal and hundreds of porters and waiters were coming and going daily. He recognized that, as a group, they were the only Negroes who traveled from place to place on regular schedules, even to spots off the beaten path. Smiley offered them a chance to increase their incomes by selling the paper.

They quickly saw the point. Before each trip, they would

gather up the bundles to drop at stops along their routes, where contacts would pick them up and redistribute the papers. Frequently they would give away copies to any Negro they saw in towns they entered for the first time. By prearrangement, some agent-correspondents who had difficulty receiving papers by mail or express met the trains, for a feeling was growing in the white South that the *Defender* should be forbidden circulation. The stage folk, too, often distributed papers in the theaters where they played.

Before the singer Anita Brown, popularly known as "Black Patti," made her yearly tours of the South, she would leave her itinerary with Phil Jones, and he would dispatch papers to meet her at the concert hall of each city where she was to perform. Then she would have the ushers place them on tables at the entrance with instructions to give every patron a copy free. Profit, mostly, was the original motive, but as the paper became more and more vigorous in espousing the Negro's cause, these people felt it a "race duty" to help distribute the paper and even became couriers bringing back the news. The arrangement eventually became a case of one hand washing the other, because the *Defender* was the unorganized railroad workers' most articulate spokesman.

Back in 1905, when the Pullman Company threatened to displace Negroes with Oriental labor, the *Defender* carried page-one stories in protest. One will illustrate:

JAPANESE TO TAKE PLACE OF COLORED MEN

As Sleeping Car Porters—Our Men Who Have Given Their Best Days to Service of America's Railroads to be Dethroned

Abbott, indulging his passion for Negro industrial education, could not resist the temptation of adding to this story an editorialized sub-head: "This Brings Booker T. Washington's Words True that the Negro Must Learn Trades."

The *Defender* was constantly alert to any threat to the welfare of the porters and waiters. Their service to the paper notwithstanding, this concern was based primarily on Abbott's belief that their grievances were valid. Moreover, anything affecting this group was news. Naturally the paper supported the porters' demand for increased wages and improved working conditions and editorially urged the Pullman Company to "First increase the porters' pay and then reward meritorious service with something more substantial than stripes." When agitation against tipping in 1915 resulted in a public hearing held before a government commission in Washington, D. C., the *Defender* reported the details and slanted the stories in favor of the porters.

The big story was the testimony of Robert T. Lincoln, president of the Pullman Company and son of Abraham Lincoln. He sorely disappointed the Negroes, as the *Defender's* headlines indicate:

WILL ROBERT T. LINCOLN
BE THE SECOND EMANCIPATOR?

Pleads Ignorance of Porters' Condition

Declared That He Is Disappointed in Progress Race Made—
Correspondent Points out Reason And Gives Interesting
Facts Regarding the Company And Its Faithful
But Poorly Paid Servants.

The *Defender* achieved a circulation of exactly 283,571— according to a promotion pamphlet issued by the paper in 1920. But the accuracy of these figures is not possible to check, for the records for the period are not complete. Moreover, the Audit Bureau of Circulations, begun in 1914 to guarantee the circulation claims of newspapers, had not as yet

extended its services to the Negro press. But from the testi-
monies and relevant facts I have gathered, I judge the *Defender's* actual paid circulation to have been in excess of
230,000—which indeed was far and away the largest ever
achieved by a Negro newspaper. Two-thirds of this was outside Chicago, with 23,000 copies being sold weekly in New
York City.

If five people read one paper, Robert S. Abbott's *Defender*
touched the lives of more than one million Negroes in the
United States. Translated into financial terms, it meant he
could write his mother in Georgia thus: "I will be sending
you something now from time to time, so that you can have
anything you wish; I want you to get a Ford to go where you
want without using the [segregated] streetcars. . . . Please
don't want for anything. Send and let me know just what
you need, *as I have the money to get all you want now!*" He
himself bought his first automobile—a second-hand Apperson
sedan.

The purpose, the mission of the DEFENDER *is to inform you, instruct you, guide you in the way, and stand with you under our flag; and, above all, stand with you against organized political banditry.*—ROBERT S. ABBOTT, Speech at St. Paul's A.M.E. Church, 1918.

CHAPTER IX

The Disloyalty Myth

THERE WERE VARIOUS indications along the way, even if only partially in focus, that must have given Robert S. Abbott an inkling of difficulties ahead. The *Defender* had drawn the white community's attention to its ebullient existence, and it faced the prospect of paying one price of phenomenal growth, prosperity and recognition—litigation. Finally, one day in 1918, Abbott received a formal notice from the Hearst organization that it was starting legal action against his paper. His perspiring face produced a painful expression as he read the bad news. Nevertheless, with prompt decision, he called Albert B. George, his Negro attorney. Meantime the staff was in something of a dither over the prospect of the *Defender* grappling with the Goliath of journalism, for upon the publisher's instructions they had had Langston Mitchell, who was employed by the Chicago *Evening American* and contributed cartoons to the Negro paper, design a page-one masthead which had now become the point of controversy.

The Hearst people charged Abbott with using the identical

masthead that appeared on their two Chicago papers, the *Herald-Examiner* and the *Evening American:* specifically, the eagle with outstretched wings and in the center a shield of the stars and stripes. They contended that the public was being fooled; and that many Hearst readers were buying the *Defender* in the mistaken belief they were purchasing a Hearst paper. Before the suit could come to trial, Abbott quickly had Mitchell redesign a new masthead and substitute a sphinx—inappropriately chosen, incidentally, for no other reason than the fact that the Egyptian figure was the only popular symbol anyone could think of at the moment. This was enough to satisfy the Hearst lawyers, and the suit was dropped.

One detail is worthy of note:

There were reactions of an unexpected sort in the Negro community. Few Negroes had demonstrated the ability to make a newspaper enterprise succeed, and therefore many Negroes whispered that, if not William Randolph Hearst himself, some white person owned a big share of the *Defender,* especially as they witnessed the paper's weekly use of the sensational type of journalism then characteristic of the Hearst publications. The implied deprecation of their own kind wounded Abbott, but he was perhaps consoled by the fact that the threatened suit suggested that the white population, at least grudgingly, acknowledged the importance of his paper. In any case, when the news leaked out circulation of the rumor came to an end.

The incident's net result: the paper's influence and prosperity as an independent organ soared, and Abbott himself gained stature as a leader.

Until now, most white people in the South were entirely unaware of the bitter and relentless criticism of themselves and their public policies; of their legal and political practices; their churches, schools, and other institutions; and al-

141

most everything else in southern civilization. But the white dailies soon took notice of the *Defender* and created a stir. The Birmingham *Mountain Eagle,* with a startled curiosity which suggested ominous implications, printed a double column story under the head: "Chicago Defender a Negro Newspaper Widely Circulated."

Such notice, incidentally, served to publicize the paper among Negroes. Then followed frequent criticism of the Negro press generally, criticism which declared it was dangerous to the interests of cordial race relations. In time, the South came to look upon the *Defender* as subversive—that is, subversive in the sense that on public questions the paper castigated, even challenged, the section's traditional ways. Abbott soon became the recipient of anonymous, half-literate threats like this one from Arkansas: "You are agitating a proposition through your paper which is causing some of your good Bur[r] heads to be killed and the end is not in sight yet. . . . You could be of assistance to your people if you would advise them to be real niggers instead of fools."

The *Defender,* said H. J. Seligmann, a white man who investigated racial conditions in the section for the N.A.A.C.P., was "cordially execrated among white men in the South," but the attitude of direct hostility frequently exhibited spoke still more impressively of the influence attributed to it by whites. As a consequence, they often charged the paper with fomenting race riots, as did the governor of Arkansas, Charles Brough. No wonder the paper's penetration of Mississippi alarmed R. H. Leavell, a government investigator. He did not mention the paper by name, but spoke of "a weekly published in Chicago, whose editor knows clearly what he wants for his people and why he wants it."

He described the paper's handling of a lynching in this manner: "It makes skillful use of a recent lynching in which the head of a dead man was severed from his body, so it is alleged, and thrown into a crowd of Negroes on the principal

Abbott's birthplace, St. Simons Island, Georgia.

Robert's childhood home in Savannah, above Rev. Sengstacke's store,

German branch of the Sengstacke family, residing in Bremen.

The Hampton Institute quartet in which Abbott (lower left) sang from 1890 to 1896.

Remodeled synagogue which became the home of the Chicago Defender in 1921.

Flora Abbott Sengstacke, mother of the publisher, at the unveiling of the Defender's first press in 1921.

Negro street. A photograph of what purports to be the head as it lies on the deserted street is published under the telling caption, 'Not Belgium—America.' . . . This publicity is a natural tendency on the part of this Negro press to minimize such justification as may exist."

If the white community was inclined to damn the *Defender*, Negroes were inclined to shout amen. The esteem in which the paper was held by some Negroes is suggested by a report that in Gulfport, Mississippi, a man was regarded as "intelligent" if he read the *Defender;* and in Laurel, Mississippi, it was said that old men who had never known how to read bought the paper simply because it was regarded as precious. The paper's advocacy of Negro rights found strong support among southern Negroes, mainly because it published news condemning the racial practices of the South in language forbidden to southern Negro journals. Moreover, it frequently defined the racial problems for them. This public reaction is abundantly evident from the volume and kind of letters that were written by the readers of the *Defender*. When Negroes had trouble of any sort they wrote directly to Abbott, usually beginning the letters with, "I ask for publication in your valuable paper." Group petitions came with the signature, "representing the influential colored citizens." Sometimes the writers merely wanted to utter a cry for justice, and often such letters served as a safety-valve for indignation boiling over some disagreeable incident—and if many were illiterate, they nevertheless were eloquent. "No longer than last week," a woman wrote, "two white men knocked and beet a colored man and then the police walk up and put the colored man under rest and let the white go free, so you Hon. [Abbott] please favor me with the knowledge as to where to go."

Following the Elaine riots in Arkansas, a Negro so fair-complexioned he could easily pass as a white person, made this report to Abbott:

143

Your special correspondent, detailed to investigate the recent wholesale killings of Negroes in Phillips County, Arkansas, quietly dropped into Helena and visited the scenes of the recent troubles, talked with scores of Negroes, overheard the conversation of many whites, read the leading Arkansas newspapers, asked and got information and opinions and left the state without disclosing his identity and even being suspected of being a news writer.

The reason for this is obvious. We did not know whom to trust. We wanted to get the news—the whole truth, not to be lynched. For in the present state of mind of the white people of Phillips County, any Negro is as good as dead if he be even suspected of writing for a Northern Negro publication. . . .

Here is the real truth about the whole matter. . . .

The writer then gave a lengthy report, and ended his communication with this:

DEAR EDITOR:

Please publish the above. You will understand that I do not dare to disclose my name. I have to give you the facts as I have obtained them, and that from the best and most reliable sources. Publish this just as if it came from your own special correspondent, so as to prevent any attempt to investigate the source of your news. I know you and wish you well. God Bless our Race and our Negro newspapers of the North. You are doing a splendid work. Tell the truth, cry aloud and spare not.

The identity of this man was of course known to Abbott—he was Walter White, executive secretary of the N.A.A.C.P. and now a *Defender* columnist.

Nearly everywhere in the South vigorous attempts were made to suppress the *Defender,* and eventually all Negro periodicals published in the North. Several cities attempted to prevent the *Defender's* circulation among Negroes by confiscating the papers as soon as they arrived. Negroes then relied upon subscription copies delivered through the mails. The letters of Negroes, whose names were deleted for safety, were published telling how they were forbidden to read Negro papers. The *Defender's* Birmingham agent reported that "Members of the local Ku Klux Klan invaded the office of the *Baptist Leader*, official organ of the Alabama Baptist denomination, and notified the editor, Rev. R. N. Hall, that unless the publication ceased making attacks on the notorious order, harm would be done."

Consequently, in some areas the paper's distribution soon became an underground operation. There were reports of clandestine circulation of copies folded into bundles of merchandise. One agent said, "We have to slip the paper into the hands of our friends, and I am trying to induce my friends to subscribe by the year. Every public school teacher is closely watched, also the preacher. I give you this Dot and you can read between the lines." Yet, said a government investigator, "A reputable Negro in Louisiana to whom I was directed by a prominent white leader, said of this paper [*Defender*]: 'My people grab it like a mule grabs a mouthful of fine fodder.'"

An Associated Press dispatch, with a Pine Bluff dateline, illustrates what happened in Arkansas:

> Chancellor John M. Elliott today issued an injunction restraining John D. Young, Jr., Negro, and "any other parties" from circulating the Chicago *Defender*, a Negro publication, in Pine Bluff or Jefferson County.
>
> The injunction was granted at the instance of Mayor Mack Hollis. It was sought following receipt here by Young of copies of the paper containing an account of the killing of George Vicks, Negro, here Thursday, Feb. 5.
>
> The *Defender's* account of the affair portrayed Vicks as defending his home, his liberty and his person, and was held to be false in its entirety by the court.

Following this action, Arkansas governor Charles Brough announced his intention of asking the Postmaster-General to exclude the paper from the mails. The Mississippi legislature, with a sharp eye on the *Defender*, somewhat obtusely passed

"An act to make it a misdemeanor to print or circulate or publish appeals or presentations or arguments or suggestions favoring equality or marriage between the white and Negro race." In a number of sections circulation of the paper was forbidden by local law. When legal action failed, such groups as the Ku Klux Klan resorted to extra-legal methods. The *Defender* carried a typical story from Yazoo City, Mississippi, which reported in part: "Threatening her with death unless she stopped acting as agent for newspapers published by her Race, Miss Pauline Willis was compelled to leave town."

Said Carl Sandburg, writing in the Chicago *Daily News,* "A colored man caught with a copy in his possession was suspected of 'Northern fever' and other so-called disloyalties." More than a dozen agent-correspondents eventually were driven from their hometowns—and at least two were killed in the act of distributing the *Defender.** Finally, in 1919, Longview, Texas, witnessed the nightmare of a race riot. Several white men were shot when they went into the Negro section in search of a Negro school teacher accused of sending a news release to the *Defender* concerning the lynching of a Negro. The town was alarmed by this show of resistance, and people poured into the Negro neighborhood determined to teach Negroes a lesson. They burned homes, publicly flogged the Negro school principal, and ran several leading citizens out of town.

Robert S. Abbott, deep in the recesses of his soul, must have sometimes felt that he had created a Frankenstein. He himself was devoured by fears of assassination by white men —and actually he was several times so threatened. The dilemma in which his violently partisan policy once placed him is illustrated by an incident of the period—one that is a re-

---

* These casualties do not include those among the representatives of the other Negro newspapers.

vealing sidelight on Abbott's psychology and not without a certain poignant humor.

The affair first developed back in a small town in Georgia where a judge, known to us only as Abernathy, was running for reelection. To win votes he made several violently anti-Negro speeches. His fellow townspeople—that is, Negroes—sent his campaign literature and a handful of clippings containing reports of his attitude to Abbott. He passed them along to his staff with instructions to "give the skunk hell!" —his characteristic way of ordering a strongly worded article. Shortly thereafter, an editorial appeared with the caption: "Judge Abernathy is a Jackass." Abbott promptly sent five hundred copies to Abernathy's hometown for circulation among Negroes, hoping thus to defeat him. But Abernathy's opponent unwisely reprinted the editorial as a campaign leaflet, blatantly acknowledging his source, and the judge was reelected.

Not long afterwards, a huge, red-faced white man wearing a wide-brim Stetson hat entered the *Defender* office. He quizzed the secretaries, and finally, much to the publisher's surprise, unceremoniously pushed open his office door. The man had the air of authority. His manner clearly indicated that he had something urgent on his mind, and Abbott detected a distinct southern accent. It boded no good. The white man flashed his badge and identified himself as Sheriff Moon, and this dialogue followed:

"Is this Abbott?"

"No."

"Where is he?"

"He'll be back this afternoon."

"Tell him I'll be back!"

The man had hardly left, when Abbott bounded out of his chair and went in search of his old friend, Dr. George C. Hall, who was well known for his rough and ready manner. Legend said he feared no white man. When Sheriff Moon returned late that afternoon, he was seated behind Abbott's desk, posing as the editor and publisher of the *Defender*. Abbott, pretending to be an underling, sat nearby. The white man, observing the southern custom of not addressing Negroes as "mister" or removing his hat in their presence, swung open the door without knocking, and gruffly demanded to know, "Is this Abbott?"

"*Mister* Abbott," Hall countered. Then he proceeded to upbraid him with, "What do you mean calling me *plain* Abbott?"

The Negro's belligerent attitude cowed the sheriff, and he announced somewhat less firmly, "I've come to take Mister Abbott back with me." Then he explained that both Judge Abernathy and the racial conditions prevailing in his town had been libeled by the *Defender*.

"Where's your papers?" Hall demanded.

The sheriff reached into his pocket, drew out a blue, official-looking document, presumably a warrant for Abbott's arrest, and handed it to Hall. The Negro physician carefully examined it and to the white man's discomfort, tore it up and threw the pieces into the trash basket. Moon was nonplussed but offered no argument—after all, he was now in the Black Belt of Chicago. Before he could recover his composure, Hall was shouting, "Didn't you know this is Illinois—not Georgia! You can't get away with that in this town!" Without further comment, the small town official made a hasty retreat. As his coattails got through the door, Abbott, silent until now, was heard loudly denouncing him as a "skunk!"

The impression this unexpected encounter made is suggested by the elaborate preparations he soon afterwards made for a quick trip to Woodville, Georgia, to see his mother, visit his stepfather's grave, and perhaps again court Catherine Scarborough. In those days the drawing room of the Pullman car was popularly called "Lower 13"—meaning whenever a Negro sought first-class accommodations he paid the lower berth rate, but was assigned the use of the drawing room, to circumvent his having intimate associations with the white passengers; if the room was already occupied, he was denied the right to purchase a berth, and had to travel in the coach assigned to "Negroes only." Even so, few Negroes traveled Pullman style because of the prohibitive price. But Abbott, who prudently watched every personal expenditure, was prepared to pay the additional charge for the privilege of traveling in the lonely privacy of a drawing room—he was afraid he might be recognized and become the victim of an untoward incident. So when he finally headed South, the ticket was bought in the name of his associate editor and he traveled as "Alf Anderson" in "Lower 13."

His sister Rebecca reports a revealing detail:

"Whenever he did come to Savannah on infrequent occasion," she says, "he would disguise himself by wearing a false mustache, because he was afraid that his paper's policy would cause him trouble in the South. He would stay in Woodville the whole time, and would do no visiting in Savannah nearby." Rebecca adds somewhat surprisingly, "He always was as frightened as a rabbit."

What the white community described as the "incendiary" policy of the *Defender,* came to a blaze with America's entrance into the First World War—"to make the world safe for democracy." Abbott quickly recognized the slogan's implications in connection with improving the lot of Negroes, and immediately stepped up his agitation for the extension of democracy. It was largely the Negro newspapers that made Negroes fully conscious of the inconsistency between America's war aims abroad and the treatment of her black minority at home. The country had hardly taken a position toward the conflict, when a race riot broke out in East St. Louis, Illinois —one of the bloodiest race riots of the Twentieth Century. Negroes were driven from the city, two hundred were put to death by shooting, burning and hanging. The *Defender,* whose first-hand coverage included a four-column picture showing the devastation, outstripped all other Negro newspapers. It denounced the white mobs in such inflammatory language that the Federal authorities took notice.

The Negro's feelings were raw and inflamed.

Yet Negroes did not lag when the government called for volunteers. The highest ranking Negro officer, Colonel Charles Young, who had been retired because of high blood pressure when war seemed imminent, tried to prove his fitness to serve by riding horseback from Ohio to Washington. But Negroes soon discovered that they were not to be accorded equal treatment. They were allowed to volunteer only as servants in the Navy, and as laborers in the Army. Quite different was the application of conscription. More than two million Negroes were registered under the Selective Service Law, and more than three hundred thousand were drafted, a number augmented by forty thousand regulars and National Guardsmen. They were organized as separate units, commanded by white officers, to form principally stevedore and labor battalions. None were permitted in the aviation corps.

Even so, Negroes wanted to read about what happened to them from day to day, and to this extent the *Defender* gave full publicity to the war. But it would pause long enough to express indignation at articles like the one which appeared in the magazine, *Outlook,* labeled "Mobilizing Rastus." Negro protests, articulated by the Negro press, brought fundamental innovations in the Army. For example, Negroes had complained against the absence of Negro officers. Led by Joel Spingarn of the N.A.A.C.P., they argued the issue with General Leonard Wood, who agreed to train such officers if two hundred college men could be found. Early in 1917, a Central Committee of Negro College Men was set up by Howard University, and within ten days, one thousand five hundred names had been collected.

Finally, at Fort Des Moines, Iowa, a Negro officer's camp was established and 639 Negroes were commissioned. The *Defender* had vigorously supported the training of Negroes as officers, but Abbott now decried the idea of a separate camp for them. The paper did indeed report the fact that Negroes were continuously insulted by white officers and frequently forced to work under unhealthy conditions. It reported, too, the friction between Negro soldiers and the white military police, and the frequent clashes between white and Negro soldiers. The conflicts between Negro soldiers and white civilians were especially acute, provoked mainly by insults and denial of service in restaurants and admission to theaters.

To counteract the low morale among Negroes, Secretary of War Newton D. Baker appointed a Special Negro Assistant, Emmett J. Scott, who had served as Booker T. Washington's secretary. Abbott was considerably impressed, especially when Scott industriously attempted to ease the racial tensions within the Army. In the summer of 1918, on behalf of the War Department and the Committee on Public Information, he called together a group of Negro leaders including, significantly enough, thirty-one newspaper publishers and editors. Abbott, along with W. E. B. Du Bois, was present. For three days they discussed the relation of the Negro to the conduct of the war, mentioning his special grievances and needs. Their recommendations were embodied in a "Bill of Particulars," which included the appointment of a regularly-commissioned war correspondent to report military operations on the Western front. Ralph W. Tyler, a newspaperman with thirty years' experience with a white paper in Columbus, Ohio, was given the assignment. The idea was seemingly proposed by Abbott. He afterwards volunteered his services as a speaker, and plugged the war effort in the paper with front-page headlines like: JUDGE TERRELL LAUNCHES LIBERTY LOAN DRIVE, and ran pictures of Negro women forming Red Cross canteens.

Upon his return to Chicago, he promptly dispatched his star columnist, Roscoe Conkling Simmons, to the European theater of operations as a war correspondent—one of the first to represent a Negro newspaper abroad. His assignment was to cover the Negro troops at the front and report their day-to-day activities. But Simmons somehow never got beyond the Paris fleshpots. When he could tear himself away, he casually interviewed a Negro soldier or two on leave in the city, and dispatched his second-hand gleanings to the *Defender*—and, to be sure, these were transparent enough for his publisher to recall him. His irresponsibility was particularly distressing, because Abbott's well-laid plans to get the jump on his competitors by eyewitness reports had gone awry. Upon his employee's return, he staged a monster mass meeting in Chicago at which War Correspondent Simmons, in a matchless performance of imagination, described his experiences abroad. The thousands who turned up at the armory—at one dollar a head—replenished Abbott's depleted coffers and Simmons carried off his role like a hero.

Fifty thousand Negroes were used in front-line combat, a fact that produced considerable good copy for the *Defender* and the Negro press generally. The best known unit was the Old Fifteenth Regiment of Harlem, renamed the 369th United States Infantry and popularly known as the "Buffaloes." Four months before it was called up the Negro commander, Colonel Benjamin O. Davis, was replaced by Colonel William Hayward, a liberal white man. The unit was shipped to Spartanburg, South Carolina. Soon after arrival the proprietor of a local hotel ordered a Negro officer, Noble Sissle, to remove his hat when he entered the lobby to purchase a newspaper, and kicked him into the street when he refused.

Rioting by Negroes was averted by the restraining influence of Lieutenant James Reese Europe, leader of the band which introduced jazz to Paris. But next morning fifty Negroes marched on the city to avenge Sissle, and only the persuasive efforts of Colonel Hayward prevented bloodshed. The regiment was quickly removed to Camp Mills, Long Island, New York, where Negroes joined white troops from Alabama and Mississippi. Trouble broke out the first night over discrimination in the canteen. The next day the troops embarked for France, one of the first units to go overseas.

These details the *Defender* reported, and when individuals performed outstandingly at the front stories were carried under such headlines as:

15TH REGIMENT SOLDIER ROUTS
TWENTY GERMANS

BRAVERY WINS FRENCH CROSS

BATTLE SCARRED HERO TELLS
OF TRIALS ON FIRING LINES

NEW YORK HONORS NEADHAM
ROBERTS, FAMOUS HERO

To be sure, the *Defender* kept its readers well-informed. But Abbott had a personal and sentimental interest in the Old Eighth Illinois Infantry Regiment, a national guard unit originally commanded by a Chicago Negro, Colonel Franklin A. Denison. The paper reported the outfit's activities in considerable detail—after all, the men had come from the South and entered the Army via the sidewalks of Chicago, and had left the city amid cheers and tears. The regiment was renamed the 370th United States Infantry, and reached France in the summer of 1918. It was equipped with French arms, and soon afterwards was sent to the front.

Before long the *Defender* carried this headline: GERMANS HALTED BY CHICAGO BOYS. When they entered the Argonne Forest, a letter from Major James R. White was quoted with the banner head: 8TH REGIMENT GASSED

153

BY GERMANS. In concert with several French units, the 370th pursued the enemy out of France. Between battles, according to a four-column picture on the *Defender's* front page, the men were now studying THEIR FIRST LESSON IN FRENCH. The paper afterwards duly reported that twenty-one men had received the Distinguished Service Cross, one received the Distinguished Service Medal, while sixty-eight received various grades of the *Croix de Guerre*.

The white Americans, and particularly the Federal officials, were anxious about the attitude of Negroes in this emergency. For, by its inflammatory utterances and truculent headlines, the Negro press perhaps created the feeling that Negroes were not entirely loyal. Robert Russa Moton, heir to Booker T. Washington's Tuskegee mantle, was forced to assure the nation that "The Negro press was a very helpful factor in the prosecution of the war . . . and whatever happened they were most loyal to the government, even when, as was sometimes true, they might have criticized with justification." Scott, as if sounding off from an amen corner, testified that "The Negro press was an asset of incalculable value in pushing the war work among colored people by publication of information bulletins."

Suspicions of disloyalty were, however, strong, and these statements failed to allay official fears. The truth is, Negroes exhibited little enthusiasm for the war—actually, their eyes were fixed on Washington, not London, Paris or Berlin. The sympathy white people felt for the invaded Belgians was not shared by Negroes, who knew too well of Belgian atrocities in the Congo. And they held British imperialism, ruling millions of their African blood brothers, was no less savage than German conquest of the Cameroons. Nor did they feel the United States was altogether virtuous. Meanwhile, the Negro newspapers had campaigned violently against racial discrimination in every form.

These reports often provoked bitter response among Negroes.

Consequently, the Department of Justice felt the Negro press bore investigation. The Attorney General, A. Mitchell Palmer, who conducted the investigations solemnly stated in his report to the Senate that the utterances of the Negro editors were "not the ignorant vaporings of untrained minds," but the sober declarations of intelligent men who were "definitely assertive of the Negro's equality." He declared that fifty educated men, who wrote in "fine, pure English with a background of scholarship," edited the Negro publications.

While Palmer dropped them all into one basket, actually these publications were not uniform in their social philosophy. However, they all stood to the left of any previous position taken by Negroes—a few even had broken the once inflexible ties to the Republican Party. Backstage, so to speak, a noisy radical press had emerged: *Challenge, Crusader, Emancipator* and *Messenger*—most of them published in New York and now defunct. Even the old and conservative Negro newspapers, such as the New York *Age*, Baltimore *Afro-American* and Norfolk *Journal and Guide*, spoke more boldly. Most widely read, and in general typical of the radical publications, was the *Messenger* magazine, edited by the Socialists A. Philip Randolph and Chandler Owen. The Lusk Committee, a body appointed by the New York State legislature to investigate radicalism, declared it "by far the most dangerous of all the Negro publications." The *Messenger* went beyond attacks on white people. Its editors also attacked those conservative Negro leaders, who during the war indulged in rhetoric and bombast to "lull Negroes into a false sense of security." But while much heat was generated, it created no serious difficulties for the *Defender*.

The Negro publications had perhaps created an unfortunate atmosphere of mistrust. Robert S. Abbott himself first came into conflict with the authorities in 1917 when the *De-*

fender published a cartoon by Leslie Rogers showing the mayor of Gary, Indiana, arrogantly sitting on the throne of the German Kaiser. Rogers, who lived in the steel town, was promptly jailed for contempt and released only after much legal palaver. Yet, though the paper was caustic about the ill-treatment of Negro troops, when a young man named McCoy, who worked in the circulation department, was preparing to leave with the Old Eighth Illinois Regiment, the entire staff was drawn up to witness his being honored for patriotism. He was presented with a watch by the publisher, who proudly concluded his patriotic speech with a line repeatedly used by the *Defender*, "We are Americans always!"

This was true enough.

Even so, the paper could not escape the scrutiny of the government. For the authorities believed that the *Defender*, if not disloyal, was dangerous for the morale of Negroes. Major W. H. Loring, who apparently had been assigned by the War Department to investigate the paper's policies, sent Abbott a confidential memorandum after his return to Washington and consultation with his superiors. He outlined the points that made the government suspicious of Abbott's policies. His letter was not found among the publisher's papers, but from Abbott's answer we can gather the points at issue. Moreover, his long and detailed reply suggests how seriously he regarded the government's charges, and indeed the implied impugning of his personal loyalty. The letter plumbs deep into his psychology and gives us insights into his philosophy of the conflict and the tactics he employed.

"I say with absolute certainty that without a doubt," he wrote emphatically, "[the *Defender*] has never at any time spoken disloyal, and is entirely guiltless of the attack centered on it." He declared that he had suspended expansion of his plant, so that he would be able to be of "service and assistance to the government amid these perilous trials." And he added, "To substantiate my sincere feelings for the great cause of

Democracy, I have made every conceivable sacrifice, and to-day my name is entered on the Liberty Loan budget for the sum of $12,000. This amount I subscribed without the slightest solicitation from our government. And during the height of the Liberty Loan Campaign, I advised my employees to subscribe to the worthy cause, and on many occasions I gave unlimited space to the publication of such matter that would aid the funds of the campaign."

He reported an "incident that will probably tend to make for loyalty," in which he presented the regimental colors to the 365th Infantry Regiment stationed at Camp Grant, Rockford, Illinois. "This flag," he continued, "was presented to that body of soldiers at the recent Douglass-Lincoln Celebration held in this city in February under the auspices of the National Council of Defense. Major-General Barry and Capt. Adam Patterson together with a company of soldiers from that regiment were there to receive the flag. I have also accepted a place on the Speakers' Committee on Public Information to further aid the government by taking the platform in its behalf and cause."

The key paragraph of his communication enables us to see the publisher's mind as he grappled with the problems of his day. He wrote: "The very psychology of our position in making known the evils of the South probably caused this objection to be filed against our publication. We have been outspoken, no doubt, from a southerner's point of view, in exposing the injustices done our race in that section; but in every case we have endeavored to avoid placing our criticism on the national administration. On the contrary, we have fought the individuals and contested their rights to brutally punish members of our race without resorting to due process of law. Especially in the states of Louisiana and Tennessee have our policies been vigorously assailed, and repeated attempts have been made to reject our paper from the mails, not only in the time of war, but when peace was supreme in our dominion.

In many cases my life has been threatened through the mails, and in some towns my agents have been forced to leave under cover of night."

Abbott concluded with, "Fairness constrains me to add that I firmly believe that our enemies are taking undue advantage of the position in which we are now placed. This is largely evidenced by their attitude shown in the past few months. It is clearly a case of a 'hand in the lion's mouth,' and I have more than once advised my staff writers to refrain from expressing their views on problems that would precipitate national strife, or inculcate in the heart of any member of my race the spirit of revolt against the laws of the national and state governments."

Robert S. Abbott loved his country as deeply as any; served her faithfully; willingly made personal sacrifices—save that of feeling and saying all was well with her Negro citizens. Now, with the perspective of time, we can see that his position was only one of confirmed patriotism—for, after all, the cardinal principle of his policies was insistence upon the use of the constituted legal and political machinery of the country to gain full citizenship for his race; and when this failed, to urge Negroes to escape the areas where they were restricted and terrorized. If the investigation was calculated to intimidate him, it never succeeded. He held firmly to his policy—as we shall see!

The DEFENDER *more than any other one agency was the big cause of the "northern fever" and the big exodus from the south.*—CARL SANDBURG, Chicago *Daily News,* 1919.

CHAPTER X

The Uneasy Exodus

IT WAS REALLY time for a change!

The nation braced itself for the day when the Negro soldiers returned from abroad—everyone expecting they would surely demand first-class citizenship. Before long government leaders launched a campaign to convince Negroes that they could not expect any great change in the race's traditional position in the United States. Newton D. Baker was particularly vocal on this point. The effect of such a policy was immediately apparent—Negroes soon became the victims of new outrages.

Robert S. Abbott had a solution.

He had long urged Negroes to escape the terror areas and come North—where, as he said, "They could get the wrinkles out of their bellies and live like men." But now he struck pay dirt, for his people were fed up with the petty persecutions of law enforcement officers, the daily insults and humiliations, the lamentably poor schooling, and the rough-handed competition of "poor whites" for low-paid jobs. Moreover, the Ku Klux Klan, revived in 1916, flourished with nearly five million members. Hooded bands of night riders, sometimes with the tacit approval of local authorities, swept through the South

flogging, branding, tarring and feathering, hanging and burning—even terrorizing white men who opposed the Klan's platform and methods. The lawlessness came to a peak in 1919,
when during a six-month period twenty-odd riots blazed, and
seventy Negroes were lynched. James Weldon Johnson, torn
with anguish, described the summer of 1919 as "The Red
Summer."

The Negro's blood ran in the gutters of the nation.

The situation produced mass dissatisfaction, perhaps despair, and the northward trek began. But the immediate reasons for leaving the South were largely economic: depression,
soil erosion, boll weevil ravages of cotton crops, and floods
had left Negroes homeless and destitute. Then a sudden demand for Negro labor in the North developed as the approach
of World War I brought a sharp decline in foreign immigration. Soon a mad scramble to draw upon the South's great
reservoir of black workers was in progress. Labor agents
traveled south, begging Negroes to come north. They sometimes carried free tickets in their pockets and distributed
them to those who consented to make the trip. They scoured
the section, bringing back consignments of blacks. The railroads, acting on behalf of employers, picked up trainloads on
the promise of a long, free ride. The great mass of southern
Negroes suddenly stirred, and nearly a million left the South
forever.

Single-handed, Abbott had set the great migration of the
Mississippi Valley in motion. For he had repeatedly cried:
"Come North, where there is more humanity, some justice
and fairness!" He had coaxed and challenged, denounced and
applauded—until finally he decided to launch a full-blown
campaign he called "The Great Northern Drive." From then
on things moved fast. The formal kick-off day was set for
May 15, 1917—a day that started the mass exodus North.
Before the appointed hour, he was deluged with letters. For

instance, one woman wrote, "Sir: I have been reading the *Defender* for one year or more and last February I read about the Great Northern Drive to take place May 15th on Thursday and now I can hear so many people speaking of an excursion to the North for $3.00. My husband is in the North already working, and he wants us to come up in May, so I want to know if it is true about the excursion. I am getting ready and oh so many others also, and we want to know is that true so we can be in the Drive. So please answer at once. We are getting ready."

This was the most ambitious project ever undertaken by the *Defender*. Consequently, Abbott did everything to aid and abet the migration. He argued, pleaded, shamed and exhorted Negroes to abandon the South. He inspired the formation of clubs composed of ten to fifty persons for the purpose of migrating, and arranged "club rates" with the railroads so the fare could be brought within the reach of many. Even schedules were set up—usually the dates for leaving were Wednesday and Saturday nights, following pay days. The congestion at Chicago's terminal points testified to how faithfully these plans were observed. The plans were so cleverly carried out that the migration assumed proportions never envisioned by Abbott. It was to have profound meaning for the Negro community.

This spectacular movement, sometimes called the "Black Diaspora," caused Chicago's Negro population to jump from roughly 40,000 to nearly 150,000 within the short space of a few years. During the period 1917–18, a half-million Negroes suddenly moved North and 65,000 settled in the city—"home of the *Defender*." According to one daily newspaper, they arrived at the rate of 2,000 every two days. Chicago, now called the "top of the world" by southern Negroes, was the logical destination of those coming from Mississippi, Arkansas, Louisiana, Tennessee, Georgia and Texas, simply because the railway lines led directly into the city. Besides, Chicago had been regarded as a place to make a permanent home ever since the World's Columbian Exposition in 1893, when the progress of the city's Negroes was dramatized in an imposing exhibit. Abbott, himself a migrant, had been distinctly influenced by the Negro's showing at the Fair. His people headed for Chicago for identical reasons—actually a push for self-realization.

Carl Sandburg observed the development and reported the details in a series of articles for the Chicago *Daily News*. He wrote, "Not only is Chicago a receiving station and port of refuge for colored people who are anxious to be free from the jurisdiction of lynch law, but there has been built here a publicity or propaganda machine that directs its appeals or carries on an agitation that every week reaches hundreds of thousands of people of the colored race in the southern states." He labeled the *Defender* as the chief single promotional agency. Actually, Abbott's campaign had now created a state of hysterical urgency. Consider these headlines, for example:

SAVED FROM THE SOUTH

Charged with Murder, but His Release is Secured
by Habeas Corpus

GOOD-BYE, DIXIE LAND

Lawyer Saves Another From Being Taken South
New Scheme to Keep Race Men in Dixie Land

EXODUS TO START

NORTHBOUND THEIR CRY

Under the head, "School Board Bad," the *Defender* argued one reason for leaving the South by reporting this grisly bit: "While in Arkansas a member of the school board in one of the cities of that state (and it is the rule throughout the South that a Race woman teacher to hold her school must be on friendly terms with some one of them) lived openly with a Race woman, and the entire Race, men and women, were afraid to protest or stop their children from going to school, because this school board member would get up a mob and run them out of the state. They must stomach this treatment." Editorially the paper harangued in this style: "I beg of you, my brothers, to leave that benighted land. You are free men. Show the world that you will not let false leaders lead you. Your neck has been in the yoke. Will you continue to keep it there because some 'white folks nigger' wants you to? Leave to all quarters of the globe. Get out of the South. Your being there in the numbers you are gives the southern politician too strong a hold on your progress."

What fears the migrant may have entertained of adjusting to the North the *Defender* simply countered with success stories of southern Negroes who already had made good in the North. The idea that the South was unfit for Negro habitation was played up week after week, and prominence was given the humiliating aspects particularly distasteful to Negroes.

The last sentence of the editorial was indeed the *leitmotiv* of *Defender* propaganda, and manifestly had decisive effect. Everywhere in the rural South the paper was greeted as "a herald of glad tidings." The movement consequently spread like a contagion. Rumors and gossip added volume and enthusiasm to the exodus, which was kept at fever pitch when the migrants wrote back to friends and relatives. The stimuli of suggestion and hysteria almost gave the migration the significance of a religious pilgrimage. Soon standards, songs and watchwords were introduced, and people declared they were "Bound for the Promised Land." Abbott, quickly recognizing this development, characterized the migration as "The Flight Out of Egypt," and the migrants sang they were "Going into

Canaan." Listen to W. Allison Sweeney, who boasted the ability to "break southerners and white folks niggers on the wheel," in one of his typical articles, "A Chicago 'Nigger' Preacher, a Feeder of The 'Little Hells,' Springs up to Hinder Our Brethren Coming North." Aroused by a "white folks nigger," he wrote:

> Such a creature has recently been called to my attention, and for the same reason that an unchecked rat has been known to jeopardize the life of a great ship, a mouse's nibble of a match to set a mansion aflame, I've concluded to carve a "Slice of liver or two" from that bellowing ass, who, at this very moment no doubt, somewhere in the South, is going up and down the land, telling the natives *why* they should be content, as the *Tribune* puts it, to become "Russianized," to remain in that land—to them—of *blight;* of *murdered* kin, *deflowered* womanhood, *wrecked* homes, *strangled* ambitions, *make-believe* schools, *roving* "gun parties," *midnight* arrests, *rifled* virginity, *trumped up* charges, *lonely* graves, where owls hoot, and where friends dare not go! Do you wonder at the thousands leaving the land where every foot of ground marks a tragedy, leaving the grace of their fathers and all that is dear, to seek their fortunes in the North? And you who say that their going is to seek better wages are insulting the truth, dethroning reason, and consoling yourself with a groundless allegation.

The South was alarmed by the exodus.

Even so, there were those who clearly saw the reasons for the movement. "This loss of her best labor," said the Atlanta *Constitution,* "is another penalty Georgia is paying for her indifference in suppressing mob law." And it correctly observed that "The heaviest migration of Negroes has been from those counties in which there have been the worst outbreaks against Negroes." The Savannah *Morning News* declared: "Another cause is the feeling of insecurity. The lack of legal protection in the country is a constant nightmare to the colored people. . . . There is scarcely a Negro mother in the country who does not live in dread and fear that her husband or son may come in unfriendly contact with some white person as to bring the lynchers or the arresting officers to her door which may result in wiping out of her entire family. . . . It must be acknowledged that this is a sad condition." The Montgomery *Advertiser* complained that "While our very solvency is being sucked out from underneath we go on about affairs as usual—our police officers raid poolrooms for 'loafing Negroes,' bring in twelve, keep them in the barracks all night, and next morning find that many of them have steady, regular jobs, valuable assets to their white employers; suddenly [they have] left and gone."

The South's parochial elements attempted to bring Negro migration to a halt—forcibly if necessary. First, Macon, Georgia, exacted $25,000 for a labor recruiting license, plus recommendation by ten ministers, ten manufacturers, and twenty-five other businessmen. Montgomery, Alabama, provided jail sentences for anyone guilty of "enticing" Negroes to leave the city. Trains were sidetracked for days. Then Negroes were threatened, even, indeed, snatched from railroad stations as vagrants. For the South had dark visions of empty kitchens and empty fields. Worried businessmen and planters resorted to conciliation, even earnest persuasion. A *Defender* correspondent wrote: "White people are paying more attention to the Race in order to keep them in the South, but the Chicago *Defender* has emblazoned upon their minds 'Bound for the Promised Land.'" Abbott, aware of the development, promptly urged Negroes to TURN A DEAF EAR and then declared:

Turn a deaf ear to everybody. You see they are not lifting their laws to help you, are they? Have they stopped their Jim Crow cars? Can you buy a Pullman sleeper where you wish? Will they give you a square deal in court yet? When a girl is sent to prison, she becomes the mistress of the guards and others in authority, and women prisoners are put on the street to work, something they don't do to a white woman. And your leaders will tell you the South is the best place for you. Turn a deaf ear to the scoundrel, and let him stay. Above all, see to it that that jumping jack preacher is left in the South, for he means you no good here in the North.

"Abbott had," said one observer, "the imagination to use dramatic means to synchronize the migration with the flow of history."

And to be sure, the *Defender* kept alive the enthusiasm and fervor with every publicity device the editor and his resourceful staff could command. For instance, he showed pictures of the best homes, parks and schools in Chicago next to pictures of the worst in the South; he gave abundant space to job offers; he ran cartoons satirizing the Negro's condition in the South, and published poems expressing the following sentiments: "Farewell, We're Good and Gone," "Northward Bound," and "The Land of Hope." One little jingle, "They're Leaving Memphis in Droves," contained these words:

> *Some are coming on the passenger,*
> *Some are coming on the freight,*
> *Others will be found walking,*
> *For none have time to wait.*

One piece of poetry which received widespread circulation was called "Bound for the Promised Land." It had arrived in the morning mail one day written on brown wrapping paper. The letter was postmarked "Florida." Beyond this, its source was unknown. It was a long poem, containing fifteen stanzas, each with eight lines. Nevertheless, the *Defender* printed it. So many requests were afterwards made for copies, that Abbott ordered it "reprinted by request," and where the word "Florida" appeared in the original poem he substituted "Georgia." A few stanzas are enough to give its flavor and sentiment:

From Florida's stormy banks I go;
I bid the South "Good Bye."
No longer shall they treat me so
And knock me in the eye.
The Northern states is where I'm bound,
My cross is more than double,
If the chief executive can be found,
I'll tell him all my trouble.

Arise, you Darkies now a slave,
Your chance at last has come;
Hold up your head with courage brave,
'Cause times are changing some.
All before this change was made
They took me for a tool.
No respect for me was paid,
They classed me for a fool.

Anyone doing the work I do
Is paid four dollars per day;
But I must lie, and steal some, too,
To get one-half that pay.
Then they pay me off in trashy mess,
And cheat me in the deal;
They force me hard to work for less
And arrest me when I steal.

Why should I remain longer south
To be kicked and dogged around?
Crackers to knock me in the mouth
And shoot my brother down.
I would rather the cold to snatch my breath
And die from natural cause
Than to stay down south and be beat to death
Under cracker laws.

Two men were reported to have been arrested in Georgia and given thirty days in jail for having the poem in their possession—the authorities declared they had thus "incited riot." Abbott cried out that in spite of such harassments the people were on their way. Consequently, his news reports were often calculated to show that a mass demonstration was in progress. For brief news items illustrate this:

LEAVING FOR THE NORTH

Tampa, Fla., Jan. 19.—J. T. King, supposed to be a Race leader, is using his wits to get on the good side of the white people by calling a meeting to urge our people not to migrate North. . . . Reports have been received here that all who have gone North are at work and pleased with the splendid conditions in the North. . . . People are not paying any attention to King and are packing and ready to travel North to the "promised land."

DETERMINED TO GO NORTH

Jackson, Miss., March 23.—Although the white people and sheriff and others are using every effort to intimidate the citizens from going North, even Dr. Redmond's speech was circulated around, this has not deterred our people from leaving. Many have walked miles to take the train for the North. There is a determination to leave and there is no hand save death to keep them from it.

THOMAS LIKES THE NORTH

J. H. Thomas, Birmingham, Ala., Brownsville Colony, has been here several weeks and is very much pleased with the North. He is working at the Pullman shops, making twice as much as he did at home. Mr. Thomas says the "exodus" will be greater later on in the year, that he did not find four feet of snow or freeze to death.

LEAVING FOR THE EAST

Huntsville, Ala., Jan. 19.—Fifteen families, all members of the Race, left here today for Pittsburgh, Pa., where they will take positions as butlers and maids, getting sixty to seventy dollars per month, against fifteen and twenty paid here. Most of them claim that they have letters from friends who went early and made good, saying that there was plenty of work, and this field of labor is short, owing to the vast amount of men having gone to Europe and not returned.

The southern dailies, attempting to discourage migration, published stories to the effect that thousands of men and women were walking the streets of Chicago, hungry and without shoes, begging for transportation to Dixie. And they warned Negroes about the rigors of northern winters.

The *Defender* had an answer: "To die from the bite of frost is far more glorious than at the hands of a mob." Under the headline, WHY SHOULD THE NEGRO STAY IN THE SOUTH?, it said: "It is true the South is nice and warm, and may I add, so is China, and we find Chinamen living in the North, East and West. So is Japan, but the Japanese are living everywhere." Then it countered southern propaganda with an article like the one entitled, FREEZING TO DEATH IN THE SOUTH. "So much has been said," declared the *Defender*, "through the white papers in the South about the members of the Race freezing to death in the North. They freeze to death down South when they don't take care of themselves. There is no reason for any human staying in the Southland on this bugaboo handed out by the white press." The following stories, which originally appeared in the white newspapers of the South, were republished to demonstrate the point:

AGED NEGRO FROZEN TO DEATH

Albany, Ga., Feb. 8.—Yesterday the dead body of Peter Crowder, an old Negro, was found in an out-of-the-way spot where he had been frozen to death during the recent cold snap. [from the Macon *Telegraph*]

DIES FROM EXPOSURE

Spartanburg, S. C., Feb. 6.—Marshall Jackson, a Negro man, who lived on the farm of J. T. Harris near Campebello Sunday night froze to death. [from the *South Carolina State*]

NEGRO FROZEN TO DEATH IN FIRELESS GRETNA HUT

New Orleans, La., Feb. 4.—Coldest weather of the last four years claimed a victim Friday night, when Archie Williams, a Negro, was frozen to death in a little hut in the outskirts of Gretna. [from the New Orleans *Item*]

NEGRO WOMAN FROZE TO DEATH MONDAY

Atlanta, Ga., Feb. 6.—Harriet Tolbert, an aged Negro woman, was frozen to death in her home at 18 Garibaldi Street early Monday morning during the severe cold. [from the Atlanta *Constitution*]

The *Defender* concluded the article with a blistering paragraph which presumably was the final word on the subject: "If you can freeze to death in the North and be free, why freeze to death in the South and be a slave, where your mother, sister, and daughter are raped and burned at the stake, where your father, brother and son are treated with contempt and hung to a pole, riddled with bullets at the least mention that he does not like the way he has been treated? Come North then, all of you folks, both good and bad. If you don't behave yourself up here, the jails will certainly make you wish you had. For the hard working man there is plenty of work—if you really want it.

"The Defender says come!"

They came—and came bringing goats, pigs, chickens, dogs and cats, wearing overalls and housedresses, a few walking barefoot; they came, bringing southern folkways, manners, traditions and habits, and some came to see Robert S. Abbott in person. The migrants, mostly from the rural areas, also brought problems of adjustment and assimilation. Thus, meeting the actual conditions of "free" Chicago brought exaltation and disillusionment.

But the flight from the South—actually a flight from a feudal to a modern way of life—created new problems for Northerners, both white and Negro, especially with the disintegration of the Black Belt into a slum. Chicago was bursting at the seams, producing aggravating problems of crime, health, schooling and housing. Negro family life, such as it was in the South, completely collapsed in the North, with a consequent high cost to the white community. Broken families and juvenile delinquency were obvious manifestations. When, during the war, Negroes were siphoned into industry, particularly munitions, iron, steel, and electrical manufacturing, new areas of conflict developed as organized labor met Negro entrance with bitter hostility.

The migrants were quickly labeled as "undesirable."

The daily papers, reflecting the popular reaction among white people, carried headlines like these: HALF MILLION DARKIES FROM DIXIE SWARM TO THE NORTH TO BETTER THEMSELVES and NORTH DOES NOT WELCOME INFLUX OF SOUTH'S NEGROES. A typical subhead editorialized in this fashion: "Negro Influx Brings Disease." One especially vexing problem touched nearly every white man personally: where were these people to live? Practically no new buildings had been erected since the war, and it was physically impossible for a tripled Negro population to squeeze into the available space. On a single day the Chicago Urban League had 664 Negro applicants and only fifty-five dwellings actually open to Negro occupancy.

The solution: segregation of Negroes in the Black Belt.

This social edict placed Negroes in the hands of exploiting landlords from whose grasp it was impossible to escape—rents for Negroes rose between five and thirty per cent, and in a few cases as much as fifty per cent. The instrument used to clearly define boundaries beyond which no Negro was to move was the residential covenant—an agreement among white property owners not to rent or sell to Negroes. Even so, Negroes overran the areas designated as "white only," and in the process developed considerable friction. Bombs were soon thrown in reply—indeed, twenty-four bombs wrecked Negro dwellings between July 1, and July 27, 1919. Jesse Binga, a Negro banker and Abbott's close friend, was bombed five times. The police only shrugged which naturally led to accusations of bias.

These tensions produced fears and suspicions, even antipathy. Racial antagonisms, suppressed and sublimated during the war, now returned to the surface. The South Side was particularly nervous. Two wanton murders of Negroes were followed by notices being conspicuously posted in the Black Belt, declaring efforts would be made to "get niggers on July 4th [1919]." Negroes in turn whispered a warning to prepare for a riot. A Chicago *Tribune* article, headlined LAWYER WARNS NEGROES HERE TO ARM SELVES, quoted a Negro as saying, "Arm yourselves now with guns and pistols." And they did precisely this. Subsequently, wherever the races had contact clashes seemingly followed. For example, recreational facilities, even semi-private ones, were taxed beyond capacity, a fact that grated on everyone's nerves. The public bathing beaches were particularly explosive points of contact, but unfortunately there was no official recognition of the acute problems caused by the mass migration. Consequently, uneasy tension blanketed the city like so much smog.

Even so, Abbott's warnings, echoed by Carl Sandburg's remarkable articles in the Chicago *Daily News,* were ignored.

CHAPTER XI

A Case of Ambivalence

CHICAGO'S LAKE MICHIGAN, once reeking with the stench of wild garlic, was only a short walking distance from the Black Belt, and Robert S. Abbott often strolled along its sweeping banks in contemplative moods. Today the lake is an ornament to the midwest metropolis, but forty years ago its marshy rim provided only rocky, ill-kept beaches, to which the city's poorer inhabitants escaped during the sweltering heat of the summers. Beyond the city, cutting the beaches and extending into the water, was an imaginary dividing "line," intended to separate white from black bathers. The "line" had come about informally, perhaps a result of long practice without legal inspiration, and had hardened into a Jim Crow custom. It formed boundaries, tacitly understood and jealously guarded, across which neither race ventured.

One hot Sunday afternoon—July 27th, 1919, to be precise— a colored boy swam across the so-called "line," or perhaps was carried by the current into the section designated as "white." He was promptly pelted with stones by the white bathers. Negroes were outraged by the utter meanness of this racial display. Before long a stone-throwing clash was in progress between blacks and whites. The boy, unable to return to shore

173

during the fracas, drowned. The tragedy sobered the crowd, and they halted battling long enough to dive for him. When his body was not recovered, there were excited whispers, "The white people killed a Negro!" Soon reports circulated that a white policeman had refused to arrest the "murderer." Negroes began to mass dangerously, and at this crucial point the accused officer arrested a Negro on a white man's complaint. The policeman was mobbed, and a riot was touched off involving upwards of ten thousand people and continuing sporadically twelve days and nights.

The riot had national repercussions.

Robert S. Abbott undoubtedly recognized the outburst as, in part at least, a sequel to resentments nurtured by his noisy agitation. But, though shocked by the explosion, he was afflicted with a curious ambivalence: *he did not view the riot as unmitigated evil, because he hoped it might focus attention upon the injustices done Negroes.* This view, perhaps shared by his editors, was of course reflected in the columns of the *Defender.* If not by inclination, Abbott was certainly propelled into this position by unspoken racial pressure—and in this sense he was a captive of his own policy, for loyalty to his race demanded this course; any other brought penalties for waywardness.

This fact was illustrated in a tragic by-product of the riot: during the conflict a well-to-do Negro, prominent in local political and social circles, was sought out as a leader and asked for an interview by a reporter from the Chicago *Tribune.* In the published interview he was reported as saying: "This is a white man's country, and Negroes had better behave or they will get what rights they have taken away." He insisted that "a lot of the trouble is due to Negroes from the South" and called upon "some representative Negroes from the same part of the country [to] do what they can to help quiet things down." He declared "Some of us forget that the

Photograph of lynching found among Abbott's effects.

Abbott at the tomb of the Unknown Soldier, Arc de Triomphe, Paris, in 1929.

Publisher's mansion on South Parkway, Chicago.

Abbott at the peak of his career.

Monument Abbott erected on St. Simons Island in memory of his ex-slave father, Thomas Abbott.

white man has given us freedom, the right to vote, to live on terms of equality with him, to be paid well for our work, and to receive many other benefits." He finally warned, "If the white man should decide that the black man has proved he is not fit to have the right to vote, that right may be taken away. We might also find it difficult to receive other favors to which we have become accustomed, and then what would happen to us?"

These statements aroused a solid Negro sentiment against him. He was derided as an "Uncle Tom," and ridiculed as a "white man's nigger." Not long afterwards his life was threatened—indeed, for several weeks he had to have police protection. He was ostracized and died in less than a year. His friends asserted that he was slanderously misquoted and that his death was due largely to the rain of criticism. At any rate, few Negroes had the courage to buck the racial tide. Publicly, say Cayton and Drake in *Black Metropolis*, "conservative" Negroes like Abbott were constrained to curb the masses who did the actual hand-to-hand fighting; but privately, despite recognition of the riot's horrors, like Negroes of all classes they justified the raging warfare as self-defense and as proof that Negroes would not supinely suffer mistreatment. As a group, according to these two observers, the "conservatives" felt the riot held "the same paradoxical elements of good emerging from evil that [President] Wilson saw in the First World War." Consequently, the *Defender* reported the upheaval with these headlines:

RIOT SWEEPS CHICAGO
GHASTLY DEEDS OF
RACE RIOTERS TOLD

DEFENDER REPORTER FACES DEATH TO GET FACTS OF MOB VIOLENCE; HOSPITALS ARE FILLED WITH MAIMED MEN AND WOMEN

175

GUN BATTLES AND FIGHTING IN STREETS KEEP CITY IN AN UPROAR

FRENCH GIVE OPINION OF RIOT

Mob action had followed by two hours the incident at Lake Michigan. The people of Chicago awoke Monday morning to learn that a minor incident had furnished enough spark to rouse the Negro's deep-seated sense of wrong and denial and even memories of injustices in the South. Overnight, crowds had gone crazy like the remnants of a defeated, abandoned, hungry army. The swift circulation of distorted rumors had quickly set ablaze the smoldering resentments against racial discrimination and lynching. Negroes tumbled out of saloons, barbershops, gambling joints, basements and poolrooms intent upon revenge. Crowds soon gathered and any white man who happened into contact with them was pummeled—in all, four white men were beaten, five stabbed, and one was shot on Sunday night. When the police tried to make arrests, the attempt served only to inflame the crowds.

Then hell broke loose.

Both white and Negro mobs sprang up spontaneously. The Negroes involved grew in number and hostility, often goaded to anger by flagrant bias on the part of the white police. They surged through the streets hurling bricks, stones and other missiles, trampling people in the mêlées that followed. One huge mob broke into bands and went in search of white men, while women stood on the fringes urging them on with oaths and cheers. Finally, completely lawless elements, both white and Negro, entered the fray, and soon armed gangs were fighting to the death. When white hoodlums invaded the Negro neighborhood, pitched battles were fought in the streets. Youthful white gangs—belonging to the so-called athletic clubs—ran amuck under the baleful eyes of the ward politicians who sponsored them. They indiscriminately raided Negro homes, institutions and business establishments, attacking the people they had long labeled as "jigs," "shines," "dinges," "smokes" and "niggers."

Even in the midst of this day-by-day disaster, the press demonstrated little restraint and pretended little objectivity. In fact, the mobs were even further incited by the newspaper accounts. The dailies, which could publish six times as much material, had the advantage over the weeklies. But having the riot in its own bailiwick, so to speak, gave the *Defender* a beat on the Negro press, for Negroes elsewhere were forced to turn to it for first-hand accounts. The advantage was naturally exploited. Both white and Negro newspapers in Chicago were guilty of inflammatory handling of the riot news, but bias was particularly pronounced in the *Defender*.

For example, the front-page statistical reports of the dead and injured, clearly identified as "white" and "Negro," appeared like box scores. It produced a feeling that the score must be kept even—that is, on an eye-for-an-eye basis. Not content with this, the paper distinctly gave the impression that a conspiracy was afoot to exterminate the Negro population, and this excited Negroes to further excesses. Its "injury done women" story was typical of the paper's reporting.

There was in fact no foundation for any reports that women and children, white or black, were killed—yet the *Defender,* to its discredit, carried this highly colored report: "An unidentified young Negro woman and three-months-old baby were found dead on the street at the intersection of Forty-seventh and Wentworth. She had attempted to board a car there when the white mob seized her, beat her, slashed her body to ribbons, and beat the baby's brains out against a telegraph pole. Not satisfied with this, a rioter severed her breast and a white youngster bore it aloft on a pole triumphantly while the crowd hooted gleefully. The whole time this was happening several policemen were in the crowd but did not make any attempt to make a rescue until too late."

Such a story must have had the desired effect.

Soon the homes of whites in sections adjacent to the Black Belt went up in flames, as Negroes retaliated for the burning of Negro property. Then blacks were snatched from the streetcars and beaten, stabbed and shot; gangs roamed the Negro area shooting at random. Automobile raids were added to the rioting. Cars from which rifle and revolver shots were fired were driven at great speeds through the Negro section. Negroes defended themselves by sniping and volley-fire from ambush and barricade. So great was the fear of these raiding parties that Negroes frequently opened fire on all motor vehicles without waiting to learn the identity of the occupants. The *Defender's* city editor, Lucius C. Harper, was caught in this guerilla warfare, and wrote a "color" story carrying the head: SHOWERED WITH BULLETS. He used his fair complexion to advantage, by circulating among the white rioters and reporting their activities. For the most part the riot was confined to the South Side and stockyards area, but in time the fighting spilled into the white residential neighborhoods with much loss of life and considerable damage to property.

Provident Hospital, a Negro-conducted institution situated on the South Side, treated both white and Negro casualties without discrimination. Its annual report for 1919 gave many revealing sidelights of the riot. "During the twenty-four hours from midnight Sunday to midnight Monday," it reported, "seventy-five victims received treatment and a number died." It was difficult to get food into the hospital, and the place was so crowded that patients had to lie on the floors. The institution itself was menaced by crowds of young white toughs, "mainly mere boys," who raided the area, "destroying, wounding and killing as they went." They even shot into the hospital. When a mob gathered before the doors, many of the nurses, "worn and tried by long hours of excitement and hard work, found human nature too weak to stand the hideous sights and bloodshed, and begged to be taken away." Except for these short spells of hysteria, the nurses stayed at their posts, "often without sleep and without proper nourishment." The white doctors, normally in attendance, were absent during the riot.

The *Defender* reported these grisly details: "Every hour, every minute, every second finds patrols backed up [at Provident Hospital] unloading their human freight branded with the red symbol of this orgy of hate. Many victims have reached the hospital, only to die before kind hands could attend them. Victims lie in every street and vacant lot. . . . Undertakers on the South Side refuse to accept bodies of white victims. White undertakers refuse to accept black bodies. Both for the same reason. They fear the vengeance of the mobs."

I have said above that the over-all situation is not easy to grasp—especially when one is dealing with masses of people in turbulent action. But the awesome reality of a race riot may be grasped through the experience of one individual—in this case, a person who perhaps had no intention of recording for posterity how a Negro felt when pursued by a white mob. The individual involved was a young man in his early twenties, son of a clergyman. Before going abroad as a soldier, he had attended college briefly. The night in question he had been at work in a plant on the outskirts of the city and, becoming ill early in the evening, was forced to leave. What follows is lifted directly from the testimony given, when official inquiry was being made into the causes of the riot. I have adhered as closely as possible to the facts related.

This is what he described.

The night was unusually hot, and there was a feeling of rain in the air. He carried his jacket over his arm and wiped perspiration off his forehead. As he approached an intersection to transfer to a streetcar heading in the direction of the South Side, he suddenly heard a crowd yelling: "There's a nigger! Let's get him!" He judged the group to number about twenty men. He quickly leaped aboard a car, but they pulled the trolley pole down from the wires, halting the car, and started in the front after him. The motorman opened the rear door, and the Negro jumped off. Moved by a reflex of his whole being, he flung his jacket away and started running. . . .

"There he goes!" someone shouted. And with that, the mob started in hot pursuit. "One, two, three blocks," he recalled, "went past in rapid succession and they still came on shouting, 'Stop him! Stop him!' As I ran someone tried to trip me, but I jumped into the gutter." He bumped into a husky fellow as he turned a corner. The man struck at him. He ducked and headed for a nearby drugstore—hoping thus to stave off catastrophe, but a white woman warned him the place was not safe, so he ran down a side street where he nearly fell on the freshly oiled pavement.

"My strength was fast failing. The idea came in my head to stop and give up, or try to fight, but the odds were too great, so I kept running. My legs began to wobble, my breath came harder, and my heart was pounding like a big pump, while they crept up on me. 'They're feeling as tired as you,' I told myself. 'Maybe they smoke and booze and their wind is worse than yours.' So I stuck, and in a few more strides they gave up the chase." But he still was nowhere near the South Side—and indeed was treading hostile territory. He heard shots ring out, followed by intermittent cracks. The sky was aflame, and fire engine bells rang. Beads of perspiration dripped from his forehead. When he was sure no one followed, he slowed down to a walk and tried to catch his breath. He soon found himself in view of an abandoned automobile, but closer inspection revealed two white men with revolvers in hand searching for Negroes—at least so he believed! He crept back behind a fence and lay down as quietly as he could reflecting on how close he had come to a beating—perhaps worse.

"Fear, which had caused me to run, now gave way to anger, and a desire to fight, and after awhile I felt nothing but hatred and a need for revenge." He tried thinking up a plan to get home safely. "I decided to wait a couple of hours. I figured the time to be about 11:30 and so decided to wait until 1:30 or 2:00 before coming out of cover. Then the injustice of the whole thing overwhelmed me—and my feelings ran riot. Had the ten months I spent in France been all in vain? What had I done to deserve such treatment? I lay there trying to imagine how the innocent victim of a southern mob must feel! Must a Negro always suffer because of his skin? 'There's a nigger! Let's get him!'—Those words kept ringing in my ears. I shall never forget them! Then suddenly I was no longer afraid, only filled with a desire to get out of danger. But I shook inside, and I began to cry. In the midst of this, I found myself praying. Then relief came—and a determination to get up and try to go through and fight, if necessary. I thought of phoning a friend to come and get me in his car, but where could I find a phone and be safe? Some clothes on a line in a yard offered a chance for disguise, but even dressed as a woman I'd need a hat."

He picked up four rocks as ammunition, and slowly headed for the South Side. He slipped from shadow to shadow, through back alleys. A barking dog nearly exposed him. The approach of an automobile made him dive for cover. Then a block away he saw the forms of men. He dropped to the ground panting. He remained rigidly still. He furtively watched them for a few minutes before he realized they were the uprights of a bridge. Fear and imagination had played tricks on him. Finally, he saw in the distance the grandstand of the White Sox baseball park and he knew he was safely near the Negro neighborhood. It was all over. The first Negroes he saw, he ran up to them and shouted: "Boy, am I glad to see you!" Then he related his experiences, and together they cussed out the white folks. "It was now nearly four o'clock—exactly five and a half hours since I started home from work. Then, a white man came along on his way to work, and my first impulse was to jump on him and beat him up. But something inside told me he was not responsible for the actions of the mobs. He was as innocent as I had been when set upon."

He shrugged his shoulders and declared to his companions: "I'm going home."

It perhaps was foolhardy, but the *Defender's* editor did a courageous thing. Alarmed by the casualties and destruction, he reversed himself and urged Negroes to exercise patience and self restraint—and thereby risked rousing Negro angers and being labeled an "Uncle Tom." Heavy risks were entailed. He nevertheless quickly ran off 30,000 handbills, enough to swamp the South Side, bearing the paper's masthead with the headline in bold type: EXTRA!! He swiftly recruited his newsboys, and pressed into service anyone else he could lay hands on, and began a door-to-door distribution in which he himself participated. The signed declaration, almost plaintive in tenor, was addressed "To the Citizens of Chicago"—meaning Negroes. The statement, in a sense, revealed the riot's anatomy.

This, in effect, was his five-point plea:

Under a paragraph captioned YOUR DUTY AND MINE he explained that the riot was being "aggravated by loose talk and foolish actions," and urged his fellows "to do your part to restore quiet and order." He warned them to "Keep Off the Streets," because usually only innocent bystanders got hurt. He advised everyone to avoid crowds and streetcars. He assured them that "The police can handle rowdies better if you are not in their way," and asked that they "Help The Police Do Their Duty." The penalty for disorder, Abbott reminded, was the "loss of life, destruction of property, loss of money for you and your families." Then in a sub-head he flatly declared: THIS IS NO TIME TO SOLVE THE RACE QUESTION! And he finally urged, "Make Yourself A Committee of

EXTRA!!

To The Citizens of Chicago.

Your Duty And Mine

The present lawless conditions prevailing throughout the city are only aggravated by loose talk and foolish actions by irresponsible of both races

We urge you to do your part to restore quiet and order.

Keep Off The Streets

Keep yourself and your children off the streets. Remember the innocent bystander generally gets the worst of it.

Riots Mean an Irreparable Loss to Innocent and Guilty Alike

Remain at home and urge your friends to do likewise. Avoid crowded street cars, and corners.

The police can handle rowdies better if you are not in their way.

Every day of rioting and disorder means loss of life, destruction of property, loss of money for you and your families, and for some of us these losses will be large and irredeemable.

This is no time to solve the Race Question

Measures are being taken now to give adequate police service and protection. This is no time to solve the race question.

Never mind who started it. Let proper authorities finish it. We must have order at once for our own good and the good of Chicago.

Help The Police Do Their Duty

We need cool heads and steady nerves. The police are playing no favorites. Follow their example.

If you do your part as real citizens regardless of your color, responsibility can be easily and more justly placed.

MAKE YOURSELF a Committee of one to make things peaceful.

OBEY ALL POLICE ORDERS
Yours for Peace,
ROBERT S. ABBOTT

Handbill distributed by the *Defender* during the Chicago
race riots of 1919.

One to Make Things Peaceful—OBEY ALL POLICE OR-DERS."

He signed this plea with, "Yours for Peace, Robert S. Abbott."

The rioters paid little heed.

Of a force of 3,000 police, 2,800 were massed in the Black Belt. But the rioting was ended only by the state militia, belatedly called after the police had shown an inability, and in some instances an unwillingness, to curb attacks on Negroes. It is sufficient to look at the news photographs, for they eloquently describe the disaster that befell Chicago. But a few statistics will document the magnitude of the riot: 38 persons were killed, 537 were injured, and about 1,000 were left homeless and destitute. Of the 38 killed, 15 were whites and 23 Negroes; of the 537 injured, 178 were whites, 342 were Negroes, and the race of 17 was not recorded.

Let us not linger over these horrible details.

Upon the heels of the upheaval, the *Defender*, characterizing the outburst as "a disgrace to American civilization," commented in this fashion in an editorial captioned, "Reaping the Whirlwind":

America is known the world over as the land of the lynchers and the mobocrats. For years she has been sowing the wind and now she is reaping the whirlwind. The Black worm has turned. A Race that has furnished hundreds of the best soldiers that the world has ever seen is no longer content to turn the left cheek when smitten upon the right. . . . For this awakening, however, the color madness of the American white man alone is responsible. . . . We have little sympathy with lawlessness, whether those guilty of it be Black or white, but it cannot be denied that we have much in the way of justification for our changed attitude. Under the promise of a square deal our boys went cheerfully into the service of the country hoping that the aftermath of the struggle could find our people in an improved social and industrial condition. . . . Industrially our position has undoubtedly been benefitted by the war. Socially it has grown worse. On all sides we have been made to feel the humiliating pressure of the white man's prejudice. . . . It is a case of "teaching us our place" and limiting our sphere. We resented the assumption. Hence the race riots.

The police searched for the answer to the Negro outburst in the saloons, barbershops, gambling places and poolrooms! But soon afterwards Governor Frank O. Lowden, upon the urgent requests of both white and Negro citizens, announced the appointment of a Commission on Race Relations, consisting of twelve members, six from each race—and, ironically, Robert S. Abbott was one of those appointed. He had accepted though he expected to derive little either of honor or profit. The commission employed a biracial staff of scholars and investigators, headed by Graham Romeyn Taylor, to probe into the causes of the riot. It made a monumental report, prepared by Dr. Charles S. Johnson, a distinguished Negro sociologist, which is now contained in a 672-page book called *The Negro in Chicago* (1922). Briefly: the commission reported that "The riot was merely a symptom of serious and profound disorders [in the society] lying beneath the surface of race relations in Chicago." It could suggest no "ready remedy," but offered certain suggestions in the hope that "mutual understanding and sympathy between the races will be followed by harmony and cooperation." Finally, it declared that now "progress should begin in a direction steadily away from the disgrace of 1919."

W. E. B. Du Bois, editor of the influential *Crisis* magazine, had warned Negroes "to watch narrowly the work and forthcoming report." For, he declared, "The Commission consists of colored men who apparently have a much too complacent trust in their white friends; and of enemies of the Negro race who under the guise of impartiality and good will are pushing insidiously but unswervingly a program of racial segregation." If this was the case, it was not apparent from the tenor of the report. The commission, even if its language was rightly restrained, made fundamental and forthright recommendations for the improvement of race relations, and Abbott personally performed with credit to himself and his race.

Of especial concern to us, are those recommendations dealing with the Negro press. The commission observed the "The *Defender's* editorials are as a rule carefully written, balanced, and critical at times, in contrast with the popular appeal of the news articles," but frankly urged more accurate reporting of incidents involving the races. The final words, in effect, concluded with a polite but devastating condemnation of Abbott's paper for irresponsible news reporting: "To the Negro press we recommend greater care and accuracy in reporting incidents involving whites and Negroes, the abandonment of sensational headlines and articles on racial questions, and more attention to educating Negro readers as to the available means and opportunities of adjusting themselves and their fellows into more harmonious relations with their white neighbors and fellow-citizens."

The *Defender's* editor and publisher signed the commission's formal report to the governor, though it contained these implied criticisms of his paper's policies. Even so, he demonstrated considerable statesmanship. Robert S. Abbott was no figurehead, nor did he allow himself to be used as mere window-dressing for the commission; instead, according to Dr. Johnson, now president of Fisk University, Nashville, Tennessee, he "seldom missed a meeting, made many useful contributions to the study, and actively participated in every discussion." The reason for his unusual behavior, Dr. Johnson believes, was because "he made a distinction between the energetic publishing of a newspaper and the long-range social goals the report recommended for achievement by both the white and Negro communities." Until now, he had primarily concerned himself with finding a haven for his oppressed people, and with protesting racial discrimination and proving the Negro's humanity. But the methodical investigations and disciplined study conducted by the commission gave him new insights into the problems of Negro crime, health, schools, migration and social behavior. This ultimately was to be reflected in a shift in the *Defender's* concerns, emphasis and goals.

Our whining, baby, dependent days are over; no longer will our shortcomings be overlooked; the test of manly worth will be applied equally to all—if anything, we must be a shade the better to get equal credit.—ROBERT S. ABBOTT, "Making Good," *Southern Workman*, 1919.

CHAPTER XII

A Magnificent Moment

THINGS HAD GONE as J. Hockley Smiley had so rashly prophesied.

The *Defender* was swiftly reaching the position of justifying the oft-repeated boast of being "The World's Greatest Weekly"—and, as a sort of bonus, Robert S. Abbott was becoming a nationally recognized figure in the Negro community. The circulation, tapering off from the artificial spurt caused by the war, had settled down to roughly 180,000 weekly. The paper now contained thirty-two pages, turned out city and national editions, and sold for ten cents. Its influence was both extensive and pervasive and was widening daily. The experimental period had seemingly passed, though Abbott still was eagerly looking for new ideas and talent. He was beginning to make money, and his paper was rapidly assuming the proportions of an institution.

This achievement alone might have been enough to satisfy the most ambitious Negro newspaperman, but Abbott was restlessly searching for something more durably concrete. A vigorous competitor had entered the field: the Chicago *Whip*, started in 1919 by Arthur C. MacNeal and Joseph D. Bibb, lately a graduate of Yale Law School. It rivaled the *Defender* in the vigor of its policy and sold for only five cents. Even this fact did not deflect Abbott from his new concerns, which had developed logically from his recent experiences, and he labeled them urgent enough for prompt action. For Abbott, indelibly touched by the race riot in his own bailiwick, was now primarily concerned with methods of implementing what he had learned during the outburst—and had learned, too, in the process of serving on the Commission on Race Relations.

Abbott had now boldly modified his point of view.

To put this new development into perspective, we must pause briefly and look back to 1916, when the Western Newspaper Union was printing the *Defender*. Circulation had bounded up so rapidly that Western's old-fashioned equipment could not keep pace. The eight-page paper was printed four pages at a time, and pages two, four, six and eight were run off on a flat-bed press, while another such press was tied up printing pages one, three, five and seven. The finished product was bundled into stacks of one hundred, and out-of-town orders were mailed from the plant.

It was a slow and tedious operation. The paper, though printed on Thursday night with a Saturday dateline, never reached the far away points until Tuesday and Wednesday, a fact that brought many agent complaints. Even local papers were late in reaching the newsstands. Phil Jones, who by now had moved up in the organization to become Abbott's right-hand man, recalls how, when he was in charge of circulation, he usually had to wait interminable hours at the plant before he could gather up the papers, load them on a horse-drawn wagon, and actually begin distribution to the dealers. Abbott eventually contracted for two half-ton trucks to speed up delivery on the city routes.

But the fundamental kinks remained.

Unable to solve them himself, Abbott sought the advice of a white man, Clarence Brown, whom he had met through his cartoonist, Langston Mitchell. Brown worked as a foreman at Drovers *Journal*, a farm newspaper which did job printing. He introduced Abbott to his employers and they offered a solution. But before making a decision the Negro publisher still had several important things to consider. For example, whenever he ran short of filler he could always buy it at Western as low as twenty-five cents a column. Western, which already printed several small newspapers, charged for type setting by the galley, and for makeup, "get ready," folding, bundling and mailing by the hour, at a figure Abbott regarded as reasonable. Even so, as already indicated, he often was pushed to meet his weekly bill.

This seems an appropriate place to interpolate an amusing incident in connection with his financial problems at Western. As a boy, Jones recalls, it was his job to carry the copy to the Western printers. One day just before deadline Abbott found himself short five or six dollars on his weekly print bill. "Unable to stall the printers," Jones says, "Abbott ditched the editorials—which in galleys amounted to the shortage—and inserted a box on the editorial page containing the following notice: 'Sorry, no editorials this week. Enroute to the printers, the copy boy let the copy fall in the Chicago River and it was too late to prepare more.'"

Drovers *Journal* had efficient routines and modern presses, and was capable of printing as many copies as Abbott needed. But the only day the plant could print his paper and not interfere with the publishing of its own, was Wednesday afternoon and night, which meant the *Defender* would be published three days before its usual Saturday dateline. Nor did the *Journal* have a variety of type faces. Anyway, they quoted a flat price for the whole process of producing and shipping 30,000 papers. No amount of dickering by Abbott could alter the price or number of copies. He hesitated, because his run was only 23,000 then, which meant he would be buying 7,000 useless papers. Yet he made the plunge, speculating on his circulation rising to meet the increase.

He again had made the right guess. The first week of this arrangement, an unexpected development pushed Negroes onto the front page of every daily in the country. As related before, the Tenth Cavalry Regiment, an all-Negro outfit, was dispatched to the Mexican border in a punitive expedition against the Pancho Villa bandits. Negroes were eager for news of them and the *Defender* fully satisfied this need. Abbott not only sold every copy of the 30,000, but had to print an additional 3,000!

Until 1919 the arrangement at Drovers *Journal* worked exceedingly well, and an amiable relationship developed between Abbott and the printers. But the race riot gave a curious twist to normal contacts. To begin with, the *Journal's* plant was located at 836 Exchange Avenue in the Union Stockyards—which was the scene of the bloodiest killings in the twelve-day disorder. News of the outburst first broke Monday morning, and had reached a peak of fury by Wednesday—the day the *Defender* was usually published. A nervous atmosphere pervaded the plant when Negroes arrived to correct galleys and make up the pages. The white printers were reluctant to work. After several conferences, they agreed to set the type, make up pages and cast the page mats—but they flatly refused to proceed with the printing.

It so happened that the plant's presses were located at street level and visible to passersby. When the rioting broke out before the *Journal's* door, no amount of persuasion could bring the men of the plant to continue working on a Negro newspaper, and they quietly urged Negroes to return to the South Side to avoid any untoward incidents. This, to be sure, involved no hostility to Abbott personally—indeed, the *Journal* had procured newsprint for him during the wartime shortages. The paper's publisher, Ward Neff, who was distinctly impressed by the manner in which the Negro handled himself in every negotiation, pronounced him "a capable and first-class man." But every white man at the plant not only feared bodily harm but also feared the place would be wrecked by the rampaging mobs.

Robert S. Abbott faced disaster.

There seemingly was no place to print the paper, even though it contained one of the biggest stories of its history. When Abbott heard this catastrophic news he threw the papers he was holding to the floor, turned wet with perspiration, and was unable to utter a word. He sank into a chair, and for several minutes no one dared speak to him. This was, of course, a dilemma Abbott had never anticipated, and if his natural somberness now seemed more cloudy than usual, there was good reason. He worriedly turned to Phil Jones and asked somewhat plaintively, "What are we going to do?" It was a purely rhetorical question, for he soon was frantically searching for someone to print the paper. He had no success. His people, too, searched everywhere.

At the last minute the situation was saved. Cartoonist Leslie Rogers, who lived in Gary, Indiana, suddenly remembered that the Gary *Tribune* had presses large enough to handle the *Defender*. Telephone conferences quickly followed and the *Tribune's* publishers agreed to print, if Abbott could furnish the paper. Then began the arduous task of hauling the huge rolls of newsprint from the Chicago warehouse some twenty miles to Gary. "The necessary quantity," says Jones, "was so great that it was impossible to find storage space in Gary, and the rolls were stacked in the alley behind the plant. Had it rained that night, we would have been sunk!"

The presses did not begin to roll until Friday evening. Abbott meanwhile was being further frustrated: Chicago's police chief had informed him that he must see the paper in his office before copies were distributed locally. If he proved arbitrary, Abbott had little alternative. For, by the time he could have taken recourse in the courts, precious hours, perhaps days, would have been lost. Nervous tension gripped him, though outwardly he remained stolid. The police official finally gave clearance, but in the process delayed the distribution several hours. Consequently, not until Saturday night, when the disorders had been in progress five days, did the *Defender's* first "riot edition" begin circulation, and then only after Abbott's old Apperson Jackrabbit automobile had been used as a truck to cart the papers back to Chicago in successive trips.

It was a tremendous performance, collectively achieved.

The riot had hardly died down when Abbott moved swiftly to solve the problems the upheaval had created. He needed little nudging to recognize the unpredictable nature of his business, which could be jeopardized so by the whims of a mob. He decided at all costs to forestall a repetition of any such development as had already plagued him, by acquiring his own plant and presses. Following discussions with Phil Jones, he conferred lengthily with Clarence Brown, the Drovers *Journal* foreman. He recognized his own ignorance of the mechanics of printing machinery, and was fully aware that his employees could offer little advice. He therefore had no reluctance in employing a white man to give such information as he needed. Thus Brown, whom he thought eminently qualified and a person of integrity, advised and formulated the plans for the acquisition of a plant and presses.

Abbott quickly put his organization into motion. He himself did much of the shopping about before he decided upon a high-speed Goss cylinder press which, after Brown's inspection, he bought directly from the Goss Printing Press Company. Then he went in search of a large building to house the machinery and the new business and editorial offices he planned. He specifically sought one within the Negro neighborhood, perhaps as a defensive measure in case of a race riot. He found such a place at 3435 Indiana Avenue in the heart of the South Side, occupied by the Globe Storage Company which was about to move. He made several inspections, noting well the possibilities for expansion, and finally decided to buy. When he soon afterwards acquired the adjoining building, he shrewdly had "Alf" Anderson go into the market as the "buyer," and thus was able to make the purchase at a reasonable figure before the seller learned that Abbott needed the place for expansion.

The building, a three-story brick structure, originally was a house of worship. It had been erected in 1899 as the *Anshe Doron* synagogue by the South Side Hebrew Congregation, and was later sold to the Globe as Negroes began moving into the area. The temple, containing a gallery, was built in the form of an auditorium, which the Globe used as a warehouse. Abbott promptly remodeled the place for newspaper purposes, but until this day the original architectural framework and stained-glass windows remain. It was, however, an imposing structure for its day.

Soon afterwards the foundation was laid for the press, and Abbott persuaded Brown to join his staff and assume the job of plant foreman, which was a revolutionary innovation for the Negro press. Upon his white employee's insistence, Abbott signed a contract with the Chicago Typographical Union No. 16, and thus established a union shop at the *Defender*, the first in any Negro newspaper. But he could hardly have escaped the irony of the situation, for this union was precisely the one from which he himself had been barred membership and consequently denied the opportunity of earning a livelihood as a printer. He nevertheless faithfully lived up to his part of the bargain. Brown was allowed to assemble his own crew—all white men, a fact that produced considerable grumbling among rank-and-file Negroes and eventually loud repercussions. And his competitors lost no time exploiting his fall from grace, racially speaking.

But let us not look ahead too soon.

Even if he had wanted to do otherwise, Abbott had no choice—because, as Phil Jones explains, a search of the entire country had produced not more than a half dozen Negroes trained as linotypists, stereotypists, and pressmen, and these were already employed and had no wish to pull up stakes and come to Chicago to work. If he had attempted to persuade them, the salary costs would have been prohibitive. But obviously the public could know none of these things.

"The employment of white men nevertheless proved a mighty good arrangement," Fay Young says. "The union guaranteed production. The contract called for the union to see that the place was fully manned at all times, so the entire crew could get sick and fail to show up, but the paper would be printed as usual." And in the bargain, according to Jones, "They were dependable, respectful and cooperative, and Brown himself played fair and square. The men often worked overtime without pay, but no money was deducted when they worked undertime. Only on one occasion did Mr. Abbott fire a white man—and that because of drunkenness, and the union upheld the dismissal as just." By and large, they worked well with Negroes—indeed, not one instance of racial difficulty was experienced by the *Defender*. Abbott himself was inordinately proud of this successful experiment in integrating the races in his plant. His, incidentally, was the only newspaper in the country, white or Negro, where a biracial staff was employed. Negroes were eventually brought into the mechanical departments as apprentices and today entirely man the plant.

The formal unveiling of the new plant was held May 6, 1921. How are we to describe Abbott's facial expression, gait, voice and behavior that day? We can simply say he bubbled with excitement, though outwardly he maintained a quiet, dignified mein. It was, to be sure, a magnificent moment for him. The invitations, personally signed by him, contained this promotional paragraph which undoubtedly was a sincere expression of his sentiment: "You have every reason to be proud and rejoice with us on the completion of this big undertaking, realizing as you must that without loyal aid and support it would have been impossible for us to have given the *Chicago Defender*—with pardonable pride we add, "The World's Greatest Weekly"—this home representing as it does an outlay of a little more than $200,000. . . . And so we want you and your friends to be with us on this date that together we may fittingly mark the greatest milestone reached on our path of progress."

It proved a lively affair attended by much bustle and animation, with Abbott happily acting the role of cordial host. In a sentimental gesture, he had brought his mother from Woodville, Georgia, to press the button and start the machinery in its initial revolutions. The photographs made of her stir something of the triumphant emotion of that day: there she stood before the presses, dressed in a long, flowing old-fashioned dress and a big, wide-brimmed hat, her happiness shining through her unsmiling face. Scores passed under the sign, "The World's Greatest Weekly," to be shown through the new building. Said the issue of May 14, 1921: "The *Chicago Defender* entertained approximately 5,000 people. . . . As one entered [the lobby], two murals by W. E. Scott attracted attention. One, on the left, showed a daughter of Ethiopia holding in one hand the *Defender,* or Light, and in the other the balance scales . . . before the oppressed of all lands and climes. . . . Under one painting the complete office equipment of the first *Defender* was exhibited, a small folding table, and a single chair."

But it was the mechanical equipment that visitors mostly came to see on the "grand opening day"—and, to be sure, they paused to gape at the white employees unexpectedly present at this celebration of Negro progress. The Negro employees were seemingly as excited as Abbott himself. Fay Young whipped off a note to Hampton's *Southern Workman* exulting that the *Defender* had moved into a "three-story, modern building with four linotype machines, a four-deck Goss straight-line press, and a print shop the like of which no colored man ever saw before or dreamed of owning." And he added triumphantly, "All this is owned and paid for by a graduate of Hampton."

If sight of the plant was not enough, each guest was handed a brochure as he left, which revealed some impressive facts and figures. Under the head, "The Chicago *Defender* Today," the items were enumerated and described thus: "Four linotype machines, each one equipped with two magazines. . . . The stereotype department is equipped with the most modern machinery. . . . The press is a 32-page and color machine, made by the celebrated Goss Printing Press Company of Chicago. . . . It prints, folds and counts the papers all in one operation at a speed of 35,000 copies per hour. . . . Five hundred and twenty-eight mailing sacks are used weekly for the transportation of the Chicago *Defender* to the post office."

It was indeed an achievement.

When Abbott had completed furnishing and equipping his plant, which included the addition of another new press, he placed its total value at a half million dollars. Every purchase had been a cash transaction made in the name of the Robert S. Abbott Publishing Company, which he had formed back in 1918. He publicly announced the cost of buildings and equipment, including the two Goss presses, as $475,000—"and indebtedness none." There was a bit of yeast in this figure—actually, the major expenditures according to his personal records were these: building, $12,000, plus $7,500 for the adjacent premises; quadruple press, $40,000, and sextuple press, $60,000. Abbott figured that each edition produced in the new plant now used 850 pounds of ink, 48 tons of paper, and 3,000 pounds of metal. Whatever the exact figures, he had made a gigantic step in the modernization of his organization—a development that was eventually to inspire every Negro newspaperman in the country.

The Negro publisher, now self-consciously aware of being a self-made success, developed a good deal of affection for his possession. He regarded it almost as a child, and demanded that it be kept scrupulously clean. He often was observed personally straightening the arrangement of chairs and inkwells on desks. Dr. Charles M. Thompson, a young dentist for whom Abbott had an affectionate regard, believes Abbott was in love with the *Defender*. He says, "We often went to the theater in the Loop. But before Mr. Abbott would go home nights, he always passed by the plant and looked at it admiringly, as if he was surprised it was still there." He perhaps suspected that his outspoken editorials would one day make his plant a target, especially if there was a repetition of the 1919 race riot.

A sidelight is worthy of mention.

About a half block from the *Defender* plant, there was a restaurant operated by a white man which frankly barred Negro patronage. Abbott passed it daily but made no attempt to fight this particular discrimination—much to the disgust of his employees. He never offered a reason for this curious decision. But, I suspect, he had become so obsessed with his experiences during the riot that he was convinced every white man was a potential mobster. He undoubtedly feared this restaurant proprietor, if angered to the point, could rouse a mob to wreak vengeance on him by physical destruction of his plant. This decision may have cost Abbott some humiliation, but probably less than his employees imagined. For he very likely felt he was protecting his stake as well as their livelihood.

The acquisition of the plant cut Abbott's printing costs more than $1,000 weekly, and the paper immediately began to surge financially. Moreover, his overhead was exceedingly modest. For example, he now had sixty-eight paid employees, and had opened branch offices in New York, Detroit, Toledo, Louisville, Philadelphia, Los Angeles and New Orleans, plus foreign offices in London and Paris. But several of these "branch offices" were merely mailing addresses of stringers paid on a space-rate basis. And he paid below standard wages, though superior to his Negro competitors. The *Whip,* for example, was paying reporters $15 weekly; the *Defender* was paying them $30. Abbott's general manager, Phil Jones, earned $100 weekly, and his managing editor, "Alf" Anderson, received $60 weekly. P. L. Prattis, now executive editor of the Pittsburgh *Courier,* was paid $20 weekly as city editor. When he discovered the janitor earned $25 weekly, he went to Abbott and offered to exchange jobs with the janitor. He soon afterwards was fired.

Abbott saved money on incidental expenses as well. For example, whenever Fay Young made a trip to cover a sports assignment, he reports, his expenses—hotel, food, railroad fare, etc.—were usually paid not by the *Defender* but by the sponsor of the event. Some salaries were as low as $5 and $6 a week, but the white men in the mechanical departments earned the prevailing union wage, a fact which did not help morale among Negroes. Abbott himself drew a salary of $200 weekly—plus, according to Phil Jones, a drawing account of $1,000 to $2,000 monthly, depending upon what obligations were outstanding. Actually, these were reserve funds and surplus which he deposited in his personal bank account.

Even so, the Negro publisher could be a penny pincher.

He did allow himself the luxury of employing his Hampton classmate and old friend, Charles "Bung" Thornton, who afterwards became the model for a popular cartoon strip, "Bungleton Green." But this sentimental hiring had its value to Abbott. Thornton was a printer, but now that Abbott had a union shop he was unable to work at his trade in the *Defender.* Before a printing shop was started, he did odd jobs about the place. One job assigned to him was an institutional operation: collecting discarded newspapers and magazines—that is, every morning he went to the railroad yards, and before the cars were cleaned, he collected all the papers and periodicals left behind by passengers. He would bundle them up and haul them back to the *Defender* office, where they would be culled for stories about Negroes.

Abbott, as yet, had not provided money for the regular purchase of newspapers and magazines!

A remarkable aspect of his operations, is the fact that Abbott made money on circulation—which incidentally is a characteristic of the Negro press generally. Without such revenue, few Negro newspapers or magazines could survive. Richard L. Jones, business manager 1923 to 1927 and now a retired brigadier general, reports this unusual fact: "Out of every ten cents the *Defender* netted one cent. With the circulation roughly 200,000, the paper earned nearly $1,500 weekly, on circulation alone. The costs of production were broken down thus: five cents a copy to produce the paper (including printing, processing, mailing, paper and salaries); four cents was the agent's share, and a profit of one cent for the *Defender*." Beyond this income, Abbott naturally earned money from the advertising space, and during this period the paper sold sixty per cent weekly—indeed, the *Defender* boasted that it carried more national advertising than any twenty Negro weeklies combined, and its Chicago edition contained twenty times more advertising than its closest competitor.

The advertising was based on a circulation that steadily held keel. When it dipped following the war, he became somewhat sensitive to any remark about the decline, however jocular. One day a lawyer, who was peeved at the *Defender's* reporting of a story in which he was personally involved, met Abbott on the street and complained. He concluded disparagingly, "Your paper don't go anywhere but 'round the corner, so I don't care what you say about me!" Abbott accepted the criticism good-naturedly, but when he returned to his office he wrote a one-paragraph notice to the effect that this particular lawyer would give ten cents to every kid who came to his office with a bottle top, and placed the story on the front page. When the *Defender* reached the newsstands that week, the lawyer's office was deluged with hundreds of youngsters bearing bottle tops and clamoring for the promised ten cents!

Once he had indulged himself in this pixie-like fashion, he wisely started a new promotional campaign to boost circulation. For example, one project involved capitalizing on the national attention being accorded Negroes chosen as All-American football players by the white dailies. In collaboration with Bill Bottom, a cafe owner, he alertly sponsored the first all-star Negro football team, and staged a well-publicized contest in the winter of 1922 between the Negro college stars and an aggregation of white stars. The Negro lineup included names excitedly on the lips of every Negro—Paul Robeson (Rutgers), Ink Williams (Brown), John Shelbourne (Dartmouth), Fritz Pollard (Brown), and Duke Slater (Iowa). By charging two dollars a person admission to the American Giants Park where the contest was played, he cashed in on the racial implications of a Negro versus white game which, incidentally, the Negroes won 7–0. Whereas such a sports spectacle attended by thousands of people might have been promotion enough for the average publisher, and the money invested in staging the affair considered well spent, Abbott not only received the obvious dividends but he and Bill Bottom actually made money.

He afterwards hired Richard L. Jones, a young man of considerable energy and personal charm, as a road representative and sent him on a tour of the country much in the manner of Roscoe Conkling Simmons' trips. When he returned to Chicago, he was made circulation manager. With Abbott's consent, he published a house organ called *Go Getter* to stimulate circulation sales. "Each agent," he says, "was given a quota based on the Negro population of his town or city. No cash prizes or gifts were given, only honorable mention in the paper, which seemed sufficient incentive to get results." In the process of handling distribution, he improved the shipping methods by using mail baggage and express instead of the old straight mail.

By now, Philip Adams Jones, whose association with Abbott began when Jones was a boy in 1910, had become the paper's general manager. He was an energetic, imaginative and impulsive man, tall and rangy, with a square jaw. His salary was small, but the position conveyed considerable power and prestige in the Negro community. As a consequence, he made many of the day-to-day decisions, and often carried the ball when Abbott fumbled. He spoke German, a fact which initially delighted his employer. Jones himself was deeply attached to Abbott, so much so that his first son was christened "Abbott." He perhaps came to have the closest relationship with the publisher of any man—but it was in fact a father-son relationship, with the older man assuming the role of Negro parent. Jones explains the association's beginning this way:

"My mother, a German-reared white woman, had a sundry store where Mr. Abbott frequently came and told her about his plans for the paper. I was attending elementary school and he persuaded her to send me to his office every day after school to keep me out of mischief. My first job carried the title 'copy boy' although the duties called for any and everything from keeping the place clean to running errands. Even from the first, the relationship between myself and Mr. Abbott was that of a father and son. Having been taught respect and obedience to my elders, and having lost my dad [a Negro] at the age of nine, this association was the first I had had for any length of time with a man. And it just seemed natural that I should look up to him for guidance and advice. As time went on, this became a mutual feeling and became more and more binding on both of us."

The mustached, wrinkled-brow Phil Jones, who gained a bull-dog reputation, lived through the excruciating formative years of the *Defender*. His rise, though rapid, was step-by-step. "From copy boy," he recalls, "I was given the additional duty of distributing papers to the newsstands. During my leisure time in the office, I would peck away on the typewriter. When I could do this well, I was handed the correspondence to answer. I often helped with the bookkeeping. Finally, the job of circulation manager was given me (given, perhaps, is the wrong word), new duties were taken over as demand warranted." He thus came to know intimately the paper's problems and publisher. He even absorbed his mentor's passions and prejudices, to the point where he personally took umbrage if any injury was done Abbott.

But as he matured he discovered his idol had feet of clay, and to him Abbott became an "ultra-dreamer," who "always needed someone to harness his dreams and make them practical." Jones now came to understand his role in the equation as that of practical organizer and tough-minded administrator. And Abbott, on his part, depended a good deal upon Jones and his judgment. He would pass along matters to him with a characteristic, "Well, Phil, handle it as you think best." Jones proved loyal and capable. I have gathered considerable testimony that tallies with this estimate. In any case, his work at the *Defender* was a labor of love, and contributed to the success of the enterprise.

His experiences as general manager give us many illuminating insights into Abbott's character in this period. His reporting, though supported by popular opinion, deserves close scrutiny. For example, he recalls that "Mr. Abbott's every waking moment was spent in preaching to the Negro to fight for his rights. An early *Defender* once carried a cartoon depicting a doctor injecting a serum into the back of a patient. The heading was, 'Back-bone Tonic,' and was intended to carry the message that the Negro should display more back-bone in his fight for equality. It is regrettable that the old man never learned this lesson himself. The fact is, he would never venture a personal move unless he knew that the path ahead was void of danger. Yes, there were times when he was afraid to 'carry the ball,' and would accept the 'forward pass' from me only after the field had been cleared for him and the goal post was only a few yards away, and he could cross standing up."

Moreover, when realities were disagreeable, he says, his employer almost always refused to face them. To illustrate his point, Jones describes the time an employee was dismissed for cause and Abbott, recalling the man's valuable service, announced his reemployment. The editorial people threatened to strike because the employee in question had been manifestly dishonest, and they somehow felt Abbott was rewarding a faithless employee to their disadvantage. "The task of personally facing the hostile workers," says Jones, "was thrown in my lap." Whenever angry delegations arrived to protest unpalatable stories and demand retractions, "Mr. Abbott would retreat and leave me to face them; and return only when they had been pacified." But Jones frankly confesses, "I found happiness in doing all these things for I wanted Mr. Abbott to be a big man. I wanted to be a big man, too, and I had sense enough to know that the only way I could reach a top rung on the ladder of success was to push him up so I could occupy the rung he had left vacant."

His words may sound a bit cynical, but the trust Abbott himself placed in his young protégé is illustrated by the fact that he not only made him general manager of the *Defender* at the unripe age of twenty-five, but he also made him a director and secretary of the Robert S. Abbott Publishing Company. Jones thus was authorized to sign all checks and drafts and make contracts, hire and fire and fix salaries. In brief, he was placed in control of the paper's business operations. When the company was reorganized and was made a corporation capitalized at $250,000, Jones received a share of stock worth $5,000. With his formal promotion, his salary was lifted to $125, plus bonuses. The arrangement worked in this fashion according to Jones: "To begin with, our relations were that of father and son; not employer and employee. [Thus] what was mine was his; what was his was mine. The funds of the *Defender* were ours." Actually, neither man recognized the need for a good accounting system. Consequently, this rather loose operation eventually caused difficulties, broken friendships and even long-lasting heartaches.

Until then, the arrangement proved an amiable one, with both men dipping into the till at will.

"My years of association with him," says Jones, "made it possible for me to read his every thought. For instance, prior to one trip, he and I visited the automobile show where a good-looking Cunningham struck his fancy. I knew immediately he wanted the car and I worked toward acquiring one for him. So, during his absence from the city, I purchased the automobile and hired a chauffeur." It was, in fact, a standard model limousine painted black, and trimmed in leather with silver mountings. The body panels were painted Cleveland gray. The carmine-colored carpets matched the upholstery. No optional item was omitted. There were two auxiliary seats, the latest type touring trunk with equipment, two extra Goodyear tires with covers, and a speaking tube to talk with the driver. Upon the doors was inscribed the monogram: "RSA." Finally, a well-tailored uniform was bought for the chauffeur. Thus, when the publisher arrived at the railroad station upon his return, Jones and a delegation of employees and well-wishers met and escorted him to the terminal entrance where the liveried chauffeur stood snappily at attention beside the imposing Cunningham. As Abbott approached, the man saluted and swung open the door. Then a parade started to the *Defender* office.

Jones, with evident satisfaction, declares, "Mr. Abbott derived a great deal of pleasure in having that Cunningham and a uniformed chauffeur—and his happiness was mine."

This little item of sentiment cost a trifling $4,400!

Young Phil Jones perhaps understood Abbott's weaknesses much better than he understood his strengths. If he had grasped Abbott's strengths, he would have seen the handwriting on the wall. For his employer subscribed to pragmatic principles. Not long after Jones was elevated to the position of general manager, Abbott ordered one of his "sayings" run as a boxed streamer across the top of the editorial page and bearing his signature. It read: "No man is indispensable, though many are valuable!"

*I cannot get into my head that I am black. I do not
know what color I am. I want to think, and I do think
that I am a citizen of the United States, and the flag
that covers the head of the white man is the flag that
covers and protects the head of the Negro.*—ROBERT
S. ABBOTT, from a speech delivered before the National Women's Protective Association, 1922.

CHAPTER XIII

Murders, Messiahs and Money

A FEW WEEKS before the *Defender* moved into
the new building, Robert S. Abbott had a long talk with his
old friend Henry D. Middleton, who was present at the paper's birth. He confided his worry about the sensational character of the news presentation, and complained that people
were accusing him of being a "yellow journalist." Perhaps he
was still smarting from criticisms of his policies made by the
Commission on Race Relations, whose report was prepared
by scholars who as a group he respected. In any case, he im-
pulsively hired Middleton at seventy-five dollars weekly to
become the managing editor and instructed him to analyze
the paper, tell him what was really wrong, and make recommendations for sweeping editorial improvements.

"I sat up until 3:00 A.M.," Middleton reports, "working over
the paper. The next morning I met him at his home early.
When we finally got down to business, I gave him a break-
down of stories and the way in which they had been treated.
Then I said, 'Mr. Abbott, you can't take a toy from a baby
without giving it something of equal interest.'

"He explained that he wanted to be friendly with everyone.

He wanted friendly criticism of people in his paper, but his staff interpreted his critical attitude toward conditions and people to mean antagonism.

"I told him the paper would have to change gradually. He agreed with this idea. But a few days before the grand opening, he told me he couldn't hire me, because Roscoe Conkling Simmons was bleeding him for money."

This was the last Middleton heard.

But Abbott, subtly and effectively, began to revamp the paper's editorial approach. His thinking during this period is revealed in an article he wrote for Hampton's *Southern Workman,* called "Making Good." He said, in part, "We waste much of our valuable time wondering what our status will be if 'Jim Crowism' in every form will be abolished, if the horny head of prejudice will rise as often as in the past, if the line so distasteful to us and to our well wishers on the other side will be erased and American citizenship be based not on color but on loyalty. To all of these things there is but one reply: Rome was not built in a day; the prejudices and traditions of the American white man must go as they came, gradually, for 'a man convinced against his will is of the same opinion still.'"

Robert S. Abbott had turned to a policy of gradualism.

There was, of course, no diminution of protest stories in the *Defender*—though he urged patience. But much of the violence subsided, and more and more emphasis was placed upon Negro achievement. Thus, for example, Sadie Mossell (now Mrs. Raymond Pace Alexander), rated a front-page, two-column picture in cap and gown when, at the University of Pennsylvania, she became the first Negro woman in the United States to receive a Ph.D. degree. Charles S. Gilpin, who made Broadway theater history in the title role of Eugene O'Neill's *The Emperor Jones,* was given considerable space when he was awarded the Spingarn medal. Under the head, "Star of French Authors, Translated Classics at Age of

Fourteen," a profile was carried of the Negro, René Maran, who had won the French Academy's literary prize.

Abbott introduced his readers to Africa's primitive art. Under the headline, MARVELOUS AFRICAN SCULPTURE DISCOVERED, he ran a six-column picture layout and story, translated from the French by his city editor, Percival L. Prattis. The sub-head adequately summarizes its content: "Wonder Works of Art Are Brought to French Museums From the Jungles of Guinea, Benin and Somaliland, and Cause Excited Discussion in Paris."

By now, he was running serially *The House Behind the Cedars*, a novel by a distinguished Negro writer, Charles W. Chesnutt. Much fanfare attended the publishing of the initial installment. The *Defender*, quoting a literary review by Dean Howells, described the book as "a gripping, fascinating $10,000 serial novel," and hailed the author as "one of the first of our group to win distinction as a novelist." This was followed by the serialization of *The Negro in Our History*, a voluminous book by Carter G. Woodson, editor of the *Journal of Negro History*, who was labeled "one of the scholars of the Race and a historian of first rank."

The staple copy was still concerned with crime, lynching, suicides, discrimination and human interest as these marvels of arresting condensation will illustrate:

TULSA AFLAME:
85 DEAD IN RIOT

KU KLUX WHIP MINISTER

'SHIMMY' TURNS TO 'SHIVER'
WHEN POLICE RAID CABARET

BEHEADS WIFE IN
LOVE QUARREL

SLAYS RIVAL IN
JEALOUS RAGE

TAKES POISON
WHEN LOVE COOLS

———

KU KLUX 'BOMBS'
CITY FROM AIR

By 1926 the new policy was somewhat set. The table below, prepared by Cayton and Drake for *Black Metropolis*, illustrates the proportion of space afterwards allotted to specific categories of the news in the period 1926–1937 inclusive:

News Category	Percentage of Column Inches
1. Crime	22.3
2. "People"	7.7
3. Interracial relations	6.1
4. Accidents	4.7
5. Community affairs	4.6
6. Government	4.1
7. Politics & political scandal	2.6
8. Human interest	2.4
9. Law suits	2.3
10. Foreign affairs	2.3
11. Organizations	2.0
12. Suicide	1.6
13. Church news	1.6
14. Labor	1.5
15. Mass meetings	1.1
16. Education	1.1
17. Sports	1.1
18. Weather	.6
19. All other news	8.8
20. Cartoons and pictures	18.8
21. Editorials	2.7
Total:	100.0

As illustrated above, there was a decline in the number of stories dealing with racial conflict and lynching, but Abbott compensated for this restraint with a noticeable increase in news involving crime among Negroes. New features were added to make the paper livelier and more entertaining and thus broaden its appeal. For instance, the theater pages, edited by Tony Langston, were expanded. There was a new approach to the sections for women and children. Comic strips were introduced, and a weekly sermon by an ordained minister. Feature articles were done on such subjects as: "Is Bobbed Hair More Attractive Than Long Hair?" Abbott even attempted somewhat successfully to make his readers concerned about Negroes elsewhere in the world, and this perhaps had its inspiration in a Pan-African movement among Negroes. He ran articles which carried provocative heads like this one: HOW THE U. S. DIPLOMATICALLY STRANGLED HAITI. Ever since, Haiti's progress and relations with the United States have been a concern of the paper's editors.

The *Defender* broke out of its limited orbit of concentrating on injustices to the Negro only, and now much space was devoted to lively articles on fashion, art, music, sports, spot news photography and shopping hints. The editorial page continued vigorous as ever but Abbott, though personally opposed to whiskey drinking, proved only a tepid advocate of Prohibition. The Negro editor now pronounced regularly on a variety of non-racial subjects in the somewhat philosophical vein of the elder statesman. A boxed streamer across the top of the editorial page, bearing a facsimile of his signature, carried his views and his wisdom in the form of epigrams. Two or three, a rehash of already popular sayings, are enough to give their point of view: "Our children should be taught that they are Americans first, everything else afterwards," and "Sown seeds often sprout where least expected," and "It's not how much you work, but how much you think while you're working that counts." Next door, so to speak, Roscoe Conkling Simmons, whose copy now showed a decline in vigor, was still doing a signed column called "This Week," but this was primarily because Abbott was simply susceptible to his personal charm and had uses for him beyond conducting an editorial forum.

Robert S. Abbott was perhaps nudged into his new position by a curious external development, which he unwittingly helped create by providing the racial climate. For few Negroes were untouched by the ebullient racial philosophy introduced to the Negro community by Marcus Garvey, a tempestuous and flamboyant figure. He was indeed Abbott's spiritual kinsman: he was squat and black, and had grown up in his native Jamaica, British West Indies, under a color caste system—white, mulatto, and black—which even as a boy had aroused his resentments, not only against whites but against mulattoes as well. It was this resentment that was translated into one of the cardinal principles of the movement he led and indeed began his Odyssey in search of a place to escape color prejudice.

The solemn-faced immigrant also bore a strong physical resemblance to Robert S. Abbott—indeed, one almost expected them to recognize a certain affinity, for the two had a great deal in common. Each had an active mind. Neither man smoked or drank. Both had notable moral courage. Each man relished the role of martyr, to the point of indulging in self-pity. Both were happiest when the battle was tumultuously hot, bored in peace. Both had excellent health and prodigious reserves of energy. Both were chips from the formless, sprawling tree of racial discontent. Both men had a dedicated and unswerving passion for the social emancipation of the Negro race. Perhaps the similarity of the two men is defined by the hero they shared: Booker T. Washington.

But from this point the men diverged.

There were, in fact, some strikingly dramatic differences. While Abbott met the prejudice exhibited by mulattoes stoically, even patiently, the black immigrant was impatiently truculent. Abbott was extremely sensitive about his black skin. Garvey, a full-blooded Negro, reveled in his blackness. Abbott was a humble man. Garvey was a superb egotist. Abbott was deliberate, often hesitant. Garvey was hasty and superficial. Garvey had a keen and penetrating mind but was given to rash decisions. Abbott was bright, perhaps intuitive rather than brilliant, his judgment usually sound. Garvey had a fluent tongue. Abbott was almost inarticulate. Garvey seldom deviated from his racial convictions. Abbott, on the other hand, often contradicted himself, even making a notable about-face. Abbott distrusted unbridled racialism. Garvey was not troubled by such scruples.

But Abbott became the black immigrant's Nemesis.

Upon Marcus Garvey's arrival in Harlem, he started the spectacular Back-to-Africa Movement, which noisily explored the fascinating abstraction of an African utopia and stirred millions of Negroes to wild enthusiasm. He declared, "I asked where is the black man's government? Where is his president, his country, and his ambassadors, his army, his navy, and his men of big affairs? I could not find them and then I declared, I will help make them!" Then he preached with wonderful zeal for a Black House as opposed to a White House; a Black Congress instead of a White Congress; for Black Generals, a Black Aristocracy, and a Black God, that swept Negroes along a mighty wave of black nationalism. His mammoth meetings, colorful parades, gorgeous uniforms, and heavy ritual received amazing acclaim and caused Black America to pour its wartime earnings into the stupendous scheme of African redemption. But his weekly newspaper, the *Negro World,* proved his most potent instrument for wielding opinion.

The character of this paper deserves a brief word:

It had a Spanish and French section and sold for five cents a copy in New York—ten cents elsewhere. Within a few months it had national circulation, and steadily pushed the *Defender*. Usually the sixteen pages of the paper were crowded with the philosophy and opinions of its editor, Marcus Garvey. Edged between his long polemic articles were essays, reports of African and European affairs, ads for patent medicines, occasionally a display of Lucky Strike cigarettes, and beauty preparation advertisements (though the *Negro World*, unlike the *Defender*, excluded ads for skin-whitening preparations). His bombastic editorials referred to the "glorious" history of the Negro, with particular emphasis on Africa's past regal splendor; recalled the slave struggles for freedom, and recounted stirring tales of heroism of such leaders of slave revolts as Denmark Vesey, Gabriel (Prosser), and Nat Turner. The exploits of long dead Zulu and Hottentot warriors who had fought against British rule were not forgotten, nor the histories of the Moorish and Ethiopian empires. Toussaint L'Ouverture's leadership of the Haitian Rebellion was stock copy.

Marcus Garvey's Back-to-Africa movement, whose central idea meant abdication of the Negro's citizenship, developed a hard core of fanatics. As a consequence, there were casualties among the wayward. The *Defender* reported one killing with this head:

DR. EASON, ARCH FOE
OF GARVEY, ASSASSINATED

The movement soon had violent overtones in Chicago—actually to the point where Abbott became alarmed. Eventually it set him in firm opposition to Garvey.

One jungle-hot day in 1920, a small group of fanatical followers who belonged to the movement's Chicago branch ended a parade in front of a cafe frequented by whites and Negroes. Following a brief ceremony, one man produced an American flag and deliberately set it afire. When he attempted

214

to burn a second one, two white policemen remonstrated but were intimidated by a brandishing of revolvers. When a Negro attempted to object he was shot and killed. And when a white sailor protested, he, too, was shot fatally. The men who did the shooting were later arrested and indicted, but three Negro ministers were attacked by white men in retaliation. Marcus Garvey's followers apparently intended the flag-burning—described as the "Abyssinian Affair"—as a symbolic forswearing of allegiance to the United States government.

The incidents nearly ignited a race riot.

But the police, profiting by their experience of the previous year, were vigilant. Moreover, there was evident restraint by both whites and Negroes and they combined to hunt down the offenders, both white and black. Abbott quickly recognized the movement's inherent dangers: while hypnotizing many credulous people, it had also attracted numerous crafty men who sought to exploit the legitimate grievances of the rank-and-file. But he was mostly outraged by the affront to his country and rose in patriotic fury to condemn the flag's defiling. Consequently, the *Defender's* position was unequivocal.

It said editorially: "We warn all agitators, whether they be white or black, that this paper, standing as it does for law and order, for justice to all men, for that brotherhood without which no country can long prosper, and for the better element of our twelve millions, that we condemn their disloyalty and will do all in our power to aid the constituted authorities in crushing them.

"The burning of the American flag by a group of self-styled Abyssinians . . . as a means of showing their contempt for the United States, and the resultant murders that followed in the wake of this demonstration, instead of accomplishing the end desired by these malcontents, acted as a boomerang. Every black face portrayed indignation. Every black arm was lifted to strike a blow at these law-breakers. This is our home, our country, our flag, for whose honor and protection we will give our last drop of blood. With all our shortcomings it can never truthfully be said that we are disloyal or unpatriotic."

Marcus Garvey had clearly demonstrated that he was a man with whom to reckon, both as a publisher and a leader of his people, but he was not a little perturbed by Abbott's opposition. Yet, ironically enough, it was the *Defender's* defeatist approach to the Negro's problems which helped to prepare the way for the man styling himself the black messiah. He had indeed leaped into an ocean of black unhappiness at a moment most timely for a savior. When he reached the peak of his influence in the early 1920's, he had mobilized two million followers nationally, and had gathered in nearly ten million dollars. He gave tangible expression to his ideas when he formed a Negro merchant marine, known as the Black Star Steamship Line, to develop trade relations among the darker peoples of the world.

More important, his propaganda assaults on whites and mulattoes incited the blacks to the point of open hostility. He made scorching attacks on mulattoes as a "hybrid group" and insisted upon the purity of the black race. In reality, though, the Back-to-Africa movement was a restatement of colonization schemes advanced on three previous occasions in the history of the United States. Each one was met by opposition— immediate, militant and widespread. The truth is, Garvey's followers might have consented to an African excursion, but the vast majority had no idea of leaving their homeland. The dream of an all-black nation had simply given a sorely driven people a new and abundant dignity, enough to squander.

But Abbott likened Garvey to "Chief Sam" of Kansas, who some years before had defrauded Negroes with a scheme to establish a Negro kingdom in Africa. He, too, had squandered money and purchased a dilapidated ship for a black exodus. Marcus Garvey took umbrage and promptly filed suit against Abbott, charging him with libel and demanding one million dollars compensation. The New York courts awarded him a one-cent victory, but he was obliged to pay court costs. He afterwards announced his intention of invading Chicago. The black Zionist rented the Eighth Regiment Armory and from its platform denounced Abbott more violently than ever. Soon afterwards he was arrested for selling stock in the Black Star Steamship Line in violation of Illinois law.

The man from Jamaica saw Abbott's fine hand in this action.

Back in New York, he claimed that the arrest had been engineered by the Chicago editor, who he said had arranged to have a Negro detective pose as an investor and insist upon buying stock directly from Marcus Garvey himself. He had been released on bail, but he never again entered the city. His parting shot was directed at the *Defender's* publisher: "Abbott," he declared, "has always through rivalry and jealousy been opposed to me, and especially through my not being born in America and my criticism of his dangerous newspaper policy of always advising the race to lighten its skin and straighten out its hair which was kinky."

The midwest publisher suddenly decided Marcus Garvey had passed the peak of his popularity. The reason: the boys around the poolrooms and barbershops were beginning to laugh at him. Before long Abbott joined those raining criticism upon the squat leader, which put the Chicago editor on the same side of the fence with W. E. B. Du Bois, editor of the *Crisis* magazine and A. Philip Randolph, editor of the radical *Messenger* magazine. Metz P. T. Lochard, Abbott's first foreign editor, quotes his chief as saying that the Back-to-Africa movement was "unmistakably a symptom of despair" inspired by the "sting of segregation," and as insisting that a program of escapist independence would only encourage racial segregation. Consequently, Abbot flatly refused to cooperate with Garvey and rejected overtures made by intermediaries. "The walls of discrimination," said Abbott, "can only be scaled with determination to fight the enemy on his own ground." His over-all position set a current event in its historical perspective.

Finally, upon the loud complaints of Negro leaders, the Federal government investigated the financial manipulations of the Black Star Line and Marcus Garvey was brought to trial for using the mails to defraud. The *Defender* simply noted the development with a factual story but carried this devastating head: FRAUD CHARGED TO GARVEY. Arthur Brisbane protested in his newspaper columns that to hold him was equivalent to "jailing a rainbow." In his summation to the jury, the psychological factors that underscored the movement were touched upon by Henry Lincoln Johnson, a Negro attorney who represented one of Garvey's codefendants. "If every Negro," he declared, "could have put every dime, every penny into the sea, and if he might get in exchange the knowledge that he was somebody, that he meant something in the world, he would gladly do it. . . . The Black Star Line was a loss in money but it was a gain in soul!"

Even so, Marcus Garvey was convicted and deported.

He had been a magnificent dreamer, but his movement set in motion what was to become the most compelling force in Negro life—race and color consciousness, which is today that ephemeral thing that inspires "race loyalty"; the banner to which Negroes rally, the chain that binds them together. It has propelled many a political and social movement and stimulated racial internationalism. It is indeed a philosophy, an ethical standard by which most things are measured and interpreted. It accounts for much constructive belligerency today. And, to be sure, so racial-minded a project as the *Defender* eventually cashed in on the new development. But Abbott did not bemoan Marcus Garvey's passing—actually, he had helped to speed him to oblivion.

The Chicago editor always kept his ears close to the ground, alert to seize any trend in Negro rank-and-file thinking, unless it compromised his basic principles as was the case with the Back-to-Africa scheme. But while his change in editorial approach might have been influenced by public reaction, among a complex of other factors, it is more likely that the subtleties of his new position of responsibility and leadership were decisive. To begin with, he was now considered a substantial citizen: actually, Robert S. Abbott had become an authentic millionaire. By 1929 he was drawing $2,000 as a weekly salary, plus his usual monthly bonuses, and had accumulated nearly a half million dollars in cash. His new status naturally brought new obligations and he rose to the demands.

He now had a precious stake in the society he so often criticized, and he was receiving public recognition for his achievements. He was in fact deluged with awards and citations; for example, Morris Brown College at Atlanta, Georgia, and Wilberforce University at Xenia, Ohio, conferred on him honorary degrees of Doctor of Letters. He was elected president of Hampton's alumni association, and the Columbus Business Association of Ohio gave him an award for his "labors and achievements" as an "advocate of justice and equal rights."

These, plus his prosperity, influenced him to oppose a defeatist attitude among his people, and he now declared: "If there ever was a time in our history when every mother's son of us should be up and doing, that time is now. Many of the larger opportunities we have sought, and for which we have fought, now are open to us. The question we must ask ourselves is, 'Are we prepared to take advantage of these opportunities, and are we fully alive to the fact that they are ours for the asking?'"

Emotionally he was a new man.

The publisher, who had not previously been even casually involved with women, had found someone to love. He had married a Helen Thornton Morrison, a widow, on September 10, 1918, as he approached his fiftieth birthday, and this fact was to condition his social philosophy further. Though he kept his marriage to her secret for some time, Phil Jones says he confided the fact to him like a bashful boy. The titian-haired Helen, a stylish and charming woman hailing from Athens, Georgia, was thirty years his junior and so fair that she was often mistaken for a white person. This marriage is extremely important to the story of Robert S. Abbott, for Helen ultimately twisted his life and warped his thinking.

A word about her follows soon.

Whatever the reason, Abbott now developed upper-class aspirations. The transition was first reflected in conspicuous consumption. Before his ambition to upgrade himself socially, he was frequently admonished about his shabby-looking appearance. His wife undoubtedly needled him too. He not only changed, he became fastidious. He now wore $150 tailor-made suits (incidentally, he hated the color black, so usually his clothes were blue, brown or gray). His favorite costume for formal occasions was a cutaway coat, striped trousers, spats and a top hat. He began smoking Havana-made cigars and using imported English walking sticks. Whenever he attended the theater, properly attired in a dinner jacket, he always purchased the best seats, not being content with anything else. His philosophy in these matters was perhaps revealed in his advice to his young friend Dr. Charles M. Thompson, when he was about to open his dental offices. "I asked Mr. Abbott how much luxury he thought the office ought to contain," he recalls. "He said, 'Charlie, put in the best, as Negroes should have things as good as white people.'"

"Now that Mr. Abbott had money," says Dr. Thompson, who spent a good deal of time with him socially, "he wanted class, and acted in the way he understood class behaved." For example, he contributed $500 to become a life member of the Chicago Natural History Museum, and he paid $100 to become a life member of the Art Institute of Chicago. And like the rich, he developed a concern for the poor as a social responsibility and annually contributed $250 to the Chicago Urban League.

He was not vulgarly dramatizing wealth.

He simply was attempting to enter the mainstream of the city's civilization, and wanted to enjoy all the good things in the society, a not ignoble desire. He earnestly wished to grow culturally; and, more important to him, he wished to demonstrate to white people that Negroes would grasp things cultural and assume their responsibilities as citizens if given the opportunity. His attendance and support of the opera had something of this inspiration, according to his dentist friend. "Mr. Abbott," he declares, "went to the opera to prove Negroes have a taste for good music."

The black millionaire always sat on the main floor, in a conspicuous place where he would not be missed in advertising the Negro's bent for culture. He could hardly have been unobserved, for crowds frequently milled about the entrance, snarling traffic, to catch a glimpse of the well-to-do Negro as he rolled up to the Auditorium Theatre, and later the Civic Opera House, in his chauffeur-driven limousine, escorting his fashionable, bejeweled, milk-white wife. He himself wore a blue homburg hat and a dinner jacket, and carried a gold-headed cane. He often met Chauncey McCormick in the lobby during intermission and exchanged pleasantries, much to the wide-eyed curiosity of the idling crowds. He liked the attention he provoked; but there is almost a poignancy to his companion's report that "Mr. Abbott liked to make believe he was a foreigner when he was attending the opera, and would babble some meaningless gibberish to impress people who might overhear him. I often had to hush him up, not to embarrass us both."

A detail is worthy of note.

The Negro publisher rarely expressed a preference for a particular singer, nor had he any enthusiasm for operatic music. It was, as his dentist friend observed, "merely art for art's sake, and that was about all." But Abbott was attracted to the extraordinary Mary Garden, who was the star of the Chicago Opera Company when he started attending the performances. He saw her do Debussy's *Pelléas et Mélisande* and *Thaïs*. He enjoyed them both. But a measure of his taste was the fact that he recognized her as more glamorous than musically talented, and in this estimate he had many critical supporters.

The well-to-do editor now sought to be accepted socially.

He began entertaining frequently in his attractive five-room bungalow-type house situated at 4847 Champlain Avenue. The prim, tree-dotted area of brick and white stone dwellings formed the stronghold of the Negro upper crust. To expand his social horizons he jointed a host of clubs and societies, among them the Appomattox Club, made up of prominent South Side business and professional men; and he became a member of Kappa Alpha Psi, a college men's fraternity which afterwards gave him its highest award for achievement, the Laurel Wreath. When his Highness Duke Kwesi Kuntu of Ashanti, West Africa, arrived in Chicago, Mr. and Mrs. Abbott were his luncheon guests at the Diamond Exhibit, sponsored by the Chicago Jewelers Association.

Colonel Roscoe Conkling Simmons was Abbott's social sponsor in the beginning—indeed, this gentleman staged his employer's formal debut into society at a spectacular reception. Simmons' social position was unassailable: he was the nephew of Booker T. Washington by marriage, a big wheel in the Republican party, and he maintained wide contacts among influential white people. Abbott was convinced that he should be launched under Simmons' auspices. Roscoe delivered on his promise. The reception guests included Irene Castle and Colonel Robert R. McCormick, plus the securely respectable of Negro society. Next morning Abbott's social mentor presented him with a whopping bill for what he delicately described as "incurred expenses." When Simmons soon afterwards bought a Kentucky farm, gossip connected the acquisition with the reception's promotion.

The publisher's intimates scoffed at his social pretensions.

Few were charitable enough to recognize that he was merely reacting to the identical illusions that feed the vanity of white men. Phil Jones, for one, was bitter about Abbott's social ambitions and he said so frankly. "I distinctly recall," he says, "several arguments we had. During his struggling days, the society people would refer to him disparagingly as 'that black man.' A standard joke at amateur minstrel shows was, 'What happened to the lights? It's dark in here. Oh, the lights are okay, but old man Abbott is just passing the powerhouse!' The unkind remarks hurt both Mr. Abbott and me deeply. The society folks ignored him completely and even when he attended their affairs it was not in the role of a guest but as a newspaper reporter. When he became wealthy, they started to bow to him. I gave him hell and reminded him of the manner in which they used to treat him, and urged him to form his own social set. But he couldn't see it in that light and became a social follower."

Even so, invitations to an evening at the Abbotts were eagerly sought by social aspirants, and every dignitary of the Negro community from the bankers, Anthony Overton and Jesse Binga, to Walter White and C. C. Spaulding beat a path to his door. He is remembered as a cordial host—he even entertained by singing himself. He often regaled his guests with droll stories like the one he frequently told about the day he wore a seersucker suit to a Savannah picnic, and when it rained and the suit shrunk, he could only remove it by cutting the garment open with a scissors. But one man recalls that "he always seemed to be on 'dress parade' and this discouraged intimacy."

Yet the black literati, whom Wallace Thurman described as *Infants of the Spring,* found a sympathetic climate in the publisher's house. Not infrequently was this group augmented by a sprinkling of Haitians, Africans, Chinese, and white intellectuals active in cultural and civic movements. But anyone who visited him had a difficult time avoiding bridge, a game he played badly but enjoyed. Dr. Thompson, who impressed Abbott with the ease with which he himself associated with white people, says, "He never reacted to bridge—win, lose or draw. Bridge was merely a pretext for conversation. And he always talked about the race question, with special emphasis on Negroes moving out of the South and coming North."

If Abbott was not a flaming success in society, he nevertheless had a canny sense of real values in other areas. To walk down State Street, then called "The Stroll," was to take an inventory of the man's riches in popularity with the rank-and-file. He knew everyone's name, and had a friendly word, nod or question for all—in short, he had not lost touch with the common man, which in fact was the key to his success as an editor and publisher. For he used to walk the streets and listen attentively and return to the office with story ideas, though he took only the most perfunctory notes. The man-in-the-street said, "He isn't stuck up; he's just plain folks." "Those that were well acquainted with Mr. Abbott," says Jones, "knew that his greatest pleasure in life came in being able to stand on the corner of 35th and State Streets, and with a fat cigar in his mouth, discuss the race problem with anyone."

The people still had unqualified respect for his opinions and responded with undivided attention to his disclosures. It was no wonder that half the conversations on State Street began: "Did you see that story in the *Defender* . . . ?" Consequently, whenever he meandered along the streets, people very often turned to him for help and advice. Widows asked him how to invest their money, and young men how to get ahead. He encouraged men to venture, to learn skills that would be lifetime assets. Middleton tells the story of a woman who came to him and complained bitterly that she was having trouble with a prominent Negro lawyer whom she had retained. He would neither return her fee nor try her case. "I told her she needed someone of great influence," Middleton reports. "So I called Mr. Abbott and explained the situation to him. I put her on the telephone to make an appointment for her to call at his office. To my embarrassment, she asked him to come to her home instead. He agreed. And though he had just a few days before returned from a lengthy trip, he got into his car that evening, saw her and contacted the lawyer and within a week she had all her money back. Not only that. He secured her a reputable lawyer who won her case."

His concerns for people naturally extended to his family, for his love for them was undiminished. As busy as he was, he found time to write his sister Rebecca thus: "Yours of to day at hand, but you didn't say whether you received the basketball outfit for your school or not; neither has [brother] Alex told me whether or not he received the football for the boys." Abbott had had a tombstone erected at his stepfather Rev. Sengstacke's grave, and afterwards wrote his mother: "I am delighted to know that you enjoyed and appreciate the monument over father's grave, and I am only too glad that I am able to show my appreciation of the wonderful things he had done for me. I hope you will have the time to get out to the cemetery often and see that the lot is kept refreshed all the time. I think it is a good thing to keep an eye on these things, as I know Father would have done the same for you had you gone first." By now, he had bought her a Model-T Ford, and was complaining, "I cannot see how Alex can exist, at least, without a Ford." Since he was sending the whole family money regularly, he was making his influence felt in family decisions.

Yet the editor seemingly could idle in the sunlight and needed no other vital interest than to stand at 35th and State Streets and watch the show go by the great crossroads. Not only did he have an inordinate and never-ending interest in human beings, but he liked to look at "his people"—and now they were making progress and the Black Metropolis had come of age. It had its own schools, newspapers and magazines, labor unions, hotels, hospitals, restaurants, churches, and a multitude of organizations and societies like the Elks and Masons. The community had the air of being self-sufficient. The Negro's rise in business and the professions was symbolized by the area. Here Jesse Binga, for example, founded his bank. The financier erected the Binga Arcade, the skyscraper of the neighborhood, which provided office space for doctors, dentists and lawyers, who themselves were becoming affluent.

The South Side's main thoroughfare measured up to everything a migrant Negro had read and heard about Chicago. There seemed to be gaiety, good feeling, and the sound of jazz. The rhythm of life seemed to beat to the clink of glasses and the thump of drums. There was prosperity, and money seemed to flow from everyone's pocket as easily as laughter from their lips. The South Side had entered an era of noisy vitality, and the intersection of 35th and State Streets was the center of this triumphant existence. The section had indeed become the capital of clowns, cults and cabarets, and brought a bumper crop of Negroes to the city, both migrants and celebrities. Whenever he was in the city, Jack Johnson made the section his headquarters. Even George Washington Carver, the Tuskegee scientist, timidly sought the camaraderie of this environment.

Briefly: the section formed the blazing rialto of the Negro community.

By now, the Negro millionaire felt he was able to afford the luxury of a Rolls-Royce automobile. One day he had his chauffeur drive him downtown to the Loop, where the showrooms were situated. He entered the place and inspected models on display. He decided on one with Pickwick coachwork—but when he announced his decision, the white salesman informed him that the exhibited automobiles were not for sale, nor could they take his order for one. He afterwards made repeated efforts to make a purchase, and each time he met stony silence. He finally learned via the racial grapevine that the company had a policy of not selling this make of car to a Negro—presumably, when a Negro possessed one the commodity lost its snob appeal and thus depreciated in value.

The Negro publisher's adequate credit rating and substantial status in the city was ignored. Not to be outdone, Abbott persuaded a sympathetic white friend to make the purchase. The man did and promptly transferred the ownership to Abbott. Thus, to hurdle this racial obstacle the Negro paid $16,109.55—but he probably paid more dearly in humiliation. His victory, albeit dubious, soon turned sour. When Negroes learned of the title transfer, they scornfully said he had bought a "second-hand job." He was hurt. But he was too proud to admit he had suffered discrimination in his attempt to acquire a luxury item; and, perhaps, too embarrassed to explain the circuitous route of final delivery. But in the process, he learned one more profound lesson about the vagaries of race prejudice—wealth is not enough to protect a Negro from racial hurts, sometimes indeed his problems are intensified!

*Robert S. Abbott was the first Negro newspaper pub-
lisher to feed the Negro articles based on living conditions in other countries, and cause the Negro to
re-evaluate his position in this country.*—BRAILSFORD
REESE BRAZEAL, professor, Morehouse College, Atlanta, Ga.

CHAPTER XIV

Eyewitness to Utopia

BEFORE HE MADE his first trip abroad—perhaps as
a belated honeymoon—Robert S. Abbott was urgently warned
of irregularities in the financial operations of his paper. To
put it bluntly, stealing was charged to his employees. Helen
complained that he was being hoodwinked, and in wifely
fashion offered some scathing opinions of his workers. Friends
urged him to check into the matter. But unfortunately Abbott
turned a deaf ear to every bit of gossip, however strident. As
yet, there was no concrete evidence, so he blithely set off for
one of the big adventures of his life—a three-month trip to
South America. It was indeed his first extended vacation since
the paper's founding, and what he observed in the course of
his journey was to bolster the new look he had already started
to give the *Defender's* editorial policy.

Jesse Binga, ex-huckster and now president of the Binga
State Bank, gave the departing couple a farewell dinner attended by the South Side's élite—a fact that suggests Abbott's
social status was now finally secure. Bon voyage toasts, trite,
perhaps, but sincere, were lifted during the evening. "To

you," said C. N. Langston, "the man, we all wish the greatest pleasure, and the return to us to continue the world of good you are so nobly doing." Dr. U. G. Dailey declared, "A good man is more to be desired than great riches. Your life personifies this!" Colonel John R. Marshall offered this sentiment: "Your modesty is only excelled by your cordiality and warmth for your friends that know you best." The host said simply, "A just cause of dark hue, is just what God has made of you." Oscar De Priest, about to grace the halls of Congress and usually voluble, was content to nod agreement.

Mr. and Mrs. Abbott left Chicago January 21, 1923, with this applause ringing in their ears. The trip proved a triumphal tour. The publisher, until now mostly confined to Chicago, learned personally the extent of his influence and prestige elsewhere in the country. Upon arrival in New York, en route to South America, he and his wife received home-cooking treatment from Harlem's prominent Negroes, and they were given a lively round of receptions and cocktail parties. The Walter Whites had them to dinner. They saw the *Ziegfeld Follies* with Grace Kellogg. The Dean Pickenses staged a theater party. They lunched at a French hotel with Dr. Louis T. Wright and his wife. They attended a party at the James Weldon Johnsons. Mrs. Abbott shopped with Madames Wilkins, Johnson, White, and Bagnall, while her husband was attending a public meeting with Chandler Owen, co-editor of the *Messenger* magazine.

The steamship lines were not quite so happy about Abbott's trip.

His request for first-class accommodations had created an embarrassing situation: few Negroes had the means to travel, so they had not had to face the decision of what to do about a Negro. When the Negro publisher applied, the companies were caught without an established racial policy, which meant that traditional racial ways offensive to Negroes were in operation. It proved nearly impossible for Abbott to procure accommodations on any line. For example, he applied to the Lamport and Holt Steamship Company and was told no passage was available. Abbott correctly suspected racial discrimination. To prove it, he had Helen personally call at the company's offices, where she was mistaken for a white person and was promptly offered first-class tickets for the identical ship on which her husband had been refused passage. He appealed to Illinois Senator Medill McCormick, who was a member of the United States shipping board and who, in turn, sharply raised the question with the top echelon of the Munson Steamship Lines. They finally provided Abbott with the accommodations he desired, and he carefully paid a premium on a Chicago *Tribune* accident insurance policy.

But when he sought to have his passport visaed for entry into Brazil, that country's consul in Chicago refused, perhaps because Brazilians wished to discourage the immigration of blacks. For, in conspicuous difference to the United States, the tendency in Brazil was to absorb the Negro. This tendency was, however, not merely a historical and biological fact; it was rather an expression of a national policy, in so far as Brazil had a policy with respect to the Negro. Black immigration was therefore a threat to this process.

Whatever the reason, Abbott was compelled to appeal to Congressman Martin B. Madden, who represented the district in which the *Defender* was situated. He was unsuccessful in having the bar lifted. The editor again appealed to Illinois Senator Medill McCormick, who had to send four telegrams to the Brazilian Embassy in Washington before he received a satisfactory reply. Two months elapsed before Abbott was able to complete arrangements. En route to New York, he stopped in Washington to personally thank the senator for his efforts.

"We discovered," he afterwards said, "that the conduct of these Brazilian consuls, stationed in several American cities, in refusing to visa anyone's passport on the ground of race is entirely contrary to the Brazilian National Constitution and shamefully at variance with the finely democratic temper of the Brazilian people." Seemingly the attitude of the Brazilians to a race problem, so far as concerned the Negro, was academic rather than pragmatic and actual.

This, however, he discovered later. Now he had had enough problems to discourage him from making the trip, but he persevered until he and his wife set sail aboard the S.S. *Pan American.* His feelings were perhaps somewhat assuaged when friends, in a gesture of affection, filled their stateroom with flowers and fruits. At sea, he was "overwhelmed by a sense of the Infinite" and "the vastness of God," and buoyantly entered into the activities aboard ship. He and his wife were dinner guests of the captain, and they met several people with whom he struck up a friendship. Helen did not share her husband's enthusiasm about traveling and was bored and seasick nearly the entire twelve-day trip. Consequently, Abbott carried on alone, but happily.

His initial desire to visit South America may have been inspired by a letter he received in 1914 from a Negro who had been a chauffeur for the philanthropist, Julius Rosenwald, and had somehow found his way to Rio de Janeiro en route to Europe. Under the headline, ABSOLUTELY NO COLOR LINE IN BRAZIL, Abbott had published his observations. The man had marveled at the mingling of the races, and "the absence of any semblance of prejudice." He found Negroes operating "gigantic coffee plantations," and working as pilots of tugboats and motormen on streetcars. Negroes drove taxis, had rank in the army and navy, managed the biggest hotels, and possessed "luxurious" automobiles. He reported his amazement at "the progress, wealth and lofty positions attained by Afro-Americans," and urged his compatriots to migrate to Brazil. He concluded, "Brazil is the real thing, I found Negroes everywhere."

This report was indeed a teaser.

At any rate, the editor's departure was announced in the *Defender* with a boxed head: EDITOR ABBOTT AND WIFE TO TOUR SOUTH AMERICA. A subhead described the trip as "15,000 Miles for News and Study of Conditions." Abbott himself had explained his mission succinctly in an astute beforehand appraisal: by first-hand investigation, he said he hoped to ascertain the Negro's social progress in a Latin context and compare it with that of the Negro's in an Anglo-Saxon environment. Consequently, though he briefly visited Argentina, Chile, Peru, Uruguay, Colombia, Panama and Cuba, he spent the bulk of his time in Brazil, a conspicuous melting pot of races and cultures where Negroes formed nearly fifty-five per cent of the total population.

Before Abbott's trip, two travelers—Theodore Roosevelt and James Bryce—who knew conditions in the United States, had made reports upon the situation in Brazil. These are particularly interesting in light of the Negro editor's subsequent reporting. Viscount Bryce, whose "observations and impressions" of South America were first published in 1912, remarked that in Brazil, in contrast to the United States, the color line is nowhere sharply drawn and that "the infusion of whites and blacks by intermarriage goes steadily on." Roosevelt, who visited the country a few years later, was more explicit. He said: "If I were asked to name the one point in which there is a complete difference between the Brazilian and ourselves, I should say it was in the attitude to the black man." This attitude manifests itself in the fact that in Brazil "any Negro or mulatto who shows himself fit is without question given the place to which his abilities entitle him."

This, then, was the background of his trip.

When Abbott landed at Rio de Janeiro, he observed "men and women of all complexions and intermedial shades mingling and moving freely in the daily currents of a full and active life." He paused to remark, "This is impressive!" But he had hardly set foot on Brazilian soil, when he was forced to exclaim: "Behold! Discrimination again!" Aboard ship he had developed a friendship with several white Americans, and they had persuaded him to join them in staying at the Hotel Gloria, which catered to American tourists. But when he reached the hotel's door the porters refused to unload his baggage piled on the taxi, and the desk clerk "politely told me no vacancies." His white companions were able, of course, to secure rooms. He finally ended up at a place frequented by Brazilians, the Hotel Victoria, "where accommodations were unhesitatingly and even graciously extended us."

The Negro Americans, innocent of the Portuguese language, arrived in Rio de Janeiro knowing no one and with no letters of introduction. Yet Abbott eventually met and talked with nearly everyone of importance in the Brazilian capital, particularly among the blacks. He somehow luckily met and developed a friendship with a countryman, a Dr. Alfredo Clendenden, a Negro dental surgeon who had left New York forty years before and now enjoyed prosperity and status. Before the overthrow of the Brazilian emperor Don Pedro II, the Negro had been the court dentist. Now he was the dental surgeon to the officers of the army and navy. It was Dr. Clendenden who introduced the editor and his wife to Brazil's officialdom and afterwards inspired the many receptions tendered them. Consequently, they soon met the nation's artists, writers and other professional people.

Because of his wealth and recognized position as a North American publisher, Abbott was given upper-class status; or, to use the Brazilian saying, "A rich Negro is a white man, and a poor white man is a Negro!" His mulatto wife was so much icing on the cake in a country where a premium is placed on the absence of color and particularly on a Caucasian texture of hair. But Abbott had the instinctive good sense to travel modestly, and not make the vulgar display of wealth expected of American tourists. He occupied an unpretentious suite in the Hotel Victoria, and demanded little service. He bought nothing of consequence. Helen herself only purchased an inexpensive set of earrings. This fact undoubtedly endeared him to the Brazilians, for before he left they offered to name a school in his honor. Thus, he was able to report, "Not only were we given to know these personages in their broad social contact, but with a grace unmistakably sincere were accorded the most cordial reception at their homes and tables."

The Brazilian Press Association soon presented him with a "journalist-police" card, which facilitated his investigations but was not enough to forestall discrimination when they visited São Paulo. "We arrived in the late afternoon," Abbott reports. "We went to the Palace Hotel, were assigned accommodations, but irritating as it may seem, during the night we were quietly informed by the proprietor that there were quite a number of American tourists in the hotel who objected to our presence, and asked that we give up our suite. The hour was late and I positively refused. The next morning I went to the Odeste Hotel."

However, the trip to São Paulo had distinct compensations, for he found that Negroes there had about the same social status as those of Rio de Janeiro. Moreover, he reports, "We had the pleasure of meeting Senator T. D. de Castro, a Negro minister of the interior of the State of São Paulo. We accepted an invitation to tea at his home. Senhor de Castro is an ardent admirer of Booker T. Washington, and named his son Booker T. Washington de Castro in honor of him. This de Castro family we found in every respect quite typical of the new aristocracy to which the republic in recent years has given birth; an aristocracy founded, not as in the days of the empire on blood and birth, but on true culture, patriotic usefulness and high moral principle."

Back in Rio de Janeiro, he attended the opera with Dr. Clendenden. The editor afterwards was invited to address a public meeting, jointly sponsored by the Federation of Coloured People and the Progressive Union, a group whose purpose was to develop understanding of the "hereditary and natural relations between the Negro peoples of the two Americas." The appealingly upturned faces looked to the Chicago editor for race relations wisdoms, and he did not fail them. Abbott, in truth, relished the role. He reported the manner in which Negroes in the United States conducted movements for democratic rights, the steady progress of the group, and, off the top of his head, offered some advice about their own affairs. They, in turn, were frank in describing their views and the conditions under which they lived.

The Rio de Janeiro press reported his remarks, and afterwards there was a run of feature articles, with pictures, about the successful North American editor. This fact perhaps influenced Field Marshall Carneiro da Fontoura, the city's police chief, to sponsor him as a speaker at a mass meeting at the Trianon Theatre. Incidentally, this gentleman gallantly gave Helen a basket of flowers. But for Abbott, the most moving experience of his trip was his attendance at the public ceremonies for the Negro poet, Cruz e Sousa—after all, a black man was being honored for distinguished literary achievement by both whites and Negroes on a day declared a national holiday in his honor.

"On this day," he reported, "throughout the republic, various societies of arts and letters turned out to pay tribute to the memory of this man, who had given so much in the enrichment of Brazilian poetry. Mrs. Abbott and I, as good fortune would have it, were in Rio de Janeiro at the time. It was out of a profound sense of duty that we accepted an invitation to assist at the solemn exercises held at the magnificent tomb of the poet in the cemetery of St. Francisco Xavier. The ceremony took place in the morning about 10:30 and about the tomb gathered artists, writers, members of the Brazilian Academy, eminent journalists, and high officials of the government. All fervent admirers of the poet!"

He was indeed so impressed that he afterwards wrote Dr. J. L. dos Santos, president of the Rio de Janeiro *Journal*, this revealing letter: "I should be very grateful to you were you so kind as to secure for me whatever pictures of Cruz E. Sousa, his family or any member thereof together with a photograph of his grave. . . . I am having one of his books translated with a view of introducing it to the American public through the columns of my paper, 'The Chicago *Defender*.' It is in conjunction with such a publication and popularization that I wish to use his picture. . . . Our libraries here in America unfortunately contain none of his works. In fact he is entirely unknown to the American readers. I want to introduce him to our public in general and to our colleges and universities in particular."

Abbott maintained a heavy schedule. He made trips to newspaper offices, art galleries and the aquarium. He formally visited the city hall. His sight-seeing included the botanical gardens, a trip to a seashore resort, and an appearance at an exposition. He even made a tour of the naval yards and prisons, and did a little mountain climbing. The presence of Negroes everywhere he went was good for his racial soul—and in his eyes, perhaps, black faces helped to make Rio de Janeiro's landscape beautiful. However, he was not too busy to write his mother. He inquired about her health, asked whether she received her checks regularly, and noted that "I have gotten much news for my readers."

Upon his return to Chicago, Abbott wrote an interpretative series of ten articles triumphantly recounting his experiences and observations. Their chief significance lay in the fact that his was the first report of that part of the world made by an American Negro journalist. Each article contained a layout of pictures to document the point of the series. Though he presented them under the title, "My Trip Through South America," the pieces were mainly about Brazil. They show a remarkable amount of leg-work for so brief a trip, and a fairly sound grasp of the social conditions. He seemingly hurdled the language difficulty successfully. But his reporting was more observant than critical, for his racial conceptions materially influenced his perceptions of what he saw. Even so, there afterwards was talk of nominating him for the Spingarn Medal on a basis of his reporting. Actually, he had returned to the missionary-teacher role he loved, and used the series as a springboard for again uplifting and inspiring his people. What he reported also had clear implications for reform in the Negro's condition in the United States.

"As a Negro and a product of North American traditions," he observed in the beginning, "my natural, logical reaction was the desire to reach some clear, positive conclusion as to the real depth and extent of the Brazilian democratic spirit, or to what degree it was truly inclusive of the Negro. And this, I feel that I have done."

What instances of racial discrimination he met were only minor swirls on the smooth stream of his course. He gave only small attention to the important fact, for example, that legislation had been introduced in the Brazilian parliament to end the immigration of North American Negroes into the country; nor did he mention that picturesque old seaport of Bahia, where the slave trade once flourished and blacks lived in abominable poverty. He came away with abundant affection for Brazil and its people, and a manifest belief in the country's ability to achieve a true democracy in which Negroes are the equals of whites.

The Negro editor had found a racial utopia!

Brazilian Negroes, he reported, had achieved status and acclaim in the arts, sciences, industry and the professions. And he ran pictures to document who these people were. For example, Dr. José das Santos was a distinguished professor at Milio College. José de Patricino, Jr., a journalist, was secretary to the Brazilian Embassy in Belgium. A two-column picture of his father was carried with this caption: "The late Senhor José de Patricino, an imposing figure in latter-day Brazilian history. Himself once a slave, he more than any other individual aroused public sentiment in Brazil against the iniquities of the institution of slavery. He stood at the side of Princess Gabel when she signed the Emancipation Proclamation in 1888. A powerful orator and writer, he is often referred to as the 'Frederick Douglass of Brazil.' "

He reported that Captain Ignacio C. Villarinho, a graduate of Brazil's West Point, was dean of the National Military Academy. For fear his readers might disbelieve this remarkable fact he was forced to add: "No doubt it requires some strain of the imagination on the part of the reader to conceive of a Race man as a high faculty member of a great military institution." No less triumphant a fact was the position held by Evaristo de Moraes, a distinguished member of the Rio de Janeiro courts. He was Brazil's most famous criminologist and director of the insane asylum. Abbott also carried many pictures showing Negroes working as firemen, policemen, and streetcar conductors—occupations then largely unknown to Negroes in the United States.

"Slavery was abolished in Brazil only as late as 1888," reported Abbott. "Yet the Negro's importance in the political and intellectual life of Brazil far transcends that of the Negro in North America. And this because there have been no obstacles put athwart his path of free development. . . . In North America the avenues of occupation open to the Negro are comparatively few. In Brazil it is altogether quite different. The trades and professions are freely open to any and every person. And one's progress therein depends not on traditions in respect to race or color, but sheer ability.

"The economic conditions of the plain people are conspicuously good. One evidencing feature is the tidy, clean appearance of the numerous children of all colors—black, white, brown and yellow—seen playing hither and thither in the parks, boulevards, thoroughfares and everywhere. . . . The man or woman who can do things never suffers the slightest handicap because of race. The trades and professions are thrown open to all persons regardless of race or color, and employment or a clientele is assured solely on consideration of one's merit."

Thus, according to Abbott, the race problem in Brazil, in so far as there was a race problem, was identified with resistance to absorption and assimilation. This, however, did not mean there were no social distinctions in Brazil; nor did it mean that there was no discrimination or that the blacks and mixed-blood people were completely satisfied with their lot. But the society's direction clearly indicated that a man of color could, by reason of individual merit or favorable circumstance, elevate his status and even achieve position in the upper levels of society. Moreover, this position would be with reference not merely to the blacks whose color he shared but to the total community.

He concluded the series with a round-up story carrying this head: BRAZIL FINDS DANGER IN U.S. HATE POLICY

Helen kept up a diary during the trip.

I have it before me. This document is marked by a strangely arid emptiness. Nothing of the excitement her husband felt for the sights and sounds of new places and the meeting of different peoples is apparent in her detailed report. Judging by the entries, the trip was a dismal bore, merely one long agony. Perhaps her negative attitude toward the trip stems from the fact that she was ill throughout much of it with grippe and fever. Yet her illness may well have been psychosomatic. At any rate, she had pounding headaches in Argentina, had to have a tooth extracted in Chile, and suffered with a painful sunburn in Cuba. Though "not feeling good" in Peru, she bought a Panama hat. She was sick abed in Colombia. But she picked up nicely as they headed homeward. When they reached Panama she attended the races, had a hunch and wagered a bet on a horse named "April Fool," which finished third.

Brazil, however, had proved the greatest cross to bear.

While in Rio de Janeiro, Helen suffered from excruciating toothaches and had to have two teeth extracted. Much of her time was spent in bed, attended by doctors and nurses. Whenever she did appear publicly, she deeply resented the spectacle she and her husband created. She afterwards complained to her sister, Idalee Magill, that everywhere they went they were observed as if they were a "sideshow." Abbott, she felt, had been pushy and had often sought to go places he was frankly not wanted, thus causing her embarrassment. Moreover, the racial indignities detracted from what was intended to be a pleasure trip, and she records the fact that though admitted to São Paulo's Odeste Hotel after being excluded from the Palace Hotel, they were further humiliated: they were not allowed to eat in the dining room and had to go to a nearby Negro restaurant, and when they left, the hotel's porters refused to carry their luggage. When they returned to Chicago, her husband developed the habit of pronouncing the country's name as "Braa-zeel"—as if it were something delicious, and this fact grated on her already unstrung nerves.

Helen was decidedly discontent.

If Abbott was aware of his wife's reactions, nothing in his reporting indicated the fact. His articles were clearly uninhibited. What lessons he had learned abroad, he now started to translate into editorial policy. Until now, he had held Negroes the equals of white men, but he had been unable to demonstrate this fact—there just were no Negro tycoons, Negro captains of industry, and Negro financiers he could point to as proof. Because Negroes were excluded from skilled occupations not only by social edict but also by actual exclusion from the unions which controlled labor in the trades, he was unable, even to himself, to document Negro ability, competence and industry. Consequently, his talk of Negro equality was based chiefly on the Negro's humanity.

Insinuations of Negro inferiority were so strong and pervasive. Even some Negroes themselves believed in the inherent backwardness of the race—a fact that early caused them to reject what they thought was the inferior service of Negro doctors, lawyers and dentists. To preserve his own manhood, Abbott had rejected this theory, though undoubtedly he too was plagued with wonderings. The trip to Brazil dispelled such notions, for he saw with his own eyes black men performing efficiently and imaginatively the identical tasks which tradition in the United States had declared Negroes incapable of doing. As a consequence, his tactics shifted from an exclusively moral plea to the pragmatic demand that Negroes be accorded equal treatment because they were fully capable of being absorbed into every artery of the society.

This led naturally to stepped-up campaigns for reforms in the police and fire departments. Next he attacked the operations of the transportation and school systems and the post office department as they affected Negro employment. Eventually, he extended his crusade to include the use of Negroes as judges, school principals and commissioners, and declared Negroes were capable of representing themselves in Congress. But his fight was not only for Negro entrance, but for upgrading and integration. Negroes succeeded in entering all these occupations—at least in Chicago. But the idea of all-Negro schools, all-Negro police stations and all-Negro fire houses galled him even if they meant increased Negro employment. He opposed any suggestion that Negro streetcar conductors and motormen exclusively be placed on runs in the Negro district—indeed, he wanted no solid Negro crews. "Mix them up, one white and one Negro," he urged.

But he was often ahead of his people in these demands.

Ida B. Wells-Barnett, a prominent crusader for Negro rights, tried to persuade him to support her candidacy for principal of Wendell Phillips High School, which was situated in the heart of the South Side. The school itself had four Negro teachers and a student body now made up largely of Negroes. Mrs. Barnett headed a movement to have herself made principal and the teaching staff made all-Negro. When Abbott sensed her motive was the creation of a "Jim Crow" institution, he vigorously opposed the idea, even though she had been an early *Defender* contributor and he admired her enormously. He waged a successful editorial fight against the move, and in the process lost her friendship. But he was always prepared to pay the price of racial idealism. He had already said, "The popular side is not necessarily the right side."

Consequently, when the firemen opposed his position of integration, he took an identical stand fully aware it was unpopular among them. Actually, a few Negroes had been working in the fire department since 1872, when the first Negro engine company was organized. This unusual development had followed after Negro volunteers during the great Chicago fire of 1871 had proved their abilities as fire fighters. When they sought regular employment, public opinion dictated their appointment. Eventually one of them became a captain. But the intimacy of eating and sleeping together in a fire house discouraged the formation of mixed units. Moreover, Negroes themselves claimed that integration would reduce their opportunities for promotion, for there was little chance a Negro would be given command of white firemen.

Nevertheless, in his pursuit of the racial ideal, Abbott ran bitter articles in the *Defender* charging the fire department with discrimination. The story heads changed only slightly from week to week. BLOT OUT JIM CROW and JIM CROW FLAG STILL WAVES IN FIRE DEPARTMENT were typical. Constant agitation was kept up for more Negroes in the department and against the discriminatory practices. When a fire department bond issue was presented to the Chicago voters, the *Defender* urged its readers to vote "no." During the election campaigns the voters were urged to support candidates who would fight against the segregation policies of the department.

Editorially, Abbott had this to say: "The city of Chicago isn't running the department to suit the social whims of any fireman. When a man or woman turns in an alarm, he or she wants the fireman to put out the fire in question and they don't stop to ask the operator whether a white or black fireman is coming. Any man, regardless of race or creed, should be eligible to secure a job. The placing should be according to the grade on the civil service list. If any man of color's name appears and he is subject to call, his name is passed over for no other reason than the hook and ladder company and the engine company crew, manned exclusively by race men, are all filled up. This violates the letter of the law in the civil service. The citizens demand that these Jim Crow practices end in the fire department."

No other city department followed openly the segregation policy which was found in the fire department. Abbott partially won his point. Chicago eventually came to employ more Negro firemen than any other city in the country, though they are now organized as seven all-Negro fire companies.

Abbott mobilized considerable popular support when he attacked the police department, for Negroes had long complained against the stupidity, prejudice and brutality of white police officers. He even struck at discrimination in Chicago's jails. He published a cartoon by Leslie Rogers that pictured a fat, red-nosed white jailer sitting before two cell doors, one marked "This Cell for White Prisoners," and the other labeled "This Cell for Negro Prisoners." But Abbott regarded this aspect as incidental. His main concern was the police department itself. Listen to a typical *Defender* editorial for example: "There is no law, municipal or otherwise which calls for the insulting of respectable Race people by these big, raw-

243

boned sapheads who are maintained by tax-paying citizens of which class thousands of our people form a part. It is hard to understand on what Basis these "hounds" of the law are accorded encouragement in their dastardly practices by station house superiors by word of mouth, and by the chief himself, by his ignoring of protests made by their victims. Something will and must be done. Bulldozers should have no place in Chicago's police department and birds of the stripe of _____ and _____ should be kicked off the force before something serious happens to them at the hands of some outraged citizen."

The Negro editor declared Negro patrolmen would help improve race relations, for the obvious reason they would enforce the law firmly but with sympathetic understanding.

This was not the whole story.

Actually, the issue was broader, and a good deal of emotion was tied to it—facts which Abbott fully understood. To begin with, Chicago police officers are regular civil service employees. The first Negro policeman was appointed in 1884, and put into uniform only for special occasions. The Negro community was not only interested in the services which officers of their own race might render, but they also were concerned with the prestige which Negro officers would bring to the race. In many parts of the United States, particularly the South, there were no Negro policemen. In the eyes of Negroes, police officers were the local government. The appointment of Negro policemen therefore meant that the race was regarded as a participant in the government.

The publicity campaign Abbott waged was credited with being primarily responsible for the later general increase of Negroes in the police department. By 1930 there were 124 Negro patrolmen, 4 sergeants, 2 lieutenants, 1 police operator, and 2 police women, a total of 133. More important than numbers was the breakthrough. But sometimes the improvements were illusory, mere token concessions to silence protest. The only time, for example, that Police Lieutenant Frank Childs, a finger-print expert, was seen on active duty was when there was a Negro parade to lead. Eventually, though, a Negro, John Scott, was made a police captain with white and Negro officers under his command. He was followed by Harry Deas and later Kenzie Blueitt.

The Negro editor lived to see many more revolutionary changes in the Negro's occupational pattern. Abbott was not responsible for the elevation of every Negro to a position of prestige and responsibility, but he stirred Negroes to demand their rights, articulated their grievances and made them conscious of the situation, and thereby helped create the social climate for fundamental change. And there were solid developments which were enough to hearten and encourage Abbott—whereas only a handful of Negroes were able to qualify for civil service positions in Chicago, by 1932 a total of 27,702 were employed by the city. Besides, there was a dramatic increase of Negro achievement all along the employment line. For instance, the editor's friend and attorney, Albert B. George, was elevated to the bench and afterwards appointed a member of the Board of Pardons and Paroles; Bishop Archibald J. Carey was chosen as a member of the Civil Service Commission; Mrs. Maudelle Brown Bousfield was made a school principal; and Oscar De Priest, already the first Negro alderman, was elected Chicago's first Negro congressman—indeed, he became the first Negro in modern days to sit in the House of Representatives.

A final detail deserves mention.

The social advances of Negroes also had profound political implications, reflecting the race's growing political strength— we shall soon see how Abbott contributed to this growth. Meanwhile, his Brazilian adventure had brought about two distinct developments at the *Defender:* there was more stress on Negro achievement in the United States; and for the next five or six years Abbott solicited articles from outstanding Brazilian journalists, and used them with particular reference to the American scene. Thus, when the newly-elected President Hoover made a goodwill tour of South America, Abbott carried this headline:

"WHAT ABOUT YOUR LYNCHINGS"—BRAZIL TO HOOVER

"Social Equality" Only Method to Thwart Racial Conflict

This story, cleverly inspired by Abbott and perhaps a source of embarrassment to America's chief executive, was written by his Negro friend Evaristo de Moraes, for Rio de Janeiro's daily *Correio da Manha*.

Abbott simply reprinted it.

The Negro editor had found racial kinsmen abroad, a fact that proved one of the notable turning points in his personal growth.

I discovered a sinister conspiracy. The paper's existence was put to a test. It was a question of whether or not the DEFENDER would survive the attacks from within and without.—ROBERT S. ABBOTT, Chicago Defender, 1930.

CHAPTER XV

Scandal Strikes

THE *Defender* now was struck by scandal.

On the heels of his return from South America, Robert S. Abbott heard devastating rumors—specifically, gossip said his employees were pocketing money and having merchandise sent to their homes, such as coal and household goods, and charging them to the paper. The thefts were said to run to thousands of dollars. The publisher refused to believe this, especially since the rumors had mostly been set in motion by disgruntled ex-employees. But the insinuations, plus Helen's needling, became so insistent that he was forced to take action—action long delayed because of his disinclination to face disagreeable realities when they touched him personally.

It was, in fact, Mrs. Genevieve Lee Wimp, the daughter of his former landlady and now the company's assistant treasurer, who advised him that there was truth in the gossip. She named Phil Jones, Roscoe Conkling Simmons, "Alf" Anderson and Tony Langston as those involved. Abbott, pushed to the wall, finally called in the auditors of the Lincoln State Bank to make a check of the paper's accounts. The discovery was soon made that J. Delos Bell, an assistant bookkeeper, had un-accountably misappropriated $900 and, according to a sworn deposition made by Phil Jones, confessed the theft. This reve-lation invited further investigation, and more irregularities were uncovered, much to Abbott's shock and disappointment.

The lack of an adequate accounting system was primarily the cause of the discrepancies—indeed, the publisher himself had taken a rather mild attitude toward defalcations. Before the completion of the building's alterations, he one evening sat in the gallery of the converted Jewish synagogue and watched one of his employees distribute papers down below. The man stood before a table in the center of what once was the auditorium performing his job of selling to agents and newsboys. Beside him on the floor was a bucket which he used as a cash register to deposit the receipts. When a woman made a ten dollar cash purchase instead of putting the money in the bucket, the man pocketed the bill and tossed a fifty-cent piece into the cash pail. The coin's jingle had hardly died away when Abbott peered down and, in his high-pitched voice, addressed his surprised employee thus: "Mr. _____, please leave some for me!"

There was also the difficulty in connection with Abbott's plan to publish a magazine called *Reflexus* ("Reflects Us"). Before Abbott left for South America, one Irving Johnson had approached Phil Jones with the magazine idea. Jones in turn discussed the project's possibilities with his chief. Abbott de-cided favorably and steps were taken to begin publication. Somewhere along the line, however, Abbott changed his mind, and Phil Jones, J. Delos Bell, Roscoe Conkling Sim-mons and "Alf" Anderson went forward with the plan, which, as it developed, assumed the proportions of a plot against Abbott in the popular mind. This fact led to charges that these men had used *Defender* monies to promote the maga-zine, which incidentally appeared only twice.

As general manager, Phil Jones was held accountable, and

indeed eventually became the fall guy, for—though he tried for ten years—he never explained what transpired to Abbott's satisfaction. Moreover, he was asked to explain decisions made long ago and long forgotten. The auditor's initial statement declared there had been no shortages—with the exception of the theft by Bell. Nevertheless rumors of shortages persisted. Then careful scrutiny of the irregularities produced charges of graft in the purchase of property, paper, ink and equipment by "Alf" Anderson. Phil himself was charged with paying an excessive salary to Roscoe Conkling Simmons, and excessively high commissions to Tony Langston.

Said Jones, "I reiterate that with the exception of Bell, I was not aware of any individual acts of dishonesty or collusion by these or other employees."

His sworn deposition (addressed directly to the publisher) gives us interesting sidelights on the *Defender's* operations during this period. For example, in explaining the theft charged to Bell, Phil observed, "It had been an office custom, from your [Abbott's] signature down, to leave a few signed blank checks in the custody of a responsible party," presumably Bell. Jones conceded that the charges of graft in making purchases might have had some validity, for "As purchasing agent, with full power to purchase all of our needs, it could have been possible for Anderson to have many hoop-ups that neither you [Abbott] nor myself could fathom." But he met the charge of paying Roscoe an excessive salary with the refutation: "When I was given the power to set salaries, I felt the amount given him was not excessive considering the contacts, influence, and following that he had. This fact is proven by the wide-spread interest in his column attested to by many commendatory letters received from both high and low throughout the country."

To the accusation that he paid Tony Langston too high an advertising commission, he countered with a devastating set of facts: "It was you [Abbott] who originally set the commission to be paid to Langston, namely, fifty per cent on all advertisements secured in exchange for services given as theatrical editor. When Langston approached me for a contract because of an increase in business, I agreed under the same arrangement. The only change this contract brought about was putting into writing an oral agreement that had existed since Langston first joined the publication [in 1914]." But Abbott had not forgotten the day he silently strolled by Langston's desk as the latter was opening mail and saw him pocket the contents; Langston, without looking up but feeling his chief's presence, remarked aloud, "One thing you can say about these show folks, when you loan them money they sure will pay you back!"

Wholesale dismissals followed, and the *Defender's* dirty linen was soon washed in public.

Abbott's neighbor, the Chicago *Whip*, repeated deliciously-contrived gossip and labeled the men involved "The Four Horsemen," strongly insinuating they were running away with *Defender* funds. Even so, Abbott soft-heartedly refused to prosecute them. The only public acknowledgement he made of the unhappy development was contained in a brief front-page notice informing the public in somewhat legalistic language that Phil A. Jonés, Roscoe Conkling Simmons, Alfred Anderson and J. Delos Bell were no longer connected with the paper. No story or editorial comment accompanied this announcement—although at that time, ironically enough, he was running a series of articles under the title, "Why the Press Prints Crime and Scandal News," by Owen Chandler, co-editor of the *Messenger* magazine.

The denouement demonstrated a curious aspect of the publisher's personality, for he was a man who never forgot an injury, and never forgave one. His subsequent behavior was therefore in character: until his death, he never again spoke to his protégé Phil—although friends pleaded with him to give the boy an opportunity to explain personally! Ten years

afterward he still was rigidly unresponsive and made no reply to this poignantly-worded telegram: "Dear Chief for the
sake of your namesake a boy you should feel proud of, will
you please grant me an audience during my stay in the city.
Phone number Normal seven one one six. [Signed] Your son
—Phil."

The charges made against Phil Jones actually followed his
dismissal, and consequently he never had an opportunity to
defend himself personally. He says, "It may surprise you that
from the day I received the letter of dismissal, dated I believe
April 10, 1925, until his death, I never had an opportunity to
talk with Mr. Abbott. The letter stated that I was being given
a vacation with pay ending July 1, 1925. A few days later
when rumors started circulating about shortages, I tried in
every way possible to contact Mr. Abbott for a talk. As a last
resort, I prepared a letter and delivered it to Judge Albert B.
George in his courtroom, and asked him to please see that
Mr. Abbott got it.

"The old man never acknowledged it.

"William 'Bill' Foster, a staunch friend of both Mr. Abbott
and myself was in the employ of the *Defender*. About two
weeks after my dismissal Foster went to him and begged him
to 'see the boy.' He extracted a promise from him that he
would see me the following Sunday at 2:00 P.M. Foster picked
me up at my home and we waited in front of the *Defender*
office from 1:45 to 3:00 P.M. He never showed up.

"The closest I ever got to talking to him was one evening
as I was en route to work at the post office, where I had obtained employment. The Indiana Avenue streetcar stopped
at 35th Street. I was seated in the forward end and somehow
happened to turn around as the car was loading at the rear.
Among the passengers getting on was Mr. Abbott. I immediately faced forward again with the intention of waiting until
he had seated himself and then going back and talking to
him. Between 33rd and 34th Streets I turned around to see

251

where he was sitting and could not locate him. It then came to me that the car had stopped at 34th Street and the old man, evidently seeing me at the same moment I saw him, had quickly disembarked."

Fay Young expresses a universal opinion: "Phil Jones did get a kind of rough deal." Based upon the father-son relationship which existed, he was perhaps guilty of youthful follies but not theft. In Abbott's eyes, though, Jones compounded the injury by becoming involved in the publishing scheme, and by testifying in Tony Langston's behalf when the ex-bartender sued the publisher for unpaid commissions. Abbott's friends say this development hurt him deeply. Otherwise he undoubtedly would have taken a different view toward Phil's peccadilloes. But Abbott felt his trust betrayed by what he presumed to be a plot against his paper and himself. For Phil it was the loss of a beloved father, for Abbott the loss of a beloved son.

The publisher never publicly unburdened himself concerning what transpired. Not until 1930, nearly five years afterwards when celebrating the twenty-fifth anniversary of the paper, did he have anything to say. And this was only incidental to recalling his "struggles to maintain this institution." Yet his charges, striking a note of self-pity, were monstrous. He flatly declared there had been a "sinister conspiracy" afoot to destroy his paper and declare him "insane."

He wrote, "I discovered that a vicious conspiracy existed, fostered by the people whom I had considered my most intimate friends who had conspired not only to destroy the *Defender* as an institution, but also to bring about my death. This was a severe shock. When this was brought to my attention there was no one to whom I could go and confide; no one to whom I could unbosom these dastardly attempts to destroy my life, and feel that I had their confidence and sympathy.

"It developed that some prominent physicians had been secured who were to lend their aid in this sinister conspiracy to have me declared incompetent to run my own business and put in an institution for the insane. In this connection, several lawyers had been engaged for the purpose of legalizing the actions of these conspirators in their effort to destroy both me and the *Defender*. This movement was so well organized that people within my employ were giving out secret information concerning my affairs to aid and abet in my destruction."

And thus ended an era.

Robert S. Abbott sadly took the helm until he could find someone to assume the duties of Phil Jones. He found such a man almost immediately, but not before his wife, Helen, offered a candidate, one Roderick Harris, a director of a fraternal organization in Athens, Georgia—indeed, she went to the pains of bringing the aspirant to Chicago at her own expense. Abbott made up his own mind, though, and chose his sister-in-law's husband, Nathan K. Magill, who was to be described as the publisher's greatest mistake. The man quickly earned Helen's enmity, and was to play Iago to Abbott's tragic Othello. But now the publisher's main concern was effecting the long-delayed and necessary reorganization of the paper's business operations. This he promptly proceeded to do— which indeed proved beneficial in terms of public relations, efficiency and personnel morale. This completed, he handed over the day-to-day management to his new man.

Now Nathan Kellogg Magill was in the saddle.

He was a very small man. Literally a small man, given to handing down peremptory orders. He had a wiry figure, the copper-colored skin and black lank hair of an Indian, and he suffered noisily with asthma. A student of hypnotism, he had a sharp, brittle mind, and the publisher admired him inordinately. Abbott eventually placed absolute trust and confidence in him, a fact that proved his undoing. At any rate, though ambitious and ruthless, Magill was undoubtedly capable. He was a lawyer, a graduate of Howard University. He had attended Boston University, where he met and became a confidential assistant to Rufus B. Tobey, founder of the Boston floating hospital. But he was practicing law in Jacksonville, Florida, when he decided Chicago offered greener pastures. He arrived in town a few months before the shake-up at the *Defender,* casting about for something to do. He approached Phil Jones with the idea of becoming a partner in the proposed *Reflexus* magazine, but abandoned the plan when he learned Abbott was interested. Soon afterwards the publisher turned to him to head his organization.

He quickly, almost instinctively, recognized his employer's suspicious nature and later exploited this weakness outrageously. It was finally Magill who, with what in fact was hindsight judgment, uncovered the irregularities. He magnified them and subsequently revealed that a plot had been in progress to wreck the paper. His evidence was largely a composite of trifling irregularities and poor judgments. When these bits were pieced together, although they matched at many points, they differed at many others; and we may ask ourselves whether it is possible to obtain or even to approach truth in a patchwork of this kind.

For my part, I believe no such plot ever existed, though there were thefts of considerable proportions. But Abbott, whose confidence had already been shaken, was inclined to believe the most fantastic accusations against his former employees. He afterwards reported, "Magill soon discovered that my affairs were in very bad shape and began at once to readjust my business. This readjustment period required a thorough study of the ills which had previously affected my business and he made the necessary changes from time to time in its personnel and management that has since redoubled to its improvement and success."

This was a premature judgment.

Thefts by the so-called "Four Horsemen" were estimated

in the thousands of dollars. Notwithstanding, the *Defender* entered a lush period financially—actually, the publisher had begun to enjoy his maximum prosperity. He drew nice bundles of cash from the paper's earnings, though his salary of $2,000 weekly was declared excessive by the Commissioner of Internal Revenue and was shaved $500. Meanwhile Magill, who had started at a $250 weekly salary plus a percentage of the gross annual profits, himself earned a bonus of $27,931.10 the first year of his employment. Abbott had given the bonus in consideration of Magill's giving up his legal practice and devoting his entire time to the *Defender*. He afterwards raised his salary in successive increases to $700 per week, and discontinued the bonus—because, as he said, the paper was "now on sound footing." Abbott further sweetened this largesse by using his influence to have Magill appointed as the first Negro Assistant Attorney General of the State of Illinois, a position he undertook in addition to his regular duties at the *Defender*.

The chief ornament among Abbott's personal possessions was by no means neglected during this lush period. Besides proudly adorning Helen with diamonds and furs, he gave her a Pierce Arrow convertible coupe. He afterwards bought her an ivy-covered, three-story, fourteen-room red brick mansion trimmed with white stone and situated at 4742 South Parkway, once the city's main boulevard. The place, including a two-car garage, was described as "baronial." The house, costing roughly $50,000, was furnished in a style that made Negroes gape when they thronged the place during socials. A few items will illustrate: a 24-carat gold-plated dinner set, deep-piled Chinese rugs, pieces of Hepplewhite, a billiard table, and an ebony-finished Mandarin living room set imported directly from China—as well as beautiful linen, costly bric-a-brac, fine glassware and china, and handsome silver services and paintings.

The upkeep of this establishment was proportional.

255

I have before me an itemized account of Abbott's personal expenses for the month of May, 1929, which is fairly typical. The items include personals, charity, gifts, loans, merchandise and household expenses. They come to a grand total of $1,800.48—and this does not include the chauffeur and three house servants who were on the *Defender* payroll. From time to time there were unexpected expenditures like Dr. M. A. Sweeney's bill for services rendered Helen's ailing dog, "Kojo," and big gifts like the purchase of a home in Athens, Georgia, for his wife's mother. Helen, who apparently was a charming hostess and managed a well-ordered household, had, in addition, personal charge accounts in such department stores as Chas. A. Stevens, Marshall Field, and Carson Pirie Scott. Her clothes often bore the labels of fashionable North Side specialty shops.

One particular detail is pertinent at this point. American folkways in those days included a refusal to acknowledge the existence of a rich Negro. Thus, when Abbott traveled to the Loop he often was mistaken as the chauffeur of his own big limousine. This was an annoying fly in the ointment. Faced with this identical problem, ebony-colored Jules Bledsoe, who sang "Old Man River" in the Broadway musical play, *Show Boat,* broke into the limelight with an expensive, high-powered car, driven by a white chauffeur in livery. He explained to the complete satisfaction of his Negro friends, that he had a white, uniformed chauffeur so that the white people could tell which was the driver and which the owner of the car. But Abbott did not go to such lengths to establish the distinction: he settled for a fair-complexioned Negro who resembled an Oriental!

The conspicuous consumption suddenly indulged in by the publisher may very well have been his way of reassuring himself and the public of the *Defender's* financial stability. For the fact is that the mass dismissals and subsequent wild charges of thievery had shocked his people. His competitor, the Chicago *Whip,* whose stories were based on Abbott's admission to its editor, Joseph D. Bibb, of robbery at the *Defender,* had played no small part in keeping the pot boiling. In any case, the scandal did not diminish the paper's vigor one iota. For example, Abbott's policy toward American occupation of Haiti had produced echoes in the halls of Congress. Two items illustrate why: he published a cartoon by Leslie Rogers showing the prostrate form of a woman representing the Black Republic pierced through the heart by a bayonet attached to a gun, and labeled it "U.S. Military Occupancy." He afterwards carried a story, typical of those that followed, which bore this inflammatory head: HAITI'S LIBERTY TRAMPLED BY PREJUDICED AMERICAN RULERS. The sub-head ran: "Capt. Marshall Cites Unjust Tactics of White Dictators."

The internal explosion produced no decline in the *Defender's* circulation. Maybe the reason is that Abbott offered the public new columnist personalities like A. L. Jackson, a young man who had achieved athletic prominence at Harvard University; and the distinguished crusader, Mary Church Terrell, who conducted a survey of current happenings called "Up to Date," replacing Roscoe Conkling Simmons' "This Week." He also introduced a farm column, dealing with agricultural problems such as feeding cattle, proper care of soil and fighting boll weevils. But his major stroke was the timely innovation of a whole page concerned with art and literature, which thus kept step with the development of a cultural movement among Negroes during this period, popularly called the "Negro Renaissance." Across the top of the page was this boxed headline: "What We Are Doing in Literature and the Arts." Below, W. M. Farrow discussed "Art and the Home"; J. Wm. Jesse Lovell made surveys "In Literature and Art"; and Dewey R. Jones analyzed "Raciality in the Short Story."

A spectacular promotional idea was developed about now —actually the payoff for the encouragement and advice Abbott had given an ambitious Chicago girl, Bessie Coleman, who had attempted without success to become an airplane pilot. She had been rejected because she was both a woman and a Negro. Abbott advised her to study French and go abroad where she could obtain aviation instructions. Soon afterwards she went to France and later Holland, where she learned to fly and thus became the first Negro woman to pilot a plane. When she returned to this country, Abbott assigned Bill White in his New York office to handle the details of her first public appearance as a *Defender* presentation. An exhibition was staged at Curtis Field, Garden City, Long Island, in which the Negro aviatrix flew a plane with 10,000 Negroes present to witness the extraordinary feat. Upon her arrival in Chicago, Bessie Coleman repeated the exhibition at Midway Airport and the *Defender* triumphantly recorded it for posterity.

The *Defender* was no less influential during the reorganization period than it had been before. A. L. Foster, an ex-social worker, relates an incident which is illustrative. He recalls that during the administration of Bishop John A. Gregg as president of Wilberforce University a bill was introduced in the Ohio State legislature providing for the establishment of a school of higher education for Negro youth at Wilberforce, Ohio. The school was to be known as "Lincoln." The bill, according to the understanding of Negroes, was introduced at the suggestion of Ohio State University, which wished to restrict its Negro student population. Negroes formed a committee and appealed to Abbott for help. He promptly carried a page-one headline to the effect that Ohio proposed to establish a "Jim Crow College." Negroes procured copies and placed one on the desk of each member of the legislature's appropriations committee. This was enough, says Foster, to defeat the proposal.

By and large the public's attitude to the disturbing developments at the *Defender* was wholly reassuring to Abbott, for he was the recipient of a bumper crop of awards and honors. For example, Governor Louis L. Emmerson (Illinois) appointed him as a member of the Lincoln Memorial Committee to plan the erection of a monument to the emancipator. He was elected a director of the Binga State Bank, which, incidentally, proved an expensive honor. Especially prized was a pen and ink sketch of him by a distinguished figure in the Negro art world, Frank Holbrook. It appeared in *Opportunity*, a Negro quality magazine published by the National Urban League. The editor, Elmer A. Carter, wrote to inform him beforehand that its publication was in connection with a story by Dewey R. Jones, "Chicago Claims Supremacy," in which the publisher figured largely.

Nathan Magill, a hard-headed realist, made money.

Yet he had neither the racial idealism nor the business intuition of Abbott, so that when left to operate alone, his first big decision was a wrong one—wrong in terms of Negro aspirations, wrong because of *Defender* policy and tradition, wrong for the economy of the Negro community, and wrong because it did violence to the publisher's sentiments.

Now Magill was a man who brooked little disagreement— in fact, when advised to take a contrary course he was not only dogmatic but ill-tempered. For instance, Benjamin W. Clayton, a Chicago attorney and his fellow graduate of Boston University recalls the time he, Magill and Abbott were having lunch and a discussion of the Illinois election laws came up. "Magill gave Abbott one quotation from the law and I gave another," he says. "When he returned to the *Defender* office, Abbott himself looked up the law, and we discovered that I had given the correct one. Magill afterwards broke off friendship with me, simply because I had proved right and he wrong."

In any case, the *Defender* had hardly emerged from a scandal, when Magill pushed the paper into a new one, for the cocky little general manager rushed headlong into a decision which proved disastrous to the institution and damaged the publisher's reputation and prestige as an idealistic race leader.

The problem concerned the Pullman porters.

Pullman porters were an American institution but an underpaid one. They had a monopoly of this employment, though there was occasional competition from Mexicans and Filipinos. There were more than 9,000 Negro porters in the United States, and nearly 4,000 lived in Chicago—but there were roughly 30,000 more Negro workers in the railroad industry whose condition was affected indirectly by what happened to the Pullman porters. The sentiments of these people were therefore clearly on the side of the porters, who had now reached an impasse in their relations with the powerful Pullman Company.

They had long had Abbott's sympathy and support for reasons both sentimental and economically valid. For nearly ten years now the porters had been agitating for increased wages, with an assist from the *Defender*. For example, when their initial plea was rejected the paper carried this headline: PULLMAN COMPANY REFUSES PORTERS HIGHER WAGES. And the story declared: "The company's failure to act, after its own admission that part of the company's huge profits were derived by under-payment of its faithful employees, can be explained only by the indifference and disregard of its wealthy directors as to the well being of the faithful employees who man the cars." Abbott despaired of the porters ever winning an increase, as this head suggests: "Porters' Hope Only a Dream."

To be sure, Abbott went overboard with the porters, but he sometimes felt the need to slap at porters who aided and abetted racial discrimination and those whose public behavior was offensive and consequently injurious to the race. Under the head, BIG HEADED, NOISY PORTER AND WAITER GREAT RACE EVIL, he declared: "It is quite the rule for Race passengers to suffer certain kinds of humiliation when traveling, but when men of their own race are the offenders it is such a pity. When traveling members of the race try to avail themselves of service and accommodations guaranteed to all, white and black alike, it is just likely that it's a man of color in the company's employ who tells you, 'you are exceeding the bounds.'" Such articles did not appear frequently.

Talk of organizing the Pullman porters had been heard for a number of years. The idea was even proposed by the *Defender*. But no serious attempts were made until A. Philip Randolph, editor of the militant *Messenger* magazine, turned his attention to the project in 1925. One of the difficulties in organizing porters was the fact that as a class, though underpaid, they had fairly steady work—and in those days even rated highly in Negro society. Randolph held a mass meeting in Harlem and formed the Brotherhood of Sleeping Car Porters. The *Messenger* furnished the movement with an organ already well known in Negro and white labor circles, and by 1927 more than fifty per cent of the eligible workers carried union cards.

The organizational campaign, which naturally centered in Chicago, was a bitter one involving frequent charges that civic leaders and ministers were being bribed by the Pullman Company to oppose union organization. But the porters as wage earners had rank and file support. Moreover, the fact that most persons in the Negro upper class were dependent, directly or indirectly, upon the economic welfare of the mass for their livelihood, tended to bend Negro opinion towards economic "radicalism." The fact is, Randolph was charged with being a "Communist," and it was seriously asserted that the "Pullman porters' organization did not believe in God."

Said Randolph: "Were it not that these idiot-oral antics are disastrous to the unthinking, they would be side cracklingly amusing."

A. Philip Randolph was an extraordinary man.

Tall, dark and brooding, one of the outstanding Negroes in America today, he was then unique among Negro leaders—he was neither preacher, educator, nor rabble-rousing politician, but a labor organizer of considerable intellectual development. He was also a man of great eloquence. Randolph was born in 1889 in Crescent City, Florida, son of a Methodist minister. As a young man he joined the migration North and entered City College of New York. The problems of earning enough to eat interfered with his studies, and he applied for a job as a waiter on the Fall River Line. He was fired on his first trip for having organized a protest against the makeshift living quarters assigned the workers. Impatient with the views of the Negro leaders during World War I, he joined the Socialist Party and later founded the *Messenger* magazine, along with Chandler Owen. A few days after Eugene Debs' arrest, Randolph was also put in jail because of his stand against this country's participation in the war. Later he was released.

He was a zealous and indefatigable worker, his racial idealism untainted. The *Defender* would have embraced the man and his movement in days past, but Magill, with an eye on the cash register, now promulgated a strong anti-union policy which rejected Randolph and labeled the porters' organization a "monopoly." Before long, under the head, "Dangers of Monopolies," the editorial position of the *Defender* was stated thus: "Much has been said about the Pullman porters and the fact that our Race has maintained an unquestioned monopoly in that particular field of labor. Efforts are now being made by the porters and outsiders to perfect an organization whereby this monopoly will become permanent. And in this step lie great dangers, not only to the Pullman porters themselves, but to laborers in every other branch of American industry.

"For years we have fought against just such steps as this. We do not believe we should have a monopoly on Pullman porters' service any more than that white people should have a monopoly on Pullman conductor service, or that Irishmen should have a monopoly on police and fire departments. We cannot hope to break down the bars that keep us from other fields of endeavor if we are going to start movements that will automatically bar others. We believe there should be black and white porters, and that there should be black and white conductors, all employed according to their abilities and not according to their race. We believe that they should all work together along all lines and not in separate contingents. . . .

"We want all workers of all races at the same place together and work together with only their ability determining their progress. Monopolies are dangerous if formed along race lines."

The *Defender's* anti-union position assumed the proportions of a public scandal. The paper, however, was not alone in opposition to Randolph's movement. The Negro press generally attacked him and the union. Randolph soon charged that the *Defender* had surrendered to "gold and power." For a while the Chicago *Bee,* owned by the banker Anthony Overton, criticized the *Defender* for capitulating to the Pullman Company. But it, too, eventually succumbed and joined the opponents of Randolph. Congressman Oscar De Priest is quoted by Brailsford R. Brazeal, historian of the Brotherhood movement, as declaring that "he was an eye-witness to the passing of fifty-five per cent of the *Whip's* stock to Daniel J. Schuyler, one of the attorneys for the Pullman Company and also for the various Samuel Insull interests."

A good deal of money was loosely splashed about. But no such charge was openly made against the *Defender*, though it supported the rival Pullman Porters Benefit Association, a company union that Randolph observed had $10,000 in the Binga State Bank of which Abbott was a director. Perhaps the approach had been indirect, for Daniel J. Schuyler was credited with having promoted the formation in Chicago of the National Negro Advertising Agency (now defunct) of which Melvin J. Chisum, an avowed enemy of the Brotherhood, was an adviser. The purpose of this agency was alleged to have been the placing of advertisements in Negro newspapers to influence their news and editorial policies toward corporations represented by the agency.

The *Defender*, seemingly impatient for concrete developments, deplored the spending of money by the porters in wrangling when "the company union has race members sitting in judgment on disputes." The porters who had been active in building the Brotherhood were advised to "forget the past and spend the ensuing years building up the service . . . for . . . who knows what recognition, promotions and salary increase the porters and maids have been deprived of by virtue of the past two years' agitation." Brazeal flatly declares: "With due allowance for the editors' anti-union sentiment, their genuine distrust of Brotherhood leaders, and their fear that Negroes would lose preference as Pullman porters through their efforts to form a union, it still appears that their fundamental reason for opposing the Brotherhood was financial, directly and indirectly."

Randolph struck back.

He labeled Abbott's paper as the Chicago *"Surrender,"* misnamed *"Defender,"* and the "World's Greatest Weakly." He told one of his organizers in a letter quoted by Brazeal, "We do not have to court any of these Negro editors any more. The organization can stand the storm of their opposition, although it is a wise policy to silence every opposition possible, either through a head-on attack or diplomatic negotiations."

He did both.

To begin with, he launched a violent campaign against the paper, urging the Pullman porters and their friends not to buy the *Defender,* and thus hit the paper's most vulnerable spot. The porters and their supporters responded by pledging not to buy the paper, and they turned to the labor and religious press to articulate their grievances. The result was almost immediately apparent in a sharp dip in circulation, which was the *Defender's* chief source of revenue.

Robert S. Abbott, in characteristic fashion, was slow in personally taking a hand in the controversy. But when he did, he moved with surprising dispatch. He had watched the circulation figures decline, but he felt more keenly the antagonism of the porters and was exceedingly distressed by Randolph's charge that Negro editors who supported the Pullman Company were traitors to their race. In any case, he finally overruled Magill in his policy toward the Pullman porters, and brought all his talents for soft talk and negotiation into play. Soon a pipe of peace was smoked between the *Defender's* management and the Brotherhood's leadership. He had chosen the strategic moment for rapprochement, for an abortive attempt to strike had shaken the porters' confidence and somewhat discouraged their leadership.

It was a notable about-face, though engineered by Abbott with considerable aplomb. Magill could do nothing but assent to his publisher's decision. Even so, Abbott made no public sacrifice of his general manager to absolve himself from responsibility, and he thereby demonstrated considerable character.

Unabashedly, Randolph was now described as "brilliant and fearless," and suddenly the paper displayed a remarkable grasp of the porters' grievances and urged they be solved quickly. Then Abbott unambiguously placed the paper on the record with this statement: "The *Defender*, therefore, takes the side of the porters' fight to organize for their rights as other workers have done and we bid them God speed."

When the organization was recognized by the American Federation of Labor, the *Defender* carried this head: PORTERS GIVEN CHARTER. Said the paper triumphantly, "The fight for recognition by the Pullman porters, which has extended over a period of years was brought to a glorious victory when A. Philip Randolph, general organizer and main champion of the cause, was notified that the American Federation of Labor, through its executive council, had granted a charter to the Pullman brotherhood."

Randolph, now a veteran of the hurly-burly of labor strife and writing with the perspective of distance, declares:

"The opposition of the Chicago *Defender* was definite, positive and unequivocal. Nathan Magill general manager of the Chicago *Defender* at that time, during a conference in which the paper and the Brotherhood buried the hatchet, informed Mr. [Milton P.] Webster and myself that the paper had received generous payments [presumably advertising] from the Pullman Company for material carried against the Brotherhood. In fact, he showed us the figures in the accounts of the *Defender*—the exact amount I cannot recall. . . .

"Of course, I have always had a kindly feeling toward Mr. Abbott and ascribe the policies of the *Defender* at that time to his lack of understanding of the nature of the fight to win recognition from the Pullman Company as a collective bargaining agent for the porters. He was not alone among the Negro leaders who attacked the Brotherhood and was manifestly antagonistic to trade union organizations as such, whether by Negroes or any other group of workers."

The Brotherhood, now firmly supported by the *Defender*, was eventually recognized by the Pullman Company. An agreement was signed which increased the rates of pay, improved working conditions, and established machinery to handle grievances. The salary increase amounted to more than a million dollars annually. By now, though, Randolph had contributed articles to the *Defender*, and when Abbott returned from a trip abroad he received a thoughtful postcard from the labor leader: "Hope you enjoyed a delightful trip to the Old World. Sincerely, Phil."

Says Randolph: "The relationship between the *Defender* and Brotherhood today, I am glad to say, is friendly."

*Those [Negroes] who go to Europe will have their
ideas about color so upset that they never will be
the same again.*—ROBERT S. ABBOTT, Chicago Defender, 1929.

CHAPTER XVI

A Man Called Kojo

AMERICA WAS IMPLICIT in the editor's observations abroad.

His unpalatable experiences as a Negro, though hidden
deeply in the recesses of his mind and perhaps a part of his
racial psyche, kept returning like Banquo's ghost to haunt
Robert S. Abbott as he traveled about Europe. He remembered incidents which contrasted sharply with the experiences offered by a continent that proved a revelation, opening windows in his mind that thus allow us to glimpse, if only
fleetingly, the things that gnawed at his soul.

One incident will illustrate.

"One cold and snowy night," he recalled, "I arrived late in
New York from Chicago and went to the McAlpin Hotel for
a room. But I was told that there were none vacant, although
there were plenty. As I turned away from the desk to go back
into the biting cold, a white man came up, followed by another and another, and all were given rooms. One of these
white men, seeing what had happened to me, turned back
and laughed full in my face—laughed to think that he could
get in and I could not.

"I have never forgotten the laugh of vindicative triumph

267

on that white man's face. As I walked into the best establishments in Berlin, Paris, Brussels, and Amsterdam, white hotel attendants rushed forward to greet my wife and myself. I wished that same man could only see me now. I can imagine the laughter on his face turning to rage if he could see me being received just as he would be received in Atlanta, or Birmingham or Jackson, Miss."

Europe was to sharply alter his racial slants.

He explained the development this way: "There is one thought that has remained uppermost in my mind during the entire period of my trip. Many, many things that I saw would keep bringing it back to me.

"And it is this:

"All my life, even from my earliest childhood, I have felt in the depths of my being that the theory that color makes the man was one of the biggest lies ever told. Now, after months of daily contact with the white man on his own soil, I am more firmly convinced than ever that I am right.

"Better, I firmly believe now that such a theory could have originated only in a madhouse among lunatics. For what do you find in the white man's own country? That a black man receives the highest courtesy and is free to come and to go everywhere. In short, he is free to do what any other human can do.

"Not the slightest restrictions anywhere."

The Negro publisher, whom the French called "M'sieur A-boot," had felt the lift and freedom of being a wealthy Negro in Europe, and he was dazzled by what he had seen and experienced. For, he reported, the Continent had much to offer which was distinctly satisfying to a Negro born and reared in the United States. For one thing, he was given a unique sort of racial experience, involving intangibles of the spirit, which enabled him to realize himself as a whole being. He stepped into the mainstream of Europe's community—a step from a feudal to a modern society, racially speaking, and therefore there was no need for him to accommodate himself to racial prejudice in the numerous subtle ways that were characteristic of his own country.

He and his wife, Helen, sailed for Europe in June 1929, bearing two trunks, six valises, eight other pieces of luggage, and $9,000 in travelers' cheques. Before leaving America he again had been the victim of racial difficulties with the steamship companies in procuring first-class accommodations, a fact that was reported in a *Defender* story with the head: [NEGRO] TOURISTS MUST FIGHT SEGREGATION AT SEA. He recalled his previous experience when planning his trip to South America and firmly declared: "There should be no compromise on issues of such discrimination on the high seas and we as one must fight to get fair and equal treatment everywhere, both at home and abroad." Finally, to escape the racial humiliations, he traveled to Europe on an English liner, the *S.S. Mauretania,* and returned aboard another English vessel, the *S.S. Aquitania.*

They were abroad five months, and covered considerable territory in that brief span. The Hotel Victoria Palace in Paris formed a sort of headquarters for them. From here, they toured Belgium, Holland, Germany, Austria and Italy, then returned to Paris. They made a brief tour of the French countryside, including a visit to the battlefields. They afterwards went to England for what proved a short and disastrous stay, and returned to Paris before embarking for the United States. Beforehand, Abbott had arranged a meeting with Joel A. Rogers, a Negro journalist and historian stationed in Paris. Rogers spoke French fluently and knew the Continent well, so the publisher employed him as a combination interpreter and reporter-guide, a fact that helped to facilitate his movements about Europe. For Abbott was of the opinion that "If you do not speak the language of a country you are almost as good as deaf and dumb."

Eventually he developed many friendships. Judging from the number of personal calling cards he accumulated, he was introduced to hundreds of people. He afterwards maintained an extensive correspondence, which incidentally contributed to his intellectual growth. But upon arrival in Paris, he first had sought and found his old African friend, Kojo Touvalou, a lawyer and a prince of Dahomey. This unusual man had visited him in Chicago and inspired Helen to name her black dog "Kojo." He, along with M. Delgarno, became Abbott's host. Maurice Delgarno, a Negro colonial official, took especial interest in the editor's racial mission, introduced him to many important figures in the French government, and opened many social doors to him. He arranged a meeting with Maurice Satineau, editor of the Negro newspaper, *Africaine,* with whom Abbott afterwards had many long and profitable talks.

A marginal comment should be made:

It was initially Prince Kojo's rosy description of Europe's total absence of racialism, which profoundly influenced the racial course of Abbott's trip. For much of what the editor saw in Paris, was under the elbow-close shepherding of Kojo —and maybe through his eyes. In any case, Kojo became the publisher's chief social mentor and, in the process, introduced him to what in fact was Bohemian Paris. Yet, in a sense, the man from Africa was as much an innocent abroad as was the man from America. Racially speaking, it was perhaps a case of the blind leading the blind.

"We took in things pretty thoroughly," Abbott reported, "seeing much the average tourist does not see, and meeting and conversing with all classes of people in order to learn their points of view."

Actually, the Negro editor never saw Europe!

The very limited concerns of the Negro traveler were illustrated by the many striking parallels and dramatic differences in the trips abroad of Robert S. Abbott and Booker T. Washington, who visited the Continent in 1910. Like his hero, the editor conceived the notion that he would like to get away from the United States and see what this America, in which he had been so long and so actively immersed, looked like from shores abroad.

What made the journeys of these two men unique was the fact that, though they visited most of Europe's capitals, they did not, in the sense of the ordinary traveler, see the Continent at all. It was evident enough that the public buildings and gardens, the painting, sculpture, architecture and music meant nothing to them, that they counted as nothing in their mental and spiritual development, but were merely things to be toyed with by people not engaged in the serious work of emancipating the Negro race.

But from this point their paths diverged:

Washington, sedulously avoiding the historical shrines and customary sights, limited his observations to the life and labor of what he described as "the man farthest down." His purpose, as far as possible, was to meet and make the acquaintance of the classes in Europe which, in respect to their opportunities, their handicaps, and their condition of life generally, were comparable with the Negro masses of the United States.

Abbott, though he visited the art galleries and places of historical interest as if on a scooter, was primarily concerned with the élite—that is, the black aristocrats. His purpose was to meet, talk to and rub elbows with the upper classes in Europe, both white and Negro. He wished to compare the social and cultural progress of Negroes in the Old World with that of the Negro in the United States; and he also wished to compare the racial behavior of the white man in Europe with that of the white man in the United States, and perhaps discover the reason for the striking difference.

What the Tuskegee educator wanted to see abroad, from the distance and point of view of Europe, was America, and not America merely but the American Negro. Abbott had an identical purpose. But Washington searched in the slums of London, hunted out the abandoned ghettos of Prague and Cracow, explored the sulphur mines of Sicily and discovered in remote villages Polish and Italian immigrants; the *Defender* editor visited American Negroes working as entertainers in Montmartre cafes, sought conversations with Negroes who held important positions in the French government, observed Negroes who were making successful careers in the German film industry, and hob-nobbed with Negro scholars and professional men prospering in England.

Briefly: Booker T. Washington's mission was essentially economic; Robert S. Abbott's purely racial.

If the Negro editor had wished, however, to escape the fact of being a Negro, there apparently was no hiding place— indeed, he had hardly arrived in Paris and settled in a Montparnasse hotel, when one morning he found a note in his pigeonhole asking him to leave. The brief request, signed by the manager, explained that the white Americans staying in the hotel had objected to his presence and that several had already left on his account.

"When I went there first," Abbott reported ruefully, "I was received with that courtesy which is characteristic of the Old World."

He decided to stand his ground.

"Had I been even in America," he remarked, "I would have stayed."

He appealed to his friend and attorney, Prince Kojo, and they, together with the Princess Behanzin, a white woman and widow of the prince's cousin, called on the manager. The prince asked the manager if he realized what he had done. The white man protested that he was losing customers at the height of the tourist season, and added, "I saw my guests leaving me because they said a black man with a white wife was here so I asked him to go." The lawyer reminded him that the civil laws provided severe penalties for racial discrimination.

The man became a bundle of profuse apologies.

"To me their objection is perfectly crazy," said the hotel manager now addressing Abbott directly. "As a Frenchman I simply can't understand why they should object to you—you who have proved to be a gentleman in every way. I fought with black soldiers all during the war and I never met finer men. I am very sorry, sir, very sorry. I really did not know what I was doing. As you saw, I was too ashamed to tell you to leave myself and so left you that note."

The Negro editor was appeased.

"That letter I now have in my possession," he reported. "As to the hotel, I stayed there as a matter of principle until I was ready to leave for Belgium, although I was sorry for the proprietor, who, after all, was a very fine man.

"The laws of France are explicit," he afterwards told Negroes. "Where a person is refused service because of his color, the police have strict orders to go in and close the place. Where trouble does arise in Europe it is traceable directly to the American people and the American government. No European feels the necessity of treating the black American with respect when he knows the American government will not protect him! The courtesy we received abroad is not due to love or fear of America, but to the sense of justice which motivates the European."

He thus was bolstered by law and tradition.

Now the racial pattern of his trip was set.

"When I learned," he remarked, "that there was a place where colored people were not served, then that place of all places became most interesting to me. I felt I must try to enter it at all costs and when Prince Kojo invited me to a cafe [which reportedly had discriminated against a Negro to appease prejudiced white Americans], I accepted the invitation eagerly. My great ambition was to see myself rejected in France. I wanted to see whether American dollars had triumphed over the blood shed by black men to save France."

La Coupole, a swank cafe which had allegedly refused service to a M. Alexis, a Haitian diplomat, was the place to which Prince Kojo's party headed. The group included Mr. and Mrs. Abbott and a Chicago singer, Roberta Dodds Crawford, all distinctly Negroid types with the exception of Helen. When they arrived, much to their surprise Abbott afterwards said, they "were welcomed with all the courtesy and politeness characteristic of the better class French establishments." The manager came forward to greet them and conducted them to one of the best tables in the place. The party was hardly seated, when the Negro editor questioned him about the reported discrimination.

The manager acknowledged the incident.

"Certain Americans," he explained, "who do not like colored people, have been paying my employees not to admit or to serve Negroes. I am very much grieved over the incident and I have taken steps to see that the offense is not repeated."

He added, "This is France and all races of mankind are welcome in my place. You may see them in my cafe at any time of the day."

Abbott learned that nearly $2,000 had been paid to La Coupole employees by white Americans to bar Negroes from the cafe; and, he reported, when the bribe was unsuccessful and they got drunk, "they were likely to shy a champagne bottle at a colored guest." The newspaperman saw a story and perhaps a noisy exposé. He cabled his office the facts and soon afterwards the *Defender* appeared with a story carrying these page-one heads: SPREAD HATE IN PARIS BY BRIBE ROUTE, and EDITOR ABBOTT EXPOSES AMERICAN METHODS.

Abbott was now convinced that the French, imposed upon by white Americans, were aggressively resisting the importation of racial prejudice. "No wonder," he exclaimed, "white people from America are complaining about the treatment they receive in France! In France they see their color lines crumble about them—they see their theories and traditions about racial segregation trampled under the feet of the wider brotherhood!"

When he visited the Bois de Boulogne, which he described as "one of the most beautiful spots in all Europe," he confessed he had "the pleasure of witnessing the great discomfiture of a group of white Americans." They were thwarted, according to him, in attempts "to interfere with the dancing of white women and dark men, and their dining together in the numerous cafes with which this wooded area in Paris is crowded and for which it is famous." And he happily watched his white countrymen as they "contented themselves with standing around biting their nails and showing their ill-breeding by making insulting remarks about the French people and their darker compatriots."

Now the tour of Europe became a succession of racial triumphs.

While in Brussels, he visited the Congo Museum where he saw exhibited primitive works of art executed by African blacks. "Really," Abbott remarked to Helen, "after all this it will be more amusing than ever to hear that story about the degraded state of the native African, for Europe has nothing of greater artistic sincerity than have these Congolese." They attended a concert that evening and somehow procured a box adjacent to the royal box in which King Albert and Queen Elizabeth were seated. Two white Americans, whom he described as having "the map of Georgia written all over their faces," occupied the stall next to Abbott's. "They drew as far back from us as they could, and I rather fancy we quite spoiled their evening," he reported with evident satisfaction. "I noticed that the handsome king and his charming queen as well as the Belgian and French aristocrats who sat near seemed quite at ease, and not in the least disturbed at our presence." They afterwards dropped by a night club, where he observed with delight "Negroes from the Congo dancing with elegantly dressed white women, and the only ones taking notice of them were the white Americans."

The Negro editor himself proved a delightful novelty in Germany.

"I was gazed at in Germany more than in any other country," he recalled with obvious enjoyment. "But let me say here that it was a different gaze from that with which I would be greeted in America, or if I had gone into some remote village of the North. It was different from what, for instance, the Americans greeted me with when we walked into the dining room of our hotel in Bremen. In short, the gaze of the German people was full of friendly curiosity. They were eager to converse with me and whenever I addressed anyone I met with the finest courtesy. So I didn't mind a bit their gazing at me. The German people, I found, are very easy to make friends with."

Had he met them during the war, he conceded, his reactions might have been very different. Nor were there enough Negroes in the country to excite his interest—he counted perhaps two hundred and fifty, and he found them "bored as the chimpanzee." He had a brief racial encounter in Charlottenburg, a suburb of Berlin, when white Americans objected to his staying at the hotel. "But there," he reported with satisfaction, "the proprietor told them that if they didn't like it to get out!" Yet he was forced to remark, "Money is winning over manners in some parts of Europe, but as I said, all that a Negro has to do when objected to is to stand his ground."

When Abbott entered The Hague in Holland, he paused long enough to send a cablegram to the Boy Scout organization, which was holding its annual jamboree in England, a jamboree to which the Prince of Wales had been invited. Abbott seized the meeting as a pretext for placing the Negro's grievances before an international body. And he wrote thus:

> To the Boy Scouts Assembled, Greetings: The Negroes of America, through their mouthpiece, The Chicago *Defender,* represented by Robert S. Abbott, its editor, now traveling in Europe, beg most seriously and respectfully to call your attention to the atrocious practice of lynching and burning. They plead with you not to accept in your august body Boy Scouts from these cities and states where lynchings are permitted and who at the same time have witnessed lynchings without protests as well as those who believe in this barbarous practice of taking human life without due process of law. They entreat you to use your influence in abolishing color segregation in your ranks by seeing that all the boys in the southern and other states be permitted to join the same brigades as is done in the North. This request is addressed to you most fittingly from Holland, the land to which come the nations of the world for amicable settlement of their grievances, and it is because we know that the basic principle of the Boy Scouts movement is truth, justice and obedience to Christ, who bade us love one another, that we confidently address you this request. [Signed] ROBERT S. ABBOTT.

The Abbotts then briefly toured Austria and Italy, and returned to Paris where the Negro publisher received his greatest lift and perhaps experienced his proudest moment. He afterwards was to speak of it as "one of the greatest pleasures in my life." Perhaps through the intercession of M. Delgarno, Abbott decorated the tomb of the Unknown Soldier in a formal ceremony attended by dignitaries of the French government, a host of Negro and white friends, and reporters and photographers representing *Le Soir, Le Temps, L'Intransigeant, Paris Soir* and *La Liberté.*

Four pictures extant recapture a bit of the flavor of that occasion: there the Negro editor stood in his English-tailored cutaway coat, striped trousers, pearl-gray vest, spats, top hat, and gold-headed cane, with a wreath of flowers in one arm. Then he solemnly marched to the Arc de Triomphe. As he approached the sarcophagus, he removed his hat and placed the wreath on the white marble slab. He stepped back, inspected his handiwork and, with head bowed, paused reverently in meaningful silence while Helen stood to one side, her face an inscrutable mask. He afterwards spoke of the gesture as "a tribute from my race, from my heart, and from my country."

The signal event was recorded for posterity:

He lost no time in sending this cable to his Chicago office: "Editor placed eight foot wreath on grave of Unknown Soldier at Arch of Triumph Thursday. First time colored American has done this in honor of the men [who] fell in defense of France." The *Defender* story, giving details of the ceremony, carried a modest headline: EDITOR ABBOTT HONORS UNKNOWN SOLDIER OF FRANCE, and reported that "the ceremony was recorded, not only by moving pictures, but by photographers."

He never forgot that day.

England was a different kettle of fish.

The trip there was memorable for a piece of discrimination that had international echoes—indeed, according to the New York *Times,* Abbott "caused the race question to be raised in England for the first time in an acute form." Back in the United States there was talk among Negroes of the Negro editor duplicating the feat of Frederick Douglass by influencing English opinion to support the aspirations of down-trodden Negroes in America. Consequently, his status as a leader soared.

The tourist agency handling Abbott's trip had made reservations in a fashionable London hotel, presumably the Savoy. When he arrived he was frankly informed that Negroes were not admitted. In the next hotel he spent one night before the manager requested his room because he was expecting a party of seventy-five which did not wish to be separated. The Haymarket Hotel required his room after the midday meal.

Everywhere he turned he was seemingly rebuffed.

He tried a stratagem. When the taxi pulled up before one hotel, he sent his mulatto wife in to claim the reservation while he remained in the cab. She was comfortably settled before he made his entrance—but he was halted at the desk with the announcement that the establishment did not cater to Negroes. They finally were forced to accept the hospitality of a Negro singing instructor, Louis Drysdale, who lived on Westbourne Road, Forest Hill, London.

This nightmarish discrimination made page-one news, both in England and abroad. The London *Daily Express,* for example, carried a front-page story with a three-deck head:

LONDON HOTELS
COLOUR BAR

ORDEAL OF NEGRO MILLIONAIRE

30 REFUSALS

"Mr. Robert S. Abbott, a wealthy American Negro, reputed to be a dollar millionaire," reported the *Daily Express,* "has been refused admission at so many London hotels that he has given up trying to find hotel accommodation in London. He is on a three months' holiday tour of Europe with his *white wife* [italics mine], and he declares that he met no colour bar until he reached England." The paper reported the following portion of the interview in italicized type, thus: "*Refused admission to thirty hotels; Compelled to leave hotel at half an hour's notice; and requested to leave another after having booked rooms for a fortnight.*"

The Negro editor, in a formal press conference, declared: "I went first to Paris, where I was accorded the highest treatment a man could have. I was received heartily at the first hotel I entered. In the cafes everything was open to me; nothing denied me. Everywhere we went—at Amsterdam, Bremen,

Hamburg, Berlin, Wiesbaden, and Cologne—it was the same."
One reporter noted that Abbott's "eyes shone and his teeth
flashed as he shook his head reminiscently." But he cautiously
qualified his remarks: "I am not talking against the English
people. I have found them to be quite as broad-minded as the
people of the Continent."

Under direct questioning, he frankly admitted, "There is
colour prejudice in the States, especially in the South. If I
tried to enter a hotel in New Orleans they would lynch me.
At least they would kick me out, and if I resisted they would
lynch me. But in England, which has millions of coloured
people under the flag, I expected different treatment."

There were loud repercussions.

The news spread quickly throughout the United Kingdom.
There was a stir among Negroes living in England. Joel A.
Rogers wrote Abbott from Cardiff, Wales, where some four
thousand Negroes resided, that the incident had caused considerable angry talk in that colored community. Abbott was
flooded with personal calls and letters, some from remote
parts of Africa. He himself cabled his Chicago office that "excitement ran so high during the past week, a member of Parliament, Mr. James Marley, called on and interviewed Mr.
and Mrs. Abbott on the affair, and was at sea to know how
an English hotelkeeper could stoop so low."

Many English people were genuinely disturbed.

Among these was the same James Marley, Labor M.P., who
after assuring Abbott of his intention of pushing the matter
in Parliament, did indeed raise the question of the color bar
against Negroes in England. Subsequently Abbott was a victim of discrimination aboard the S.S. *Aquitania* and so informed Marley. When the international actor and singer, Paul
Robeson, reported that he too had been refused admittance
to the Savoy Hotel, although he was to be entertained there
by white friends, Marley wrote a sharp note to Prime Minister Ramsay MacDonald. He received a letter in answer say-

ing, "It is not in accordance with our British hotel practices, but I cannot think of any way in which the government can intervene."

The Negro editor was no crepe-hanger and it is even likely that he enjoyed himself immensely. The reason: notwithstanding the humiliations, he had attracted much attention to himself and dramatized the race problem. How he reacted behind closed doors among Negro friends is suggested by a letter he received a few months after his return to Chicago, in which his London host, Louis Drysdale, wrote: "Whenever both your ears ring furiously, it is because we are speaking of you and the pleasant and happy atmosphere you brought with you while with us." News from home was enough to lift his spirits. Sandwiched between business details, his general manager, Nathan Magill, had reported: "The newspapers and particularly the Chicago *Tribune* had front page stories of the affair. This morning's paper stated that the Government was making an investigation and that they deplored very much the accusation you made against the proprietors."

A few days later Magill wrote, "I had a fine cartoon made this week in which you and Mr. MacDonald and Mr. Marley are breaking down the doors of the hotels in London which refused to serve our people." Abbott must have swelled with pride when he received Magill's final roundup of developments back home: "The newspapers everywhere have given you a lot of space because of your experience in Europe, and we are all very glad to be able to say that the whole civilized world knows you are in Europe. If you did nothing more than have the English government aroused because of their discrimination, you will have accomplished great service to the American people as well as to the English people and to civilized people everywhere."

The British people, at least those concerned, moved to repair the damage done. People in Scotland invited Abbott and his wife to spend their remaining holiday with them. The

Society of Friends called a conference and set up a joint council of representative Negroes and white sympathizers to deal with the issue. This was followed by a movement, in which Abbott's aid was solicited, to establish hostelries for colored people. "You will appreciate the difficulty of finding lodging or hotel accommodations in London for Negroes," Marley wrote Abbott, "and will no doubt be interested to learn that I am associated with two Negroes to secure a Hostel in London for the residence of African students and the colored traveling public."

A wry expression crept into Abbott's face.

England was eyeing segregated hotel accommodations— at least in a modified form.

Upon his return to Chicago, Robert S. Abbott described his experiences in twelve *Defender* articles titled, "My Trip Abroad," calculated to encourage and inform his people. Much of the leg-work and research was done by globe-trotting Joel A. Rogers, who says he "showed the two Paris and went with them into Belgium, Holland and Germany. I left them at Cologne, and returned to Paris, but later joined them in London." Abbott's reporting struck a triumphant, even rapturous note. In the absence of America's elaborate racial etiquette, he declared, he enjoyed a self-respect, dignity and personal worth unknown to his fellows in the United States. Yet, oddly enough, his European pieces did not receive the universal applause accorded his South American racial revelations, though his articles served to reinforce the Negroes' popular picture of Europe as a racial paradise.

He had fallen in love with the French. Consequently, the bulk of his reporting was concerned with racial developments in France—indeed, he omitted mention of Austria and Italy altogether. This reticence in itself was revealing. But he did, in a swift roundup, make a few pertinent observations concerning Holland, Belgium, Germany and England. For example, under the head, "American Color Prejudice Finds Hard Times in Holland," he briefly described the liberality of the Dutch. He found that "Germany Honors Art of All Races" and "Scorns Color Line." This story was accompanied by a layout of pictures labeled "Berlin Open Arms to Achievement," showing one Louis Brody, a popular Negro motion picture player, surrounded by a bevy of beautiful white girls. The caption declared: "This, incidentally, isn't our Hollywood —it just couldn't happen like this in America. Is Herr Brody popular? Well, just look at the picture and draw your own conclusion." He dismissed Belgium with merely the remark, "Although this country has a deservedly bad name in the Congo, yet here at home she makes no difference, a Negro, no matter how dark, goes everywhere he wishes."

His critical observations were reserved for Great Britain, which he described as "A White Man's Land." Under the headline, ENGLAND, LIKE AMERICA, UNDER YOKE OF RACE PREJUDICE, he reported: "The average Englishman feels that England is a white man's land and that a black man has no business there, except as an occasional tourist." He paid a left-handed compliment to his white countrymen in writing, "Nearly every Negro I talked with was bitter against England and said that he much preferred the American white man, who at least was not a hypocrite." Yet he was inclined to place the onus for prejudice in London largely on his compatriots. "The great influx of white Americans," he asserted, "has been given as one of the chief reasons for the growing discrimination in this city, and has started official London to investigating conditions with a view to wiping out these practices."

But while preparing his articles, he received a letter from a Negro living in London who had provided him with much racially derogatory information. The man pleaded urgently. This hapless fellow, who described England as "the worst country in the world for coloured people," had three children and wanted to return to his native land and was fearful Abbott might write something to implicate him. "The paper, Chicago *Defender*," he wrote, "is in great demand in London by Black and Whites. I don't want my name and address to become public, for one day I'll want to return to the West Indies and I don't want trouble getting my passport. These people are just the people to keep an account of your articles, and they will not issue a passport to any Negroes to go back to his land of birth so enlightened."

Abbott respected his request for anonymity.

Across the Channel things had been happily different.

Under the head SEES FRANCE AS HOME OF ALL HUMANITY, Abbott observed: "Not only are dark Americans received cordially and treated as are any other persons in France, but I saw them in the clubs and living in flat buildings with the French people, and even working with them. Wherever I visited I was greeted with open arms and with the genuine hospitality for which European people are noted." He then remarked: "The United States and France are both republics, but when it comes to treatment of the black man, no two nations could be more unlike in their conduct."

However, he was not wholly taken in by the shiny appearance of things—spectacular, racially, as compared with the United States. He recognized French liberality as being inspired by self-interest. He wrote, "The French government is firmly opposed to color prejudice. It needs the services of the black man, and, unlike the English or the American, it is far-seeing enough to realize that it cannot antagonize the black man and have his cooperation at the same time."

French policy, or perhaps lack of policy, extended racial liberalism to nearly every aspect of French public life. To prove this triumphant fact, Abbott brought back documents which he described as "photographic evidence that a man may rise in France, just as high as his ability." Thus, he illustrated each article with a layout of pictures which read like a *Who's Who of Negro France.* For example, René Maran, shown with his white wife, was reported as the winner of the French Academy's Goncourt Prize for literature. Habib Benglia, a Negro actor, was pictured in the roles of *Othello* and *The Emperor Jones,* which he played at the Madeleine Theatre. Etienne Attuly, "a dark Negro," was revealed as the chief official of the French colonial penal system. Raoul Cenac-Thaly, a Negro professor of mathematics, "had all white pupils" at the Michelet Lycée where he taught.

Negroes also figured prominently in the military affairs of France, according to Abbott's report. General Briere de l'isie, "a great Negro engineer," was described as the conqueror of Indo-China. Camille Mortenol, "a very dark man from the West Indies," commanded the civil air defense of Paris during the World War. France's most distinguished Negro general was Alfred Amédée Dodds, who conquered much of France's African empire. He commanded the Allied Forces in 1901 during the Boxer Rebellion, was a member of the War Council during World War I, and later became Inspector-General of the Marines. For background to these developments, Abbott recalled the military career of Alexandre Dumas, père, as a general under Napoleon.

The Chicago editor counted four Negroes in the French Parliament—one senator, and three deputies. A Negro, Henri Lémery, he reported, was the first Undersecretary of State during President Poincaré's administration. He later was appointed Minister of Colonies. Incidentally, Blaise Diagne, a Negro member of the French Chamber of Deputies, was elected president of the Pan-African Congress. Since 1849 Negroes had served in the French Chamber of Deputies, followed by Negro cabinet ministers, a Negro minister of justice, and five colonial governors. Germain Casse, a Negro, was one of the founders of the Third Republic. And before Abbott's arrival, Gratien Candace had been vice-president of the Chamber.

What perhaps was the highlight of the series and proudly

published, was a six-column layout of pictures under the
boxed head, FRANCE OFFERS HOSPITALITY TO ALL
RACES. They showed Abbott himself being served in the
fashionable Lido barbershop of Paris. The caption read: "Although no shop in America compares with this for elaborate-
ness, the policy observed here is 'first come, first served.' "
Incidentally, these pictures caused considerable grumbling
among Negroes. Even Abbott's staff was reluctant to print
them, fearing they might backfire—and backfire they did. But
no one I have talked with has been able to explain why. In
any case, the layout showed a white man shining Abbott's
shoes, a white man trimming his hair, a white man shaving
him, and a white woman manicuring his nails.

This was true liberalism in Abbott's view, pragmatically
exhibited. No wonder he was upset when an American Negro
came to him with an idea that had the sound of racial heresy.
"I met a colored man while in Paris," he reported somewhat
aghast, "who informed me that he had made plans to open a
barber shop for white people only, and that he was told by
Frenchmen not to do it. He was given to understand that Paris
wanted no such shop—that an institution of this sort would
be looked upon with disfavor by the private citizens as well
as the officials of Paris and the rest of Europe. He immediately
altered his plans."

Abbott was equally upset when he visited the famous Bal
Negre, a Negro dance hall, originally situated on the Rue
Blomet, which had moved to a place on Boulevard Blanqui.
White persons were admitted only if escorted by a Negro.
The editor regarded this as discrimination against Caucasians
and his angry resentments against such a place subsided only
when "the sponsors of the place declared [to him] that it is
not an attempt to draw a color line, but only to keep back the
crowds."

He concluded his series with this racial pledge:
"I have returned with a stronger determination to plunge

into the fight and never to rest until our people shall receive the same treatment that I, a foreigner, received in the white man's country—that treatment a white foreigner receives in America, the land of my birth." Then he added, "But we Negroes in America must awake. We must make a more determined fight, for things are never going to be as easy for us as it is for the French Negro; not that things have been so easy for him either. He has had to compete with some of the cleverest white people in the world for the position he holds."

His pledge was concretely reflected in *Defender* policy.

The trip was a ghastly experience for Helen. She was frequently ill, a fact that contributed to her irritability. Upon her return, she poured out a tale of miserable happenings to her sister Idalee Magill. She reported that Abbott frequently embarrassed her during the journey. To illustrate, she told of an agonizing incident on the beach at Cannes. Her husband strayed away from his party to join a group of thinly-clad white women; but as he sought to share their company, the women ignored him and walked away. Helen was mortified. Her South American experiences were repeated in Europe: they were again treated as racial freaks and gaped at by people. Everywhere they went the spectacular difference in their color attracted attention and caused comment.

The London experience particularly distressed her, and perhaps sharpened their incompatibility. She was unable to accept the racial indignities with the quiet calm and patience of her husband. Helen was frankly humiliated. When the London *Daily Express*, in reporting the hotel discriminations, described her as a "white woman," Helen was indignant. She appealed to her husband to correct the misunderstanding. But Abbott stubbornly refused to ask the newspaper for a correction, nor would he permit her to divulge her true racial identity, for he enjoyed the idea of his wife being mistaken for a white person. She developed a contempt for him which she never quite overcame, principally because she believed her husband placed a greater value on her mulatto skin than she herself did!

As a woman, she intuitively grasped the nuances of social relations which escaped Abbott completely; and as a mulatto, actually a quadroon, she saw things from a different racial perspective. Whenever Helen was presumed to be a white woman, and this was frequent, she overheard remarks intended only for the ears of whites. Had they knowledge of her racial ancestry, the French would have labeled her a *sang-mêlée*, or mixed blood. At any rate, what often escaped Abbott was instantly seen by his wife. The total came to two vastly different estimates of race relations in Europe. Consequently, if only instinctively, Helen quickly recognized the fact that there was indeed a deep strain of racial prejudice toward Negroes running through the cultural fabric of the Continent, often so subtle that it was not always seen by the naked eye.

Even sophisticated Negroes were captivated.

But though relations between the races in Europe were less cruelly degrading than in the United States, actually racial prejudice was no less real. The evidence was to be found simply in the fact that the Continent's white men possessed Negro colonies, which formed the cornerstone of their economic well-being, and consequently had concocted a body of folklore and propaganda about Negro inferiority to justify subjugating black people. If, as Abbott believed, only Englishmen and Americans inspired racial prejudice, the French in particular managed to accommodate themselves nicely whenever profitable.

The chief reason why Abbott perhaps escaped the more nauseating aspects of Europe's racial prejudice rests squarely upon the fact that he, like most Negro Americans, enjoyed a unique status while abroad. He, accompanied by his mulatto wife, was a glamorous novelty and perhaps excited the taste for the bizarre which this sort of thing seemingly inspired in the European. To put it bluntly, Europe thought Negroes "exotic" and were intrigued by their physiques, skin-colors and hair textures, plus their reputations as gifted singers, musicians and dancers. Moreover, Negroes were infinitesimal in number and therefore never in competition with white men socially or economically. Above all, Negro tourists were dollar-carrying Americans who benefited by the tradition that the customer is always right.

The story was quite a different one for the Continent's home-grown Negroes and black colonials. For white men abroad often reacted to the same racial illusions that fed the vanity of white men in the United States, and held tenaciously to a belief in the superiority of the white race—though manifestations of this belief rarely were crude, blustering or heavy-handed. For example, the French mentality toward Negroes was sharply etched in the experiences of Prince Kojo, Abbott's close personal friend and Paris host—indeed, the Chicago editor had a hand in the man's racial undoing.

This Negro was tall, smooth and shiny as ebony.

He was born in Africa, educated in Europe, and was fluent in French, German and English. He was the darling of ultra-chic Parisian circles when Abbott arrived. His friends included titled personages, officers of the army and navy, actors and actresses, painters and singers. Sophisticated and suave, the French regarded him as something approaching a rare piece of primitive sculpture, and smart circles spoiled him outrageously. But he was no pretender. He was in fact a member of the family of Behanzin, deposed King of Dahomey whom the French had exiled to Algeria.

Prince Kojo had the good taste not to mix politics and racialism with smart bohemianism. This fact alone cemented his universal popularity. Before Abbott's arrival in Europe, he had made a trip to the United States where he first met the Chicago editor. He soon embraced Abbott's racial idealism and came to share his hostility to racial prejudice. "In your Chicago," he told Abbott, "I visited the zoo in one of the parks. There I saw a chimpanzee and the chimpanzee saw me. So overjoyed was that animal, shut up as it was in a cage, that it leaped about frantically until I walked close enough to shake hands with it through the bars. That, my friend, was the most hearty welcome I received anywhere in the United States."

Kojo afterwards made a long visit to Harlem, where he was feted and somehow became involved with fiercely race-conscious Negroes, who urged him to strike a blow for his black countrymen. He returned to Paris with notions of liberating Dahomey. Abbott's arrival in Paris restimulated his resolve. His racial reawakening, nudged on by the Chicago editor, unfortunately dovetailed with countrywide strikes among the natives of French West Africa, which caused hardships among the coupon-clipping Parisians. Back in Chicago, Abbott learned that Kojo was publicly humiliated when he advanced the proposition. Paris newspapers attacked his personal affairs. He was declared a faker and swindler. He was "exposed" as a bogus prince who had borrowed large sums of money and never repaid them. He became *persona non grata,* and was quickly driven into obscurity. He had committed the unpardonable sin of talking about freedom for colonial blacks in a country dependent upon the income and markets of Africa.

The development was disenchanting to Abbott.

I have an uneasy feeling that the DEFENDER *has become an organ of individualists, each person doing pretty much as he wishes without regard to the whole pattern.*—DEWEY R. JONES, Letter to Robert S. Abbott, June 10, 1935.

CHAPTER XVII

The Totem Pole of Negro Woes

THE MARKET CRASH of October 1929 was one month away when the first copy of *Abbott's Monthly*, a magazine published by Robert S. Abbott, appeared on the newsstands. Though it arrived under the cloud of economic depression, nearly 50,000 copies were immediately grabbed up. It was the first popular-style periodical published for Negroes and consequently had found a ready market—a fact that again illustrates Abbott's genius for combining satisfaction of the Negro's racial needs with sound business. It was to fill a definite place, and proved the forerunner of today's eminently successful *Ebony* magazine, owned and edited by John H. Johnson.

To stimulate their interest in racial advancement, Negroes already had the *Crisis* and *Opportunity* monthlies; for their religious, fraternal and educational interests, about sixty less potent journals; and for general Negro news, some 110 weekly papers. There had been two or three short-lived attempts at popular magazines at the beginning of the century. But until now, for magazine reading the Negro had to turn to the white press. *Abbott's Monthly*, edited by Lucius C. Harper, was a curious mixture. Its features ranged from book reviews to "true confessions" and sketches of successful Negroes, and was intended to be the all-inclusive Negro publication. But the magazine's content clearly reflected the things the publisher had learned and was deeply touched by abroad—in a sense, the new organ was a lively extension of the *Defender*, seasoned by his recent experiences on the Continent.

The first copy, except for the dedication to the Rev. John H. H. Sengstacke "whose early influence in the life of the publisher made this magazine possible," was typical of all subsequent issues. The red, yellow and lavender cover carried the picture of a pretty girl. There were six special features, four stories, eight bits of verse, and a short biographical sketch of the publisher, with a full-page picture of himself and his mother over the caption: "Mother of Publisher Gets First Autographed Copy of Magazine."

Among the features was an article by Whitelaw Reeding, "Will Britain's Dark Subjects Crumble Her Mighty Empire?" The sub-heads of this piece read: "What Was Once a Protest Now Develops Into a Crusade" and "Government Based on Color Difference Now Threatens British Supremacy." The story was illustrated with pictures which included. one of a French colonel consulting with a bemedaled Negro captain of the French Army. The legend declared: "Unlike England, the Republic of France recognizes no distinction of color. Equality is its motto." There also was a picture of a uniformed Negro police officer directing traffic at a busy street corner. The caption observed pointedly: "Traffic officer in Rio de Janeiro, Brazil, who could not secure such a position if he were a citizen of London, England."

Then followed an "exposé" of United States' rule in the Virgin Islands by Rothchild Francis; an account of primitive African musical instruments by N. Clark Smith; and pick-pocket operations were revealed by "Ex-Convict" Rev. William Lyles. Joel A. Rogers, Abbott's legman in Europe, did a profile of Alexandre Dumas, père, and Arthur Schomburg did a sketch of Ignatius Sancho, "the forgotten [Negro] man of letters." There was an argument against birth control with detailed objections to contraceptives; a debate, "Is It Possible for the Church to Serve the Modern Youth?", and a featured piece, "Why I Won't Marry—A Bachelor's Confession," by Nathan Hopkins.

The secondary items included a pen sketch of Paul Robeson and his family; a few pieces of partially draped cheesecake, and two short stories with the provocative titles, "Mortgaged Soul" and "Bacchante," by Ernestine Patterson and Jacland Mumur, respectively. A theater piece by S. Tutt Whitney compared the talents of Florence Mills and Aida Overton Walker, and a layout contained pictures from the Broadway musical play, *The Green Pastures*, featuring Richard B. Harrison who had achieved stardom. Jokes were included as well. But an unusual departure was the occasional use of dialect. This was alien to the older and graver types of Negro journalism. Sample: *Big Congo Chief*—"Waiter, where's that roast white meat I ordered an hour ergo?" *Congo Waiter*—"The missionary ship is an hour late, sir!"

The first issue also announced forthcoming articles, including one by Clarence Darrow, "John Brown—He Struck the First Blow." But the *Defender's* staff actually wrote the bulk of the material that appeared in *Abbott's Monthly*, though articles were solicited from both white and Negro contributors. Abbott himself conducted extensive personal correspondence with people in France and Brazil, soliciting manuscripts for which he paid five cents a word. Sandwiched between the jumps were a handful of ads for Listerine, Murine, Dr. E. A. Walters' Tooth Powder, and so on.

The ninety-six page magazine made a noisy splash.

Frank "Fay" Young, the magazine's managing editor, told a reporter of the Chicago *Daily News*, "We are circulating all over the world. Besides providing a market which did not exist before for the work of talented Negro writers and artists we intend to create a medium which will tell white and Negro people of the United States what we are doing."

The Detroit *Independent*, a Negro newspaper, gave a typically enthusiastic report of the new publication. "It is really different," this paper exulted editorially. "There have been many literary ventures of this sort, and magazines upon magazines, but not of the caliber of *Abbott's Monthly*. It has outstripped the imagination of all and upon perusal proves to surpass any other endeavor. . . . Mr. Robert S. Abbott and his staff of efficient co-workers are to be complimented on blazing the trail in this field of journalism."

But not all Negroes heaped praise upon the publication simply because it was by and for Negroes. Said the widely-read columnist critic, Theophilus Lewis of Harlem's *Amsterdam News:* "Probably it will be an interesting magazine when it makes up its mind just what type . . . it wants to be. Its first issue is a mongrel affair . . . should have prominent writers among its contributors. . . . The only explanation [of the crude art work] I can suggest is the somewhat improbable one that Editor Abbott himself drew the pictures."

Even so, *Abbott's Monthly*, described in the masthead as "A Magazine That's Different," achieved a circulation of roughly 100,000. But suddenly it made a headlong dive and never recovered. The reason: black workers were now unemployed by the millions, and could hardly afford the luxury of buying Negro publications of any kind when they were actually standing in breadlines. The *Defender*, too, was to feel the drastic effects of this development, and indeed now headed for some of the roughest going of its career.

Beginning in 1930, Negroes faced actual starvation as the race was crushed under the Great Depression. Conditions in the North varied only in degree from those in the South. For example, by 1935 more than thirty per cent of Chicago's Negro population was on relief, while in Atlanta sixty-five per cent was in need of public assistance and eighty per cent in Norfolk. In the South—where widespread unemployment struck white and black alike—there were differentials even in poverty. More important, soil erosion, the boll weevil, and the southwestern shift in cotton cultivation created mass starvation. Tobacco, sugar and cotton had been depressed on the international markets.

This development accelerated a new movement of Negroes to the North. There were three main streams of Negro migration: one came through the tobacco fields, rice swamps, and sugar farms of the Eastern seaboard and flowed into New York; another came from Mississippi, Alabama and Georgia and ended in Chicago and Detroit; and a third came out of Texas, passed through Arkansas and Oklahoma, and poured into St. Louis and Chicago. Before 1930 there were but two northern cities in the entire country with a Negro population of more than a hundred thousand. By 1935 there were eleven, and, oddly enough, Abbott now reversed himself and urged Negroes to remain in the South.

This time they ignored his counsel.

The migrations sharpened the problems of the North. Consequently, as Abbott observed, when southern Negroes reached the North they were little better off, because "a tenement," said Thomas Sancton, "was a hundred delta cabins, plus tuberculosis." The Negro population in Chicago as elsewhere became "slum shocked." Chronic unemployment produced dependency, discrimination, delinquency, disease and crime. Men lost their self-respect and independence, with a consequent loss of authority in the family. The result was broken homes and desertion. Able-bodied men, unable to support their families by their own toil, turned to petty crime and vice; they played the "numbers" and "policy," hoping to gain through luck what was denied them through labor. Women turned to shoplifting and many to prostitution. Negroes consequently became irritable, touchy and frequently belligerent. That was true of white slum dwellers as well, but there was this difference: Negroes bore the double cross of indigence and discrimination.

Few were untouched by the depression.

Abbott himself faced cruel adversity. To begin with, his health suddenly failed. "There is nothing to be alarmed at," he wrote his aged mother. "My sickness was on account of the flu, which has been an unwelcome guest in Chicago for the past three or four months." He was trying to relieve her worries, but he was absent from his office twenty months between 1930 and 1932, and during this period the *Defender* lost money for the first time in its history—to be precise, $66,383. No wonder he sent a sharp note to his sister Rebecca when he received a past-due bill for $2.50 which she had failed to pay.

"I think," he wrote irritably, "I am sending enough money home that little bills of this kind can be taken care of. It looks as if you folks are just eating up the money each week. It is very strange that the man has to send here to me to get his money. I hope you will look into this thing. It grieves me to see that I am trying to help and do all I can to make life easier for you all. Yet, I do not seem to be doing enough. You have got to look out for yourselves. I am not going to be here always, and after I am gone, you will have to look out for yourselves. If I get down and out I will be in a fix and will have no one to look out for me, I will have to look out for myself."

His illness soon became progressively worse, though he managed to return to the *Defender*, if only for a few hours a day. Yet he had his chauffeur drive him to the Loop, where he purchased a shawl for his ailing mother. "I hope," he wrote her affectionately, "you will use this wrap to come up and down the stairs each day and at night when the radio is going. You can now wrap up properly and sit and enjoy it."

One Sunday morning in church, Daisy Dickerson, a trained nurse who was to attend Abbott as a gesture of friendship, heard him coughing and observed him repeatedly spit into a handkerchief. As an old family friend, she approached his wife and told her that she thought Abbott was seriously ill. Helen urged her to tell him. Instead, Mrs. Dickerson, a firmly efficient woman, persuaded him to see a white specialist, Dr. Benjamin Goldberg. The physician soon diagnosed his ailment as tuberculosis—a disease which, incidentally, had killed his Aunt Celia and his father, Thomas Abbott. The doctor gave Abbott treatments which included pneumothorax, an operation in which the lung is collapsed by the injection of air into the lung cavity. But soon he was afflicted with Bright's disease, which necessitated the taking of insulin injections.

Meanwhile, Abbott lost his greatest source of comfort and strength. A telegram from his sister Rebecca had sent him hurrying to Woodville, Georgia, to see his mother, Flora Abbott Sengstacke, who was thought to be gravely ill. He returned somewhat shaken and not long afterwards did, in fact, receive word that his mother had died September 21, 1932. Illness prevented him from attending the funeral, and she was buried alongside her husband in the colored section of Laurel Grove Cemetery, Savannah, Georgia. There is not a virtue that can abide in the female heart that Abbott did not sentimentally attribute to her. He had often said that she was the delight of his heart, the sweetener of his toils, the comforter of his sorrows. In all his struggles, she had offered never-ending support. His letters and public statements bear abundant testimony to the love and veneration which he felt for her, and of the influence she had exerted over him and the solace she had given him. His wife, indeed, was left to him,

but with the death of his mother a great and warmly benef-
icent influence went out of his days.

A footnote is pertinent at this point:

Mrs. Dickerson firmly observes, "No patient could have arrested tuberculosis with the problems Mr. Abbott was bur-
dened with during this period!"

The fact is, his worries were rapidly mounting. He was not
only plagued with ill health at a crucial moment in his career,
but the *Defender's* stability was imperiled, a fact that prevented him from going to the dry climate of Arizona as his
doctor had ordered. The depression had not only knocked the
props from under *Abbott's Monthly* but, more important, it
nearly engulfed and washed away the *Defender*. How desperate the situation had become, not even Abbott's employees
quite understood. The one exception was, of course, his general manager Magill. Consequently, what followed seemed to
them like sheer capriciousness.

Abbott allowed the magazine to fold in 1933, as he tried
desperately to keep the flagship of his enterprises afloat. The
reason was simple: the *Defender's* circulation had dropped
to a dangerously low point. To grasp fully the meanings of
this development, we must recall that circulation was the paper's principal source of revenue. From a peak of roughly
200,000 in 1925 (meaning 40,000 sold in Chicago and 160,000
nationally), circulation now had dipped to less than 100,000,
a decline of fifty per cent. By 1935 only 13,000 were being sold
in the city, and 60,000 nationally. Even Abbott's sturdy and
vocal competitor, the Chicago *Whip*, would eventually give
up the ghost and expire.

Its passing would cause him no feelings of elation for, meanwhile, his own personal finances were receiving some mighty
heavy jolts. Abbott's extensive personal records have somehow disappeared—but fragments I have gathered reveal the
fact that his financial affairs were in bad shape, and indeed he
was beginning to scrape the bottom of the barrel. For exam-

ple, he was compelled to procure a loan of $1,470 on his policy with the New York Life Insurance Company. More serious, perhaps, was the fact that the two Negro banks in which he had been a depositor, stockholder and director had failed, sweeping away the careers, resources and reputations of two old friends, Jesse Binga and Anthony Overton. His own savings in them also went down the drain. The banks were placed in the hands of receivers and Abbott, as a stockholder, found himself with considerable liabilities. One receipt shows he paid $3,400 toward liquidating the Lincoln State Bank indebtedness. The Binga Bank failure involved him in long and expensive litigation. But the passing of Negroes as bankers was perhaps a more telling blow to his morale.

The publisher, along with Magill, had incorrectly attributed the decline in the *Defender's* circulation to his employment of white men in the mechanical department, which had now become an inflamed issue in the Negro community. But the depression was one of the real causes, plus the subsidiary fact that vigorous Negro papers had emerged in various key localities where they naturally displaced the *Defender*. Louis Schooler, Abbott's New York representative, wrote him: "I have attempted to find out what has been wrong with the falling off of circulation. It seems there are many reasons. . . . But you must consider this—according to the depression of the times the sale of foreign newspapers in New York has fallen off considerably." Beyond this, Schooler seemingly was unable to account for the sharp dip. Actually, though, New York's *Age* and *Amsterdam*, covering local happenings completely, had a resurgence of energy and influence at the expense of importations like the *Defender*.

New York was typical of a countrywide development.

More important, though, was the fact that there was a noticeable decline in the *Defender's* editorial quality—a fact directly traceable to Abbott's long illness and frequent absences from the office. While away from the paper on a leave of absence the city editor, Dewey R. Jones, a graduate of Columbia University's School of Journalism and a man Abbott regarded with considerable affection and respect, had noticed this development with some alarm. He wrote his chief a confidential memorandum in the hope of reversing the trend. Make-up and editorial content, he observed correctly, had not kept step with the modern trends in journalism. There was laxity in choosing type for heads. He pointed up one week's edition in which there were five different styles of headline type that seemingly had been thrown at the paper without any thought of order or importance. The theater pages were "a hodge-podge of jumbled words and uninteresting stories. That decorated line across the top of the two pages is absolutely out of place in a newspaper today." He thought the *Defender* editorials, while usually timely, much too long and wordy. "Naturally," he concluded, "I lament this situation which is no less than a calamity when we consider how easy it would be for the *Defender* to be so far ahead of other papers that it would not be possible for them to touch it."

But the publisher first moved to reduce the *Defender's* overhead. Magill, with characteristic ruthlessness, had already purged the organization—some say he fired only those who opposed his policies. In any case, he had written Abbott while the publisher was abroad, "Anyone who does not work in harmony and for the good of the company will not be here when you return. Each one must understand that he or she is to produce and earn what they get. All of this is necessary to keep this great business running at a profit." His stick was long enough to reach anyone in the organization. Consequently, the axe had fallen on several veterans—including sports editor Frank Young and columnist Roscoe Conkling Simmons, who, incidentally, had been rehired when the scandals involving theft had died down.

Nevertheless the paper's personnel was again drastically reduced, and the salaries of those who remained were accordingly cut exactly in half. Abbott reduced his own salary to $200 weekly, plus his usual bonuses, if there were any. He afterwards little by little poured his life's savings back into the paper to keep it alive. The transfusions started with small doses and eventually increased to colossal sums. By 1935 he had transferred from his personal bank accounts to the *Defender* exactly $261,751.40!—until today, a fact unknown to the public generally.

The one exception to the salary reductions had been the thirty-five white men working as linotypers, pressmen, stereotypers and mailers—actually, when Abbott attempted to reduce salaries they had appealed to their union, the Chicago Typographical Union No. 16, which forthwith threatened a strike. In addition, the union threatened to halt the *Defender's* paper supply by calling out the white truckers in a sympathy strike, thus preventing delivery. This was a serious situation, and Abbott had to move cautiously. Incidentally, unlike the musicians' union which graded the places where its people worked and established a wage scale accordingly, the printers' union applied the same wage scale to the *Defender* as it did to the Chicago dailies—a manifestly unfair arrangement in the face of the superior earnings of these giant organs.

The situation also was destructive of morale among the Negro employees—for reasons quite different from those affecting management, but reasons, nevertheless, with which Abbott had to deal. Not only did the union bar Negroes from membership, but the white men averaged from $20 to $40 more a week than the Negroes. For instance, the whites averaged $85 weekly whereas, before the reduction, Frank Young, sports editor (until fired), drew $65 a week; Leslie Rogers, cartoonist, $65; Dewey R. Jones, city editor, $40; and David W. Kellum, assistant city editor, $40. Reporters ranged from $20 to $30 weekly. The managing editor, Lucius C. Harper, earned $78 a week until reduced to $39, but the composing room's white foreman drew $99 weekly. Thus, the already yawning gap between the two crews was widened by the reduction of one and not the other group.

While Abbott was grappling with these problems, a Jobs-for-Negroes campaign was launched which was to directly affect the *Defender*. For it served to dramatize the unemployment problems of Negroes and served as well to further stimulate racial unity. The movement was national in scope but had its first expression in Chicago. The campaign reached terrific, often bloody, proportions in this city, where it was led by the Illinois Civic Association. The movement soon gained the support of the entire Negro community, and particularly that of the aggressive Chicago *Whip*. The *Whip* even gave the movement an emotional slogan: "Don't Buy Where You Can't Work!" The objective was to persuade, perhaps even force, white merchants doing business in the Black Belt to employ Negroes. Picket lines became a noisy feature of life in the Negro community and served to keep feeling at fever heat.

Abbott was placed in an untenable position when concentrated attention was focused on the labor relations aspect of the *Defender's* operations. The public's reaction, to be sure, was wholly racial. It was understandable. While there were thousands of Negroes walking the streets unemployed, a Negro institution gave employment to white men, whereas white employers would not (and some could not) give Negroes jobs. Abbott soon heard the demand that Negroes replace the white workers. Organized protests crystallized and had countrywide repercussions as Negroes sent up the cry: "The *Defender* is unfair to Negro workers!"

What further complicated matters and indeed stirred new racial emotions was the fact that for efficiency the paper's distribution had been placed in the hands of a white agency at the expense of Negro distributors. Moreover, the paper's national advertising was handled by a white man, W. B. Ziff, who had cornered the Negro press generally by persuading it that as a white man he had greater facility for gathering national advertising accounts. He received from thirty-five to fifty per cent commissions, but he opened new advertising doors to the Negro press, guaranteed payment, and thus eliminated the problems of collection. Even so, Negroes were only made more hostile by the knowledge of these facts—for, after all, it implied a deprecation of their own kind.

Under the pressure of these developments, Abbott moved to fire the white workers in the mechanical department—a fact that probably violated his sentimental attachment to these capable white men long in his employ. But Magill, who had strongly urged the firings, was touched by no such feelings—in fact, his motive was plainly to employ Negroes for the purpose of procuring cheaper labor and removing the anti-Negro onus which had been placed on the *Defender*, which he believed was the chief reason for circulation's decline. In any case, Abbott first appealed to the union to admit Negroes, so his plant could be manned by members of his own race. The union turned a deaf ear to his pleas, though the union's president, George J. Chiles, admitted the paper had a right to employ Negro employees if it so decided.

When negotiations failed, Abbott secured the services of Paul Jervay, a Hampton printing instructor, and sent him on a countrywide tour to find skilled Negroes. He successfully recruited enough men from trade schools and Negro newspapers to man the plant. Then, with one swoop, Abbott fired the entire white crew and installed Negroes who, of course, were hired at wages below those paid white men. Magill was satisfied that the payroll saving was impressive. The union, however, claimed its members had been "locked out" and promptly flung picket lines before the *Defender's* doors.

Abbott was a captive of his own racialism.

Yet he was quite prepared to pay this price to appease the mounting angers of his readers and recover their good will. But the printers' union brought the case to the attention of the Chicago Regional Labor Board. The union representative contended that the main issue at stake was the question of paying union wages. The importation of Negro non-union help, however, complicated the situation. At any rate, Magill offered this statement in rebuttal: "There is no argument or misunderstanding between the labor unions as such and the *Defender*. The question is that of an employer's right to dispense with the services of an employee. The question of wage scale has nothing to do with the situation and that has been clearly and repeatedly stated to representatives of the union in various conferences held for several years. The Chicago *Defender* has been unable to satisfactorily explain to its readers and supporters why those readers and supporters could not secure employment in the publication and distribution of the paper. In a field of competition, the failure to answer such questions satisfactorily is not only detrimental but shortly totally destructive of its existence."

The *Defender* eventually was sustained, but Abbott ruefully viewed the wreckage of his interracial experiment.

Now Robert S. Abbott was deluged with letters appealing to him for financial help, usually beginning with some such phrase as "Years ago when you needed help, I put my hand in my pocket and gave you money. . . ." He was forced to reject these pleas, simply because he himself was a victim of the depression. His employees, too, made insistent demands. The requests were not without merit. For example, Dewey R. Jones, upon his return from a leave, had ignored Magill and sent the publisher a confidential memorandum.

"My position on the editorial staff is that of assistant managing editor," he wrote forthrightly. "The present salary of the managing editor is $40 a week. My salary is $20 a week. There are persons on the staff receiving a salary higher than $20, and most of them receive not less than $20. . . . I should be earning more as an assistant editor than numerous others whose chief claims are merely the fact that they work here.

"I have had ten years actual training in your shop and under your direction, coupled with all the theoretical training available. I mean no disrespect, am not disgruntled, and am as loyal and just as anxious that our institution succeed as ever I was. I merely believe that the change I suggest would make for a little more hope and respect on my part for myself, for Negro business in general and the Chicago *Defender* in particular, certainly for renewed effort to give all I have to help perpetuate your monument. If, on the other hand, you do not feel that my claim is a just one, or that it merits consideration, I know of no reason why I should prolong the day when I must inevitably find this out."

Dewey Jones' stay was not prolonged.

Abbott had long had a reputation for being penurious, but during the depression it became legendary. There is, in fact, an abundance of stories, many no doubt apocryphal, to illustrate what was described as his miserliness. For example, when advised to have all his employees who handled money bonded, he objected on the grounds that premiums cost money. He soon renewed the habit of picking up pins, string and pieces of paper. He often said, when on such forays, "We must pick up these pins and things, we can't throw them away. They represent money."

A typical story about Abbott's tight-fistedness involved Jack Johnson, former heavyweight champion who was himself a master of the small touch. He once declared: "Thank God, I had no money on me when I talked to Abbott!" Johnson had attempted to borrow fifty dollars from him, but when he heard the publisher's own hard luck story, he felt the need to give him a helping hand.

As Christmas approached, so say his employees, Abbott usually reduced the number of his visits to the business and editorial offices. Whenever he was seen he would display, perhaps simulate, anger. "You would be afraid to say good morning to him," reports one man. This behavior, his employees believed, was calculated to prevent them from asking for pay raises or taking advantage of the holiday seasons to demand bonuses. When his managing editor, Harper, perhaps in jest, once asked him for five dollars to buy a turkey for his children, Abbott replied: "A turkey! I myself might have to catch a bullfrog for my own Christmas dinner. I can't even afford to buy a turkey!"

Before one Christmas, Harper told one old employee with a straight face that Abbott was going to give everyone a handsome bonus. He said each share would be about two hundred dollars. Elated, the man worked very industriously as the holiday approached, and had nothing but praise for the publisher. He afterwards made a shopping tour and bought one hundred dollars worth of gifts in expectation of receiving the bonus. But Christmas eve arrived and Abbott failed to put in an appearance at the office. Harper, who had shared the joke with other members of the staff, announced mournfully, "The old man has let us down—we're not going to get a thing." The man was so enraged that he broke a typewriter, kicked a hole in the partition separating the offices, and tore up as much stationery as he could get his hands on.

Not to this day does he know that Harper was merely pulling his leg—but the incident reinforced Abbott's reputation for being a skinflint in this man's mind.

David W. Kellum, a *Defender* employee, relates what he regards as an illustrative incident:

"Mr. Abbott," he says, "had been complaining that 'Things are so bad, I think I'll have to eat some rabbit for Christmas.' Well, one day soon afterwards, I joined [city editor] Dewey Jones and went to a confectionery store nearby the office where the staff frequently lunched. I wanted to play the slot machine, because I owed a nine dollar electric bill. As we entered the place, Mr. Abbott was seated at a table eating.

"I walked over to him and asked him if he would let me

have some money to pay the bill, explaining my difficulty. He said he was very sorry, but he was broke and all he had left after paying for his lunch was a twenty-five cent piece. He got up from the table and walked over to the slot machine, tinkered with it a bit, and inserted a quarter—and he hit the jackpot, with twenty-five dollars in coins tumbling out! He stood there and carefully counted them to see whether he had the correct number. Then he walked away leaving me standing there—without my electric bill paid."

Under adversity, Abbott was outwardly calm.

But those who observed him closely during these days say that he bore the look of "a totem pole of Negro woes!" His personality was further complicated by his illness. Once a week he still had to have the doctor puncture his side. This proved a very painful operation for him, and it brought about very severe, seemingly traumatic, emotional reactions. He afterwards would often be incoherent, morose or petulant, and all the deep racial bitterness in him would come to the surface. Moreover, by now he had reached the point where his decisions were frequently affected by his depressed mood.

How he functioned under the pressures in the office is reported in considerable detail by Agaliece Westbrook Miller who had been his personal secretary since 1931. She had hardly begun her employment with the *Defender* when one day "I looked up from my work to find Mr. Abbott standing at the office door gravely looking about at the workers like a ship's captain checking to see if 'all hands were on deck.'" Though new and inexperienced, he soon chose her to do his personal work.

"The first thing each Friday morning, as soon as the presses started," she reports, "copies of the first run of the paper would be brought to Mr. Abbott. He had become a master at scanning a page and spotting make-ups and techniques not to his liking. Then he would be on the telephone inquiring and protesting to his editors. He was quick to spot what he thought to be a 'hustle,' [or what he believed was a story published in consideration of a gratuity]. Whenever the paper failed to meet his standards, he would call in the editors and lecture them about the type of make-up that featured big headlines, snappy captions and short stories.

"He said to me many times," she says, "that Negro newspapers had been built up on the 'big headline—short story' method, 'but those fellows upstairs want to write an entire galley on a subject that could be taken care of in one stick.' He often cautioned them to write a 'little bit about a lot rather than a lot about a little.' He would fuss and fume and pace up and down the office complaining that he couldn't get anyone to do what he wanted—everyone thought that they knew more about the paper than he—he who had founded it!"

"Taking dictation from Mr. Abbott," she reports, "was quite difficult. He talked very rapidly and my shorthand training was no match for him. I made up with memory what I lacked in skill. His dictation during those days was colored with tales of his visit to Europe and I found myself struggling with French and German names that almost ended my career. Nevertheless, I would take pages and pages of notes covering personal letters, business letters, news stories and editorials, and return to my desk to type them up—not always what I had in shorthand, but what I could remember and improvise. He knew that I was not transcribing verbatim, but he must have liked what I wrote for he soon developed the habit of asking me to answer his letters."

Between these chores, she recalls, "Mr. Abbott loved to talk about South America and Paris. Every speech and every occasion that gave him opportunity to express his opinion to a group, and especially to a white group—was filled with the 'freedom of the black man' in Paris and Brazil. Particularly do I remember the school groups who used to tour the plant—elementary, high school and university students—and Mr. Ab-

bott striking a familiar pose by leaning against the reception-
ist's window in the lobby of the *Defender,* availing himself of
the opportunity to get his favorite lesson across to the young
people.

"To Negro students, his plea was that they strive for higher
education—that they prepare themselves. He warned often
against the tendency of Negroes to seek the professions as
a career—such as doctors and lawyers. He emphasized time
and again that if all young people sought the professions, the
fields would become over-crowded and other equally de-
sirable areas would be neglected. He said Negroes should
also seek to prepare themselves as carpenters, mechanics and
bricklayers.

"He said that it was a mistaken idea for Negroes to feel
that the only avenues which offered success or which required preparation were medicine, law and dentistry. It is
just as necessary, he said, to study and prepare for trades. He
offered his own life as an example. He said that his mother,
wiser than he, had urged him to study printing, realizing that
he might not be able to spend the years of study and the
money necessary to become established in a profession. She,
he said, advised him to learn a trade first, and then he could
earn enough money to pursue other studies if he chose.

"This was his constant and often repeated message to Negro youth.

"To white youth, he used the opportunity to talk about
equality of opportunity for Negroes. He spoke of the freedom
offered the Negro in other countries. I remember how embarrassed the *Defender* people would be on such occasions
as he drove home his point to a 'captive' audience. But then,
he was a man who lived a purpose—who had an all-consum-
ing desire to be free and to gain freedom for his people. He
never missed an opportunity to drive home that point to any
white person who came into his presence.

"Weak and sick as he was during most of the years that I

knew him, he would deliver that message when his voice was weak, he was gasping for breath, coughing between every sentence—but it seemingly just had to be said. He could not come into contact with a white person without touching upon his fight for freedom. Because of this tendency, we strove to limit his contacts during his visits to the office, because once having gotten into a conversation, he would talk beyond the limit of his endurance."

One morning, while he was signing checks, he suddenly turned to his young secretary and asked: "Agaliece, why aren't you in school?"

She explained that her father had been hard hit by the depression, and though he was willing to make the sacrifice to send her to college, his health was not good and the family needed the help she could give by working and earning money. Abbott then said that if he had not lost so much money, he would have sent her to school and afterwards financed a European trip for her, for he felt that, given an opportunity, she could attain success and make a distinct contribution to his paper.

"When I had money," he said, "I made many contributions to young people who I felt had less to offer and they did nothing with the opportunity given them."

He then asked her how much it would cost for her to attend school evenings. "I told him that I didn't know, but I would find out. Later he asked me what I had learned and when I told him, he said for me to go out to school and register and make out a check for his signature."

For approximately two years he paid her tuition at Northwestern University, and adjusted his own schedule to enable her to reach her classes on time.

"I was very grateful," she says, "but whenever I would mention the fact to Mr. Abbott, he would say: 'I wish I had my money. The *Defender* needs smart young people to carry on my work after I am gone.'"

He had begun thinking of death.

The highest product of social evolution is the growth of the civilized home—the home that only a wise, cultivated and high-minded woman can make.— ROBERT S. ABBOTT, Chicago *Defender,* 1934.

CHAPTER XVIII

The Women : White and Black

Now SIXTY-FIVE years old and a person of substantial status in the Negro community, Robert S. Abbott faced the prospect of divorce—a fact that proved a cruel development in the midst of serious illness and financial setbacks. The relationship between himself and Helen had been rapidly deteriorating lately, and some such action was inevitable. He wrote his sister Rebecca a long description of detailed grievances he held against his wife. He concluded firmly, "I hope to get free of all my entanglements. . . . I must be *free*. . . . I have stood all I can." Two years later he vigorously opposed her filing suit for separate maintenance.

To grasp fully the meaning of this situation and of his subsequent curious actions, we must understand the background of his relationship with women before his marriage to Helen. We must also understand the influence women had on the *Defender,* if only indirectly. Not until he was fifty years old did he begin regular associations with women—during this almost celibate period not even one jazzy Jezebel crossed his path. The extent of his feminine social contacts was occasionally to escort a girl to a public dance. One was a pretty darkskinned lass who hailed from somewhere in Mississippi. Before launching the *Defender,* he was seen with her fairly often. One evening, calling at her home, he was received by the mother and invited into the parlor. When the mother went into the kitchen announcing his arrival, he overheard the girl giving instructions to say she was not at home—adding the cutting remark, "You know, Mom, I don't deal in coal!"

He never forgot this disparagement of his color and afterwards frequently offered the incident as the reason he did not associate with dark women. He came to believe that as a group they were profoundly hostile to his black skin, a belief that reinforced his persecution complex. In any case, he afterwards became acutely concerned with the plight of the tragic mulatto and the *Defender* carried such heads as THE FOUR MILLION MULATTOES IN AMERICA, which had a subhead: "May We Ask the Champions of 'White Supremacy' to Explain This?"

"Whenever I went to a dance as a young man," Abbott told his foreign editor, Metz P. T. Lochard, "the only women who would dance with me were the fair-complexioned girls." But his other associates declare he was "color struck" and perhaps believed in the Negro folk-saying, "White is Right!" Abbott's dentist friend, Dr. Charles M. Thompson, says, "I have to admit that Mr. Abbott admired white and fair-complexioned people primarily, I suppose, because the dominant group of the society is white." He adds, "This of course was in a period when the Negro race had not developed to a point where Negroes had feelings of worth in their own eyes. Maybe Mr. Abbott was a victim of the era in which he was born."

At any rate, Abbott found solace in a white woman when rejected by a dark girl. By some curious twist of fate, she happened to have been Phil Jones' German-reared mother, Louise. She had been born in Alsace Lorraine and had migrated to this country as a young woman. She was working as a maid to Alfred Foreman, president of Foreman Brothers

State Bank, when she met and married Phillip S. Jones, a Negro male nurse. Together they founded the famous Manassas Society for the purpose of creating a congenial environment for interracial couples.

The publisher first saw Louise at a dance given by the organization of which her husband was president. When the latter died, Abbott began visiting a sundry shop she operated on Cottage Grove Avenue to support her three children. The attractive widow proved a sympathetic audience and Abbott lingered—indeed, Phil believes "Mr. Abbott's first interest in me, was a means of strengthening his suit for my mother's hand." Though Abbott saw her frequently for several years nothing came of the relationship. "To her death," says Jones, significantly, "she wore a pendant around her neck, displaying for all to see, a photograph of Dad."

Not more than one month before meeting Helen Thornton, Abbott, firmly purposeful, had traveled to Savannah, Georgia, to see his childhood sweetheart, Catherine Scarborough. His beloved "Miss Cathy" had lately manifested uncommon concern about his mother, often bringing her fruits and flowers. Rebecca recalls, "I once casually told her that Robert wanted her to return the watch he had given her as an engagement present years back, but she wouldn't give it up." When Abbott was informed of these developments, his love for her was perhaps reawakened and he was emboldened to again propose.

Miss Cathy's folks, who had so cruelly rejected him as a youth because he was black and penniless, were now dead. Her ne'er-do-well brother, Joseph, was employed periodically by Abbott and frequently borrowed considerable sums from him. The mulatto Catherine had meantime been married twice, but not well: her first husband was a drayman and her second a barber, both mulattoes. Now widowed, she had a ten-year-old daughter to raise by herself. Even so, for nearly thirty-five years Abbott had danced attendance to her and between husbands had paid her court, a fact that must have flattered her outrageously. Her daughter, Cecile Callen, recalls him often sending boxes of candy and visiting her mother whenever he was in Savannah.

The widow Catherine, now Mrs. Alonzo Hazard and no longer youthful, agreed to marry Abbott in the spring of 1918. The ceremony was set to take place in Savannah a few weeks hence. Overjoyed, he chose his old local buddy, Albert Jackson, as his best man. This gentleman promptly purchased a new suit for the big occasion. Abbott had meanwhile returned to Chicago, but before he could arrange his affairs and entrain for Savannah, Catherine capriciously wrote him that she had changed her mind. Her daughter says, "Mother never actually believed Mr. Abbott could support her in the style she felt she deserved." To offset any suspicion she might have that he was merely boasting, he tried to persuade her to come to Chicago and see for herself how well he was doing, but she stubbornly refused. He suspected the old bugaboo of color. His parting gesture was to send her a paid-up subscription for the *Defender*.

He soon married a replica of his first love.

Helen, like Catherine, was a quadroon. She had blue eyes, delicate features, and what was described as "a regular Georgia woman's titian hair." Tall and slender, she was always carefully groomed: her monthly bills from Chas. A. Stevens' beauty salon included manicures, massages, shampoos, permanent waves and pedicures. Her favorite costume was black silk lounging pajamas, figured with flaming yellow and burnt-orange birds and flowers. She was rather cold and aloof in her manner and rarely exhibited her feelings. On occasion —when she was greeting guests, for instance—she did simulate spontaneity, but even in her diary she was frigid and never once made a warm or affectionate entry about her husband—she referred to him only as "Mr. A," and in chilly wifely letters addressed him as "Dear Mr. Abbott" or plain "Mr. Abbott."

Dr. Thompson doubts that Helen ever loved him, for, as an intimate, he never saw any show of affection between them. Joel A. Rogers, who was the couple's guide and companion during the tour of Europe, doubts that she even respected him. Yet she could manifest a concern which at least suggested affection. Richard L. Jones, Abbott's advertising manager who describes himself as a "wet nurse" to the family, recalls the day when Abbott was involved in an automobile accident. "When I heard about it," he reports, "I jumped into a car and rushed over to the place where the accident happened. I picked him up and took him home. Meantime someone had called Helen. When I brought him in, she broke down and wept convulsively, though Mr. Abbott was only slightly bruised. From what I observed, I assumed she thought a good deal of him. As a matter of fact, she never went anywhere without him."

Helen was a first-rate enigma.

Her parentage was exceedingly modest. Her family lived in the mill section of Athens, Georgia, and, for whatever reasons of snobbery, was not invited to the homes of upper-class Negroes. Even so, they lived comfortably and the Thornton girls, resembling Caucasians in every physical particular, all seemingly made good marital connections: Helen, of course, married the publisher of the *Defender;* Helen's sister Idalee wed lawyer Nathan K. Magill; and her sister Lucille won William A. Fountain, Jr., president of Morris Brown College, Atlanta, Georgia. Helen attended Knox Institute in Athens, and afterwards taught school briefly. Her old professor, R. W. Gadsden, remembers her as a smart, shy and likeable girl who did not mingle with the students.

Helen was herself on the rebound when she met Abbott. Her first marriage had ended disastrously. Her husband, Lacy Morrison, had taken his own life by shooting himself with a revolver. Gossip placed quite a different interpretation upon his demise. Abbott himself apparently gave credence to the rumors, for I have before me a long, anonymously-written letter, postmarked January 24, 1919, which he received a few months after his wedding and kept until his death. Moreover, his subsequent behavior suggests that he was definitely influenced by its scurrilous contents. For example, Idalee Magill recalls the evening he came to her home for dinner along with Helen and, when served, refused to eat until his wife removed his plate and gave him hers.

This incident occurred when the relationship was already about to collapse. But when Abbott first saw Helen he was immediately captivated, and a whirlwind courtship followed between her daily chores as a saleslady in Carson Pirie Scott's department store where upon arrival in Chicago she had secured employment by passing as a white person. Helen became the show-piece of his existence, and she did grace his home with considerable charm and assume her civic responsibilities by dabbling in welfare work. The marriage might have been a tempestuous one had they been volatile people. It never reached stormy proportions because both had considerable self-control—and this very fact perhaps served to sharpen the creeping conflicts. At any rate, Abbott was seemingly jealous and once discharged a *Defender* executive because he was overly friendly to his wife at a public dance. He afterwards said to his friend and nurse, Daisy Dickerson, "The day I fired X——, you would have thought there was a funeral in the house!"

The publisher's marriage to Helen was not universally popular, and he was flooded with mail which held that as a *Negro leader* he had failed the race. "The South," said a typical letter, "has lost faith and admiration for you since you married a white face." Nor was the marriage popular with the Abbotts —a legion of black-skinned nieces, nephews, cousins, aunts and uncles with whom he had lately resumed contact. His strong-minded cousin, Randolph, speaking for the Abbott clan and today still somewhat irritated, declares, "We tried to show him that he would be much better off with a black woman. But he was 'color struck.' The truth is, his white wife was embarrassing to us. For it was humiliating to go out publicly with them. People were always looking and staring, and making nasty remarks. He could never come to his birthplace in St. Simons Island with her, because the white people would threaten him because she was white. Maybe she was a Negro; but she was white as far as we were concerned."

His mother, whose own husband had been a distinctly mulatto type, was singularly detached. Rebecca, who idolized old Rev. Sengstacke, was initially pleased. To be sure, Abbott himself was delighted with his wife's milk-white complexion, but the color question eventually became a bone of contention between them. She never forgave him for his extraordinary behavior in London, when she had objected to being disparagingly labeled the "white wife of a black millionaire" by the newspapers and he had refused to seek a retraction in her behalf. But neither did he forgive her for what he believed was her color discrimination against his relatives. His mother and sisters were rarely guests during her stewardship of the Abbott household. In justice to her, the reason might very well have been a purely womanly disinclination to share her home with in-laws.

Whatever the reason, Rebecca recalls the time Helen visited Woodville, Georgia, and, when she was about to return to Chicago, strenuously objected to her brownskin sister-in-law accompanying her to the depot. Rebecca undoubtedly reported this to her brother. But Helen, who usually passed as a white person when traveling alone, faced a curious dilemma: had she allowed Rebecca to accompany her to the station, she would have been identified as a Negro, and therefore would have been compelled to ride the "Jim Crow" coach and accept the inferior accommodations provided Negroes in those days. Unfortunately she chose comfort and dignity at the expense of her husband's sister, a fact Abbott could hardly forgive.

Nathan Magill, who by now was styled the "Little Napoleon" and was later divorced by Idalee, had for a long time poured subtle poison into his chief's ear. For more than a year Abbott had listened, without answering but also without discouraging. Magill needled him particularly about paying an unmanlike deference to Helen. But Abbott was already becoming weary of her: he had married an ornament and now wondered why he had no intellectual companionship. He declared Helen had no appreciation of beauty and culture. He charged her with being disloyal and grasping. He kept in his billfold a yellowed news clipping with the revealing headline: "Tactless Wife Can Put a Big Crimp in Husband's Plans."

As for her, she thought Abbott abysmally ignorant and insensitive in social relations, and declared him incompetent to run the *Defender*. Her sensibilities were particularly violated by his personal habits. And as was natural in a wife, Helen's implacable hostility was reserved for Magill, who she felt unduly influenced her husband and was an enemy of her marriage. Even so, her friends say she was reluctant to divorce Abbott.

He, though, lost his mental and emotional poise.

Suddenly he abandoned his home and went to live with Mrs. Genevieve Lee Wimp, daughter of his old friend, for he had now come to believe his wife's motive was to destroy him. According to Lochard, he suspected that she somehow had infected him with tuberculosis by something she had put in his food. Then he charged her with hiring paid killers to murder him. He even wrote his niece Gwendolyn, "It seems to me that she [Helen], her two brothers and Mrs. [Idalee] Magill want to get a nurse that will give me knockout drops." Among his effects, I found a Chicago *Defender* envelope with the following statement scrawled across the face in his own handwriting: "Should foul play be done me in Chicago, these two men whose cards are enclosed, should be questioned as they know something about it. R. S. Abbott." The envelope contained the business cards of two men, presumably white, who represented established insurance companies.

One detail is worthy of note.

Abbott had already been plagued by threats to his life and by attempts at extortion, blackmail and kidnapping. The demands had ranged from ten to fifty thousand dollars. Incidentally, sometime after his death a Negro racketeer, Edward Jones, belonging to the infamous Jones Brothers combine, was kidnapped by white gangsters and one hundred thousand dollars was paid in ransom to secure his release. Abbott's own home had been mysteriously broken into by a prowler early one morning, and when the police could find no theft motive, Abbott concluded that an attempt was being made on his life. Mostly he feared being poisoned.

This unexplainable behavior may have been a reversion to the superstitious environment of his childhood. In any case, his friends and associates were inclined to dismiss his fantastic charges as figments of his imagination. Yet Lochard believes that if he had pointed this out Abbott would never again have confided in him. "A look of intense sadness," he says, "would have crossed his face, and he would have acted as though he were being treated as an ignorant oaf." Today, however, his friends firmly declare there was not the slightest foundation for his suspicions. "To understand him," says Idalee, "you must know that he comes from that part of Georgia, where people believe in crazy things. This explains this constant suspicion of my sister Helen and the belief that people were trying to kill him."

Fourteen years of marriage had come to an end.

When the childless Helen finally told her story in court before Superior Judge Phillip Finnegan, her charges against Abbott were equally fantastic—a fact that provided the Negro with a field day: The Pittsburgh *Courier,* now the *De-r's* liveliest national competitor, carried a bold streamer: RT S. ABBOTT SUED FOR DIVORCE, and related the delectable details. For Helen declared that he was a man of violent temper, that he had threatened her, used vile language, and struck her. She accused him of peccadillos with one of his nurses, and asked his removal as publisher because, she asserted, he was letting the paper go to ruin through neglect. Her lawyer, Robert E. Cantwell, Jr., demanded an absolute divorce, a receivership for the paper and one hundred thousand dollars, plus a property settlement.

Abbott was stunned—not only by the magnitude of the demand, but perhaps even more by the break-up of his marriage to a woman whom, in truth, he still loved. He had a sentimental regard for the home and had once even written an article entitled "Home Sweet Home." He had written many editorials like "Broken Marriage Vows," bemoaning the break-up of marriages and urging the stabilizing of marital relations. He even suggested a course of conduct for this purpose. However, his ideas about women were sentimental and old-fashioned, actually Victorian. He insisted that women study the arts and attend finishing schools only, not attempt to compete with men. Their place was clearly in the home. He himself was always gallantly protective of females.

Now when the chips were down he tried to extricate himself as cheaply as possible. His thinking is revealed in a bit of advice he gave young Dr. Thompson. "When I told Mr. Abbott," Thompson reports, "I was divorcing my wealthy wife, he emphatically declared I should sue her for support—because, after all, she had more money than me." At any rate, Abbott specifically cautioned his attorney, ex-United States Senator Charles S. Deneen, to make it distinctly understood in court that Helen was "a colored person." He was, perhaps justifiably, fearful that a white judge, presuming her a white person, might be partial to her plea and render a racial verdict in her favor.

When he appeared in court, the publisher declared his inability to meet his wife's excessive demands but admitted that the *Defender* had picked up after its depression slump and was now making a little money. "Dough-faced and grizzled court attachés," wrote a reporter covering the trial for the Associated Negro Press, "were almost stunned when Nathan K. Magill, general counsel and general manager for the Robert S. Abbott Publishing Company, took the stand to testify what he knew about Mr. Abbott's assets. He admitted under questioning that the publisher had in excess of $335,000 cash in two Chicago banks. Judge Finnegan also seemed to be startled when Mr. Magill uttered this large figure. The general counsel then described other assets, consisting of a Rolls Royce automobile, a Pierce Arrow, a Cunningham, and a fleet of Fords, of real estate including a mansion, some bonds and some stocks."

What made Helen insistent upon a financial settlement, was the discovery that everything they were supposed to own jointly—house, automobiles, furniture, etc.—had been bought in the name of the Robert S. Abbott Publishing Company and therefore she had little protection as a wife. Upon her lawyers' advice she consequently pressed for tangible possessions. The fact is, she had no precise knowledge of her husband's actual worth. The reason is seemingly contained in a remark Abbott made to one of his employees, Birdette Augustus (Trigg). "When I got married," she reports, "Mr. Abbott told me, 'You're entering a new life, but always have some money of your own that no one knows about!'" His cousin Randolph complained, "He was so secretive that he hid his affairs from his own wife. He was always saying, 'Don't let Helen know!'"

The wrangling in the No. 1 Negro publishing family titillated the public for nearly a year—though when the Pittsburgh *Courier* sought an interview Helen declared, "I should hate to have reports of our affairs circulated which would embarrass him or me or injure his influence with the public." Helen was awarded temporary maintenance of three hundred dollars monthly, use of the mansion, the Pierce Arrow, Arthur the chauffeur and Rosalee the maid. She finally was granted a divorce decree June 26, 1933, and the court awarded her fifty thousand dollars, an additional five thousand dollars for lawyers' fees, the Pierce Arrow and the home furnishings—perhaps the largest award ever granted a Negro woman. Abbott's own attorney's fees cost him an additional fifteen thousand dollars.

To be sure, the decree shook Abbott to the foundation of his personality. He was especially upset by the ugly manner in which the mansion was stripped, with the crowds gaping as four moving vans carted away its contents. Continually goaded as he was, and not seldom thwarted, bitterness and invective became more and more evident in his utterances. It is by no means needful to ascribe this, as was often done, to irascibility or pettiness of temper. In fact, he afterwards observed to Myrtle Sengstacke, his nephew John's wife, "I didn't have to give her a dime. But she bore the name of Robert S. Abbott, which made it my duty to see that she lived in the style she had become accustomed to."

His severest test came when he had to make a decision as to how the story would be handled by the *Defender*. From the beginning, he had played no favorites. When a well-known minister was charged with homosexuality he carried the story. He wrote up the misadventures of his closest friends and his family just as thoroughly as he wrote up anyone else's. A number of times he had to report his own difficulties, and thus, when Helen had filed her suit in the Chicago courts and when the decree was granted, the story appeared on page one.

In 1934 the publisher received this telegram: "Boyfriend,

wherefore art thou? Hast thou forsaken me? Without your cheery letters, life is a pallid thing! Thine own, BEATRICE A——."

Robert S. Abbott somehow had developed a new romantic object—actually, it was a strictly platonic affair since he was to never meet this girl personally. Beatrice was presumably a white person, young, and light-hearted. He had published her poems in the *Defender*, and in appreciation she had sent him a thank-you note. This had led to regular correspondence between them. Then she sent him a photograph of herself and afterwards remarked cryptically, "Thus we each enjoy ourselves—after our own fashion." The relation was of brief duration, but in her many letters she toyed with the idea of marrying Abbott—despite, according to her, "age, color, creed." Finally she began analyzing the problems involved in inter-racial relationships:

"In cases where a white person loves a brown person," she wrote forthrightly, "it is fatal when misunderstanding comes up. One always imagines that the other is fed up. Given time and enough of this: 'What's the matter?' a person will get fed up. I don't go silent for spite. I just can't help it. And I wouldn't help it, if I could. It may be selfish. But a person has to escape the mundane once in a while! But if, while I'm in one of these vile silences, you were to think I'd ceased to care, I'd get peeved. Then you'd be sure it was the age, color, creed thing. And I'd be too peeved to see that I was acting in a way that really made it appear as the race nonsense were to blame."

Abbott was delighted with her letters and described her as "My Great Big Beautiful Doll." He wrote her, "That photograph of yours was just what the doctor ordered and when I tell you that I have it among my souvenirs, you will certainly see how I value it. It has come up to all my expectations." He playfully threatened to one day make a trip to her New Jersey home to see her. "I have been planning all kinds of ways to come East," he told her, "but up to now my devilish doctor and satanic nurse have kept me straight in front of them. I can't even get anyone to kidnap me." He offered fatherly advice to problems she confided to him. He urged, for example, that she attend business college, encouraged her to continue writing poetry, and discouraged her flight at writing lyrics for songs. He signed these letters "Your boy-friend, Bob."

This was a new and somewhat reckless Abbott.

The Negro publisher was perhaps flattered by this white girl's attentions, but he never thought seriously of a permanent alliance. The truth is, he was now enamored with a stunningly handsome woman, Norma Sewell (now Mrs. Naylor). When he met her, she was in her early thirties and an elementary school teacher in Washington, D. C. She had a white velvety skin, a shapely figure, considerable allure, and spoke with a voice of cultured timbre. Those who knew her intimately described her as "undoubtedly one of the most beautiful women in Negro Washington." She had first come under Abbott's admiring gaze in Chicago during the summer of 1933, shortly after his divorce from Helen. He soon developed considerable affection for her and, according to Lochard, offered to marry her. Upon her return to Washington, he deluged her with telegrams and long distance calls.

But Norma soon discovered that, underneath, Abbott had become cynical about women. She tried studiously to combat this development by kind deeds and affectionate concern. She showed considerable interest in the *Defender's* progress, and often complimented him on his articles. She frequently urged him to do this or that "since you are the Boss." She suspected that he was "greatly influenced and controlled by two people, your physician and manager." She cautioned him to be careful, because "the almighty dollar is the best friend you have on this earth." She had shrewdly recognized his basic frugality and, in requesting him to telephone her long distance, assured him, "It will only cost $1.40 plus 15 cents tax, if you make the station to station call which is much cheaper than if you ask for the person to whom you wish to speak."

Abbott by now was feeling the infirmities of age and was further troubled by diabetes and advanced myopia. When he consulted his physician, Benjamin Goldberg, on the wisdom of marrying at his age and in his condition, the doctor firmly advised against the step. Tired, disappointed and discouraged, Abbott reported the situation to Norma. He asked her to be patient, for his recovery was not far distant, but from this point on the relationship deteriorated and finally came to an unannounced end. Abbott's intimates say that he was sincerely in love with Norma and that he regarded the denouement as Paradise Lost. Once again, curiously enough, he had been attracted to a woman who, in complexion, was strikingly like Miss Cathy of Savannah.

Norma had hardly drifted from his mind, when in the summer of 1934 he met Edna Denison, a widow with four grown children and two grandchildren. The ailing Abbott had been invited by his old friend, Edward H. Morris, to visit him at his country place near Benton Harbor, Michigan, and there he made a delightful renewal of an old acquaintance. He had been a friend of Edna's late husband, Colonel Franklin A. Denison, a distinguished United States Army officer. Back in 1924, Abbott had persuaded Senator Medill McCormick to intercede with President Coolidge in securing Denison an appointment as a member of the Mexican Claims Commission. Abbott and Mrs. Denison consequently had much to talk about and shared many experiences during his brief stay. Not long afterwards they were married at Crown Point, Indiana, August 7, 1934—and, in the process, he ignored his physician's advice.

The new Mrs. Abbott's beginnings were misty.

Born Edna Brown in Winnepeg, Canada, April 1, 1891, she was first seen in Chicago as the twelve-year-old niece of Harry and Ida Brown. She attended the Keith School and afterwards worked as a stenographer. Her obscure parentage in no wise affected her South Side social status, for she eventually married the prominent Colonel Denison. He had been attached to the famous Eighth Illinois Infantry Regiment, saw overseas duty in World War I, and had retired a brigadier general. He was also a lawyer and, for a time, Assistant Attorney General of the State of Illinois. She bore him five children: Franklin, Dorothy, Denise, George and Jacqueline. When her daughter Dorothy died, she assumed the care of Dorothy's two children, Edna Rose and Anita.

Edna, who after marriage to the publisher bore the nickname "Lady A," was as completely white as any Caucasian—she was in fact literally a white woman. She had a rosy complexion, with not a blemish on her skin. She stood about five feet five inches in height and weighed some one hundred and fifty pounds. She had tiny bones, small feet, small hands with exceedingly long fingers. Her hair, which she was careful to have waved regularly, was beautiful, brown and slightly curled. Her taste in clothes was conservative but smart. Her bills at Carson Pirie Scott's department store frequently included such items as gardenias and perfumes. Her jewels, though modest, were the envy of Chicago women.

But like Helen, Edna was a frigid person. Rebecca Styles Taylor, a *Defender* columnist, once spent a revealing night at her house. She declares, "Edna had none of the mannerisms of colored women. She had an air of reserve and fixed habits, and was studiously cold. Yet she never left anything undone in the way of courtesy." During her stay, Edna had thoughtfully placed a copy of *Rebecca* at her bedside and a bunch of luscious grapes—"and withal," says Taylor, "there was no warmth in the gesture." Yet she was adored—not only by her children, but by Abbott as well. Edna was especially attractive to men, often rivaling her attractive daughters for their admiration and compliments.

Edna, though giving the appearance of being lighthearted, was basically secretive, prudent and remote. The manner in which she told her children of her engagement to Abbott was therefore in character. Her son George recalls, "One day she showed us a diamond ring, and said in a casual way, 'Look what I have.'" She was undoubtedly persuaded to marry Abbott by his offer to educate her children. (He kept his word— indeed, he developed a genuine affection for them, particularly for Jacqueline and George who, themselves, returned his affection.) On his part, Abbott decided to marry Edna principally because he was childless and she had a ready-made family.

At one point, it seems, Abbott may have hoped for children of his own. His personal secretary, Agaliece Westbrook (Miller) remembers reading a letter from his close friend, Dr. William Marshall, in which the latter assured the publisher he was not too old to have children.

But whatever hopes the marriage may have contained, it proved to be far from idyllic for either party.

Discretion dictated silence about women.

To be sure, for many months after his divorce and remarriage, Abbott had taken the greatest care to express himself cautiously in both written and spoken word. Suddenly, without any apparent excuse, he exploded a veritable bombshell— one which, nevertheless, was in character: several times before in his life he had distinguished himself by dealing a bold stroke which was as unexpected as it was daring. So, beginning in early 1934, he prepared (with the assistance of his foreign editor, Metz P. T. Lochard) and published a series of twenty long articles under the title, "The Search for Culture," which, though intended as a program of racial improvement, was in fact mostly a transparent reflection of his disastrous marital experience with Helen.

The articles revealed a curious cynicism and perhaps

served as a catharsis, but an explosion inevitably followed. He was deluged with protesting, even shrill letters. A typical one labeled him "Robert 'Uncle Thomas' Abbott," and another "Blundering France Abbott." No series the *Defender* ever published received more articulate reaction, perhaps because he had exposed a lack Negroes were highly sensitive about. Moreover, the series was regarded as somewhat obtuse in the midst of the depression, when the race faced actual starvation. For a time his popularity among women was greatly lessened, as was his reputation for sound judgment. He himself pretended that publication of the series did good by making people argue the question, but we can regard that as merely spurious balm for a self-inflicted and unnecessary wound.

He perhaps felt he was expounding from a position of strength and unassailable prestige—after all, he had been abroad, had seen what he regarded as the citadel of culture. Only a few weeks before, Abbott had been elected to permanent membership in the *Institut Littéraire et Artistique de France*, a fact that delighted him no end. Under the three-column head, EDITOR ABBOTT IS HONORED BY FAMOUS FRENCH INSTITUTE, the *Defender* had given the fact much fanfare. In his letter of acceptance Abbott said in part: "My editorials have been responsible for many social and legislative reforms. I have fought social inequalities, racial injustices and religious bigotry fearlessly whenever and wherever such evils protruded their demoniac heads in our midst. I have championed the cause of humanity at large irrespective of creed, race or color. Such virile militancy of course, is not always in harmony with established order, but I care not what order is disturbed, though it may represent centuries of consecrated ideals and vested interests—aggressive, determined, systematic and consistent prosecution of truth and the principles predicated upon it is my first and last preoccupation."

The *Defender* introduced the culture series with this note: "Mr. Abbott, a keen student of human affairs, has given much thought to the part our [Negro] women have played, and are destined to play, in the development of our cultural life, and he is of the firm conviction that much needs to be said about the type of training which will fit them for their roles." The first article, bearing the head FINISHING SCHOOLS ARE NECESSARY, SAYS EDITOR ABBOTT, pretty much set the tone of the whole series. He began by citing the historical examples of Hannah More, Madame de Maintenon and Mary Lyon, women who helped form culture patterns abroad. "Unfortunately with us in America," he wrote, "the institution of slavery, though abolished more than 60 years ago, left us still with a vague sense of what truly constitutes the icing of the cake."

Then he firmly declared: "The mammy type must be transformed into a respectable society matron. She must forego her culinary predilection for the more exquisite and pleasurable art de salon." He bemoaned the fact that "Our professional men are actually handicapped by the glaring lack of adequate knowledge, on ordinary points of culture, exhibited by their wives at public functions." He observed that "At receptions which call for the best decorum and evident ease, most of them dress and look like home folks from nowhere lost in a modern art gallery." How often, he asked, "do we hear wives call their husbands Bill, Joe, Steve or Butch in the presence of company." He reminded his readers that "Ladies are not fashioned in the kitchen or washtub. They come, like rare flowers, from another soil—the parlor or finishing school, if you please, where correct breeding is assimilated and cultivated." He declared "There should be no hesitancy as to what step to make, what dress to wear, and what spoon or fork to use at a formal gathering."

The publisher was clearly unhappy about the lack of a genuine society among Negroes or, to use his phrase, "No sharp line of demarcation." "In truth," he wrote, "what we have is nothing more than a ghastly admixture of Tom, Dick and Harry, without either precedent or tradition." Even the young girls, he felt, were "growing up beautiful and elegant, but a close-up soon dispels the magic effect of their seductive make-up for they have neither grace nor poise, neither refinement nor dignity. There was a time when school girls were carefully escorted or chaperoned. That time is gone. Now they go and come at all hours of the night, and do as they please. They smoke, drink and even spend the night out. Social graces cannot be acquired from schools, summer camps and playgrounds."

Under the head, "Old Slaves Were Well Bred," he observed that "The old slaves may not have been tutored in metaphysics and geometry; they may not have known the rules of rhetoric and advanced syntax; they may not have been able to quote Aristotle, Shakespeare and Victor Hugo, but they reared families in a manner more commendable than the sophisticated fathers and mothers of today. They had first-hand information about polite manners. They were in daily contact with the master. They observed his speech, his general decorum, his table manners and all of the minute details which good breeding requires. Now that we have no masters to imitate we must rely on finishing schools to recreate the lost atmosphere of refinement which permeated society in olden days."

He held that the colleges and universities had failed to produce ladies, and he declared in a head, EDUCATION FUTILE WITHOUT CULTURE. However, he hastened to add that he was not opposed to higher education for Negro women. "But," he said, "what does it avail us to have a superabundance of women with masters and Ph.D. degrees, women so highly trained as to frown upon the biological functions of their sex and ignore such basic aspects of the society as marriage and the family?" He asserted that "Highly specialized training seems to incubate female deserters of the nuptial foyer, and what is more deplorable and alarming is that a great deal of sweet feminine essence is drained off to be replaced by masculinity. If by some accident such a woman marries, the man must be a first-class imbecile with the docility of an Egyptian ass in order to get along with her."

Abbott conceded that intelligence in a woman is a good thing—but, he observed, "wit and brilliancy of intellect in a woman provoke ⸺ ⸺eous admiration when with these sparkling q⸺ ⸺ins the refreshing attributes of her sex. To be w⸺ same time womanly, is to wield a tremendous i⸺ may be felt for good in the lives of generations⸺ hen quoted Dr. David Starr Jordan of Leland ⸺ ⸺sity, who once said: "It is true, as I have else⸺ ⸺, that you cannot fasten a $2,000 education on ⸺

His sharpest ⸺s were directed at marriage.

"We find in this 20th century," he wrote, "that the entire [female] sex has gone violently insane, and imagines that all men owe women a living for which they need give nothing in return. Little indeed most of them give. . . . As for dignity, there is no such feature to modern marriage. Stripped of engagement ring, white veils, wedding marches and the ritual, what is there dignified about the woman contracting to sleep with a man all her life provided he will first bind himself to pay all her expenses? Marriage is no longer a sacrament, but a sale—ex parte, unilateral, and a one-sided contract. You bind yourself to give one woman, not alone an excellent living for a life time, but half of what you have, and you agree in addition that if your conjugal conduct is not perfect, she may plunder you legally and torment you all your days."

Essentially, Abbott had the high-minded purpose of uplifting his race. He was fully aware his series would create a chorus of howls, for he observed in the beginning, "I trust that I may not be misunderstood in my efforts to bring about a much needed evolution"—but most assuredly he was! He nevertheless held firm. To illustrate, he replied to one particularly caustic letter thus: "It is hoped that a candid survey of the problems affecting our cultural status, will awaken in the mass the desire for an introspective examination of the characteristics which have caused malicious observers to label and libel us. . . . It is not by closing our eyes to our shortcomings culturally that we shall find an escape from our troubles. . . . The continuation of the series is contingent upon the abatement of the evils which I deprecate."

The fact is, he followed up this series with a campaign to improve the public conduct of Negroes. It was the first such campaign launched by a Negro newspaper, and it was afterwards adopted by other papers. Until now, as a rule, Negro behavior was generally considered to have extenuating circumstances, viewed as it was against the whole social background. But Abbott felt each Negro must be held accountable for his own behavior if the race was to progress. "Sometimes," he remarked, "I am inclined to think that many discriminatory gestures on the part of white people are due to a belief that we are not cultured. Our lack of emotional control, consistent dignity and appropriate poise has profoundly affected our interracial relationships. We are simply lacking in those fundamental things that make for culture and it is about time that we make an about face.

"We should polish our manners as well as our nails!"

Mr. Abbott was almost pathetically loyal to the American system of government, clutching desperately to the hope that America might some day extend democratic practices as well as words to her darker citizens.—METZ P. T. LOCHARD, "Race Leader," *Phylon,* Second Quarter, 1947.

CHAPTER XIX

The Racial Radical

Now WE TURN to an episode far more important than his too obvious petty personal traits, one in which Robert S. Abbott displayed his capacity for independent judgment, assumption of sole responsibility, and courageous action. He had grown suspicious of Nathan K. Magill, his general manager, but the trouble did not come to a head until one day late in 1934, when Abbott's bank called him about a check and he discovered that the "Little Napoleon" was attempting to deposit a *Defender* check in his own account. Meanwhile, an audit of the paper's accounts—inspired by the divorce action—revealed shortages. Abbott had transferred nearly $300,000 of his personal funds to the Robert S. Abbott Publishing Company, and when he sought a return of the money, he discovered it was mostly spent. Magill was unable to give a satisfactory explanation and the publisher promptly dismissed him.

Among Abbott's papers was an envelope marked "RSA Personal" containing a brief memorandum presumably prepared for his attorney. According to these notations, he charged Magill with rifling his safe deposit box at the Continental Illinois Bank and Trust Company and removing its contents; personally profiting at the expense of the paper from the East-West baseball games staged in 1933 and 1934 by the Negro National League and the Negro American League; failure to repay $3,800 he was advanced for purchase of an automobile; the loss of revenue in sales through delaying publication of *Abbott's Monthly* two weeks to run an apple-polishing story of a politician; and, finally, an attempt to buy the *Defender* plant through a dummy purchaser. Whatever Abbott thought, the loose business operations of Magill were characterized in the office thus: "All the money that comes into the *Defender*, Magill throws against the wall —and that which sticks belongs to Mr. Abbott!" Beyond his hearing, his city editor, Lucius C. Harper, observed: "While Mr. Abbott is picking up pins off the floor, Magill is carrying money out of the office by the bucketfuls."

Yet Magill frequently reassured Abbott during his illness, "Everything will be done to safeguard all the money as well as everything else so that you need not give yourself any concern or worry whatever, but enjoy yourself to the fullest extent and come back full of new life and vigor, ready to put over this great program." Whether or not he was guilty of actual theft, is still in the realm of speculation. But he did contribute significantly to the destruction of his chief's marriage—for, indeed, it was he who first planted seeds of suspicion in Abbott's mind. He even went to the extraordinary lengths of sending flowers to Abbott's home, addressed to Helen anonymously. Yet, at the same time, he flattered Abbott outrageously. One method was to run his picture in and out of season, though these were mostly dull and repetitious handshaking scenes. Consequently, the following jingle developed from the popular rejection of the too frequent publishing of Abbott's and Magill's pictures:

Robert S. Abbott and Attorney Magill—
I'll run my picture, 'til I get my fill.

"Whether or not he robbed Abbott," says Magill's divorced wife Idalee, "I do not know. But I would believe he did something that got him into trouble, though I know that after he left the *Defender* he never had any more money." Magill soon sued Abbott for unpaid wages—for, in truth, he had drawn no salary since 1932 when the paper had financial reverses. But he had a drawing account, a fact that perhaps made for abuses. In any case, Abbott brought a counter suit to recover $300,000, and received a court judgment of $17,000. He never collected, for by now Magill had declared himself a bankrupt. Yet Magill's assets seemingly were solid and indeed an open book, for in 1932 the Pittsburgh *Courier*, in recounting his meteoric rise, had reported that he owned three automobiles (including two Pierce Arrows), plus two six-flat buildings on Michigan Avenue and a prosperous real estate firm, which, incidentally, had managed Abbott's holdings.

The publisher, though infirm, resumed direction of the paper. With surprising vigor, he reorganized the enterprise. He rehired many of the people Magill had fired. For example, Fay Young, his old sports editor who had gone to the Kansas City *Call*, was brought back and made managing editor; Dan Burley, a purged reporter who had subsequently introduced a popular gossip column, "Back Door Stuff," in the Chicago *Bee*, was rehired and made a gossip columnist; "Bung" Thornton, his old buddy of Hampton days, was returned to the payroll, as were Roscoe Conkling Simmons and A. N. Fields, a columnist. But the publisher soon dismissed his old friend's daughter, Genevieve Lee Wimp (now Mrs. Ridley) who as assistant treasurer was charged with incompetently handling funds. A remarkable fact about this particular case, according to Abbott's secretary, Agaliece Westbrook (Miller), was that a relationship reaching back to 1905 was terminated in less than five minutes, and the publisher emerged from his office as though nothing untoward had happened.

His most significant appointment, perhaps, was that of his nephew and heir, John H. H. Sengstacke, who had only recently graduated from Hampton Institute, as vice-president and treasurer of the Robert S. Abbott Publishing Company. The next year he made him general manager. If this was nepotism, it did not extend to the point of over-paying his relative. The young man received a salary of $2,675 a year to start, which later was increased to $3,600. Upon the recommendation of his nephew and attorney, Euclid Taylor, he employed the energetic Valoris J. Washington, now director of minorities of the Republican National Committee, who eventually rose to general manager. And later, from Savannah, Georgia, he brought Rebecca Styles Taylor, who had established a reputation as secretary of the National Association of Colored Women, to write a column and to help develop the woman's pages. But he outstripped his competitors with the appointment of Metz P. T. Lochard as the first foreign editor in the Negro press.

A word about Lochard is pertinent.

By now, he had become Abbott's confidant, and perhaps had developed the closest relationship with the publisher of anyone during this period. Brisk, bright and black, he often was described as "a brainy, little big-headed man." He was first seen in the United States when he arrived in 1918 as an interpreter for General Foch, commander-in-chief of the French Army. He afterwards taught languages at Howard University, Washington, D. C., and Fisk University, Nashville, Tennessee. Lochard first met the publisher sometime in 1932 when one of Abbott's nieces invited him to play bridge with Abbott. The discovery that he spoke French delighted Abbott, as did the revelation of his background of scholarship during a period when Abbott was placing considerable emphasis upon culture.

Lochard had been educated at the University of Paris and at Corpus Christi, Oxford, England. A firm friendship developed between the two men, and, after the divorce from Helen, Abbott invited the Frenchman to live with him as a companion. He soon was translating the publisher's extensive correspondence from abroad and, in time, began writing his speeches. He thus came to know Abbott quite intimately. Abbott soon developed annoying habits: for example, while relating a story to a white group he would point to his companion and say such and such was "as black as Lochard"; and frequently he hid his cigars in the Frigidaire so Lochard could not indulge his own taste for luxuries. Even so, the publisher admired him extravagantly. He was indeed entrusted with the task of tutoring Abbott's nephew, and heir, John, and advised a course of education to prepare the young man for assumption of his duties as editor and publisher. Lochard, who has a brilliant and supple mind, eventually became the editor-in-chief following the death of the publisher.

With Abbott giving day-to-day supervision, the *Defender* sharpened up and began to resume its characteristic vigor. He became a rugged taskmaster, though his health was rapidly declining and he was suffering with advanced myopia, which meant that someone had to read to him. His secretary, Agaliece Westbrook (Miller), observed his demoniac drive during these days. "He felt," she says, "that too many people wasted too much time when there was so much to be done. I think he was fond of me—almost as if I were a member of his family—but he would push me to the limit of my strength and endurance. He never wanted me to do his personal work during the hours I was carrying on my work assignments for the paper. He would wait patiently until I had completed eight full, hard hours, and then ask me if I would stop by the house on my way home and take some letters.

337

"And Saturday afternoons (my regular time off) was the time he wanted my services for his personal work. He would stand at the door of his office every Saturday at noon, and when I punched the clock and came through the door to cross the lobby, he would say in that voice that was always impossible to say 'no' to: 'Agaliece, could you come out to the house and take some letters?' Because I just couldn't say 'no' to anything he asked of me, some Saturdays I would sneak out through the press room and down the alley so that I could have a Saturday afternoon off. And then I could be sure that he would call me at home on Sunday morning and I'd have to work Sunday—and no extra pay.

"He was the same with the other employees. He felt that everyone should have the same driving urge to build a great *Defender* that he had—even if it meant working seven days and all hours. He thought that employees should be willing to work until the job was done—otherwise, they were guilty of disloyalty. Nothing annoyed him more than to see people rushing out at closing time. 'Look at them,' he would say. 'All they are interested in is getting out of here. How do they ever expect to get anywhere in life with that attitude. Why, when I was a boy . . .' and again he would talk of his struggles and the hardships he endured to make possible the job which we all held."

Yet he was jealously protective of his people.

When heavyweight boxer Joe Louis was training for his first fight with the German challenger Max Schmeling, Alfred E. "Al" Monroe, then the *Defender's* sports editor, drove from New York City to Joe's training camp accompanied by three white sports writers. When they arrived at a hotel in Lakehurst, New Jersey, the Negro was assigned accommodations in the basement. He protested but the management declared it was the best they could do and offered to refund his money. Monroe sent a telegram to his Chicago office reporting the discrimination. Abbott was angrily indignant. But he did not leave his reporter to his own devices; instead he immediately dispatched a 500-word telegram to Walter White, executive secretary of the National Association for the Advancement of Colored People, asking him to take action. Then he sent a blazing wire to his New York lawyer, instructing him to investigate the discrimination and take steps to sue. Result: before long, "Al" Monroe was transferred to the best suite in the hotel to the accompaniment of profuse apologies from the management.

"Be sure," Abbott was cautioning his reporters, "you're right—then give the skunks hell!" He revamped the handling of headlines with the observation that they were merely "'sponges' to absorb space and deprive readers of what they have a right to expect in a ten-cent newspaper—real, pithy items of information." Thus these marvels of condensation were produced:

JUDGE FREES LYNCHERS

SEN. TYDINGS SILENT ON MOBS; SCORES HITLER

WAR DEPT. FIRES BRUTAL LEVEE CAMP BOSS
USED LASH TO PUNISH WORKER

KENTUCKY INAUGURATES LYNCHING SEASON

Though mainly concerned with the stern affairs that affect Negroes, the *Defender* was not by any means a mere crepe-hanging sheet. The paper now contained a few comic strips, humorous cartoons, and two gossip columns—no doubt to soften the blows dealt by a tough front page. Society news was a breezy and prominent feature in which the doings of colored café society was recorded for the edification of those

in the hinterlands. Much of this output was done in the manner of the Broadway gossip columns, and it often contained
the flavorsome vernacular of the curbstone. Considerable
space was devoted to lively articles on fashion, shopping hints,
music, theater, book reviews, always with an abundance of
names quoted. The large number of columnists carried by
the *Defender*—who conducted what was frequently sound
and thoughtful forums—testified to the new emphasis placed
on personal journalism.

To be sure, the style was flamboyant.

When scratched, the paper's content now laid emphasis
on personalities—which indeed was a new development in
the *Defender.* The race had developed new heroes during
the 1930's, consequently Negro personalities now had a special "racial" significance. Cayton and Drake analyzed the
Defender's 1933–1938 period for *Black Metropolis.* The ten
persons, according to them, receiving the most prominent
page-one attention were as the table below indicates:

Person	Nationality and/or Race	Significance	Incidence of Display
Joe Louis	American Negro	Race Hero—first Negro to hold world heavy-weight title since Jack Johnson.	80
Haile Selassie	Ethiopian	Race Hero—leader of nation with which Ne-groes felt kinship, dur-ing attack by a white nation, Italy.	24
Oscar DePriest	American Negro	Race Hero and Leader —First Negro Con-gressman since 1901 elected by Negro voters. Reputation for being fearless.	20

Person	Nationality and/or Race	Significance	Incidence of Display
Jesse Binga	American Negro	Race Hero and Leader —Home bombed by white persons who objected to his living outside the Negro community. Banker whose bank failed during depression. Jailed for embezzlement.	16
Arthur Mitchell	American Negro	Race Leader—Successor to DePriest in Congress. Often charged with lack of aggressiveness.	15
Edward Kelly	American white	Mayor of Chicago, considered a "friend of the Negro."	15
Colonel John C. Robinson		Race Hero—aviator. Served in Italo-Ethiopian War.	11
R—— J——	American Negro	Criminal—committed sensational crime.	9
Benito Mussolini	Italian, white	Race Enemy—leader of attack on Ethiopia.	9
Dr. Mercer	American Negro	"Big Negro"—died mysteriously.	8

The *Defender* was still having a tough time financially, for there was little profitable advertising. As usual, the chief revenue came from the sale of the papers, which retailed for ten cents. Much of the advertising was reminiscent of that in the general papers of the '80s and '90s, before advertising developed into a competitive art, and included many sucker items such as lodestones, zodiacal incense, books on unusual love practices; products that purported to turn black skin white, or straighten kinky hair. The hair dekinking process had, indeed, developed into a sizable industry, which, besides catering to Negro women, had found vogue with crinkly-haired white women. Much of the big advertising copy that appeared in the *Defender* came from such sources.

About this phase of his operations, Abbott was extremely sensitive. He had indeed made determined efforts to eliminate such copy from the *Defender's* columns. By now, Negro readers themselves had become particularly critical of the paper in this regard, but Negro businesses—none too large— could hardly buy the space necessary for operating a large newspaper plant like the *Defender*. Moreover, white firms discriminated against Negro newspapers generally when earmarking funds for advertising. Thus the *Defender*, like its competitors, was forced to snatch whatever it could get. Not until the next decade did white advertisers recognize the value of the Negro press, and it is only fair to say that the first venturesome advertisers cashed in handsomely on a meager investment—for such direct appeals to the Negro community do produce tangible results. After all, the Negro's mass buying power exceeds that of a country like Denmark.

Robert S. Abbott now discovered that much of the good will he had so carefully built up during the years had been destroyed by Nathan K. Magill. Especially was this true in the political arena, where his general manager's machinations had been particularly unsavory. To begin with, Abbott was an independent Republican; whereas Magill became almost a lackey for the Democratic party when Edward J. Kelly was elected mayor of Chicago. Moreover, Abbott had laboriously earned the reputation that the *Defender's* editorial support could not be bought. His position before the 1924 presidential elections is illustrative. He had attacked the Republican party frequently. This devastating headline appeared in 1923: RE-

PUBLICAN PARTY TO TRY NEW TRICK TO KEEP OUR RACE OUT OF POLITICS.

Nevertheless he supported the party's candidate, Calvin Coolidge. He had accepted $45,000, according to Phil Jones, in political advertising from supporters of the Republicans, who indeed were fully aware of the influence Abbott wielded. Even so, in 1928 he refused to support Herbert Hoover for president, and instead brought the weight of the *Defender* behind the Democratic candidate, Alfred E. Smith. He was convinced that Hoover's record in terms of Negroes was suspect. When Hoover became president he proved himself decidedly not sympathetic to the aspiration and progress of Negroes, especially when he attempted to cultivate Southern supporters. Thus Abbott was able to crow in the *Defender* with these headlines:

HOOVER FOR LILY-WHITE PARTY

REPUBLICANS MAKE BOW TO DIXIE RULES

PROVE DEFENDER RIGHT
IN PROPHESY

The decision not to support a Republican presidential candidate was a revolutionary departure for the Negro press. Abbott afterwards liked to assume much of the credit for the Negro's final achievement of independence in their break with the Republican party. Carl Sandburg, who conducted a weekly "Notebook" for the Chicago *Daily News,* was enthusiastic over the development. "One of the best features of the late presidential campaign," he wrote in 1928, "was the independent stand of the Chicago *Defender.* Robert S. Abbott, its editor, told his readers to break away from the Republican Party if they felt that way. He intimated plainly that both parties were long on promises and short on the keeping of promises. This is the first time so independent a break has

343

happened in Negro political viewpoint. Hitherto the outstanding Negro spokesmen have been chained to the Republican Party chariot. Mr. Abbott and the Chicago *Defender* should have no regrets over their declarations. Such independence can be a healthy current in the Negro body politic."

The publisher himself had a disinclination to have any truck with politicians, although back in 1908, he was prepared to take the stump in behalf of the Republican party. He wrote his old mentor, at Hampton, Dr. Frissell, "I am slated to speak during the National Campaign [for Judge Taft's candidacy] and am required to have letters of recommendation. I send to ask will you kindly send one for me by return mail." He had ambitions of procuring a federal appointment, but his efforts came to naught. His disenchantment permanently conditioned his attitude toward politicians. Thus he said, "If we are depending on them to solve our problems, we shall wait a long, long time." Loosely, his policy became: support friends and punish enemies.

Until he employed Magill, Roscoe Conkling Simmons—who allowed it to be assumed he was the protégé of Mark Hanna—was Abbott's pipeline to the Republican politicians. But when Magill became general manager he assumed the job of dealing directly with the politicians, and indeed their underworld supporters whom Abbott had studiously avoided. Julius J. Adams distinctly recalls the day when he was the *Defender's* managing editor and Magill called him into his office ". . . and gave me instructions to lay off the numbers racket. Mayor Kelly would go along, he said, if the *Defender* would go along too." Adams is convinced this decision was made without Abbott's knowledge. In any case, things went along nicely for Magill until the election of Mayor Cermack (who heartily disliked Negroes) started the drive to end the black-and-tan character of the South Side and end the Negro's control of policy.

As with everything, Abbott judged politics by the degree

to which racial equality was practiced and racial progress was made. For example, he began to actively support Mayor William Hale Thompson only after Thompson had banned the showing in Chicago of the anti-Negro motion picture, *Birth of a Nation*. However, Abbott had been aloof in the beginning because Charles S. Deneen, who headed the opposing wing of the local Republican Party, had vigorously opposed lynching when governor. Incidentally, these two factions were represented in the Black Belt by the powerful subchieftains, Edward H. Wright and gambling king, Daniel M. Jackson, men with whom Abbott maintained excellent relations. During his administration Mayor Thompson turned City Hall into what was often derisively described as "Uncle Tom's Cabin," and made precedent-making appointments of Negroes. He was afterwards labeled the "Second Lincoln."

Abbott's aspirations for the race led him to give unqualified support to Mayor Thompson. He apparently felt justified, for shortly after the death in 1928 of Congressman Martin B Madden, who represented the Negro district, Mayor Thompson was in a position practically to dictate the nomination. Thompson's account of his position was later stated in a public meeting at the South Side's Wendell Phillips High School. If he said nothing more, Abbott would have perhaps gone along with him, for his language contained uncommon racial frankness for a politician.

"I used to come to you," Mayor Thompson declared, "and say to you that Bill Thompson would be the last one who would put his hand on a Negro's head to prevent him from rising higher. Yet I used to ask you to vote for a white man for Congress—the Honorable Martin B. Madden, Calvin Coolidge, Len Small, Bill Thompson; why did we keep him there, because of the great work Madden was doing. When he died there came some Judas from Washington and said to me, 'We don't want a Negro Congressman. You're the man that can keep a Negro out of Congress.' I said, 'If I'm the one who can keep a Negro out of Congress, then, by God, there'll be one there.'"*

Thus was Oscar DePriest nominated for Congress.

He had already been elected the first Negro alderman in Chicago in 1915. Abbott was only lukewarm to him in the early stages of the campaign, for he felt the Negro community should be represented by an unfettered leader not a politician. He already had demonstrated his attitude, when he supported Wendell E. Green for appointment as a Civil Service Commissioner in preference to his old friend Louis B. Anderson, because the latter was too intimately tied to politics and, in Abbott's view, might be tempted to give political preference to candidates for jobs. The election of Oscar DePriest to the United States Congress—the first Negro in the twentieth century—symbolized the political development of Negroes in Chicago. He was succeeded in Congress in 1934 by a pallid Negro Democrat, Arthur W. Mitchell, who charged on the floor of the House that the Republicans were "trying to buy back the Negro votes." Congressman Hamilton Fish queried: "I want to know whether the gentleman believes the Negro vote is for sale." Mitchell responded: "I may say to the gentlemen that every vote in the United States is for sale, not for money but for rights and privileges." This indeed was an echo of Abbott's position in the *Defender*.

The seat in Congress was a symbol of Negro achievement. It stood for the recapturing of a banished hope. It meant that the Negro was part of the national government. Consequently, the eyes of all Negroes were focused upon their single spokesman in the national law-making body. But this development was the result of the great interest shown by Negroes of Chicago in politics, and a result, too, of a strong racial solidarity, which Abbott almost single-handedly developed. Moreover, the influx of Negroes to Chicago had steadily increased the Negro population to 233,903 by the

* Gosnell, Harold F., *Negro Politician*, 1935.

1930's. It was these new voters, Republican by tradition, who, crowded into the Black Belt, supplied the base of operations for the Negro politicians and gave to the latter power in the city's politics.

Abbott never abandoned his suspicions about the motives of politicians. He advocated a unified demand for unrestricted political participation. He urged that this demand be made before the elections, when parties were hunting votes. Negroes, he declared, should be independent and use their votes as a bargaining weapon. Briefly: he advocated crass opportunism. His position led him to oppose President Roosevelt. Thus when two Negroes were barred from eating in the Congressional restaurant he held the New Deal wing of the Democratic party responsible. Incensed, he published a signed editorial on page one, IS THIS THE NEW DEAL? "The New Deal," he held, "is either a fact or a fallacy. It is either to be carried out impartially to every citizen alike or it is a hypocritical pretense fostered and prompted by hypocrisy and insincerity. . . . Congress must determine once and for all. We are either a united country or a nation of hyphens." He said nothing about the New Deal's economic programs. But he felt deeply enough to accept appointment as campaign publicity director for the Colored Division of the National Republican Party in the 1936 campaign.

With the Italian assault on Ethiopia in the winter of 1935, a tailor-made issue arose for the *Defender*, one cut in precise racial proportions. A black nation had been invaded by a white nation. Here, at long last, was some sort of tangible ideal—certainly a legitimate issue—around which the Negro could rally. Abbott did indeed rally a great section of the Negro population. When white liberals and radicals took up the cry of Fascist aggression, the prestige of the *Defender's* editorializing was given a decided boost. The fact is, the conflict stirred considerable emotion among Negroes. For example, when news reached Negroes that Ras Gugsa, a cousin of Haile Selassie and a general in the Ethiopian Army, had sold out to Mussolini, there was dismay. But the *Defender* immediately created a term to describe what was later called a Quisling: "Gugsacrat," meaning a Negro who sold out the race to an enemy. The term never quite caught on perhaps because it did not have roots in American Negro experience.

The *Defender*, however, personalized the conflict for its readers by dramatizing the aviation exploits of a Chicagoan, Colonel John C. Robinson, who had joined the Ethiopian Air Force, such as it was. Foreign editor Lochard himself became "Operator 202" and ghosted stories about the war with an Ethiopian dateline, using the daily newspaper reports as a springboard. But it was the publisher, stirred by the racial meanings of the invasion, whose imagination came to flower. One evening he told Lochard he had received information that the Italians were marching on Ethiopia's Adowa, historic scene of Menelik's great defeat of the Italians in the previous century. According to the report, Abbott said, a Coptic priest had contrived clay receptacles, with escape holes, and in them kept tsetse flies. As the Italians came on the Ethiopians unleashed these insects and stopped the advance. The casualties were considerable. Lochard duly wrote the story—in fact, several dailies picked up the story and republished it as, presumably, an authentic report. It was, actually, a figment of Abbott's imagination. But following the publication of this article, such an incident actually happened, delaying the capture of Adowa!

When Emperor Haile Selassie went before the League of Nations at Geneva, Switzerland, to make an appeal to brand Italy as an aggressor, Lochard suggested to Abbott that this was a rare moment in history and that it would be a red-letter day for the Negro press, if he had the foresight to have his own correspondent on the spot and report the proceedings. Abbott jocularly replied: "Before a Negro could get to Geneva, the Chicago *Tribune* would have the full story, and for two cents we can get the story." He meant, by this, that the *Defender* staff could rewrite the *Tribune's* story and this would suffice. Moreover, he declared, "A Negro would not know what they were talking about anyway, because of a chronic linguistic deficiency." His elaborate rationalizing, Lochard felt, was to avoid spending the money entailed in sending a correspondent abroad. But, then, he was unaware of Abbott's prior experiences with Roscoe Conkling Simmons' trip abroad in which the publisher lost money and received no stories.

However, according to Lochard, "Anything that meant the crushing or suppression of freedom, whether freedom of thought or freedom of person, was abhorrent to Mr. Abbott." For example, back in the early part of the century he decried the so-called lynching of Leo Frank, and now denounced the Nazi atrocities against the Jews of Europe. When, in 1933, Charles Walgreen, of the drugstore chain, attacked Robert M. Hutchins, then president of the University of Chicago, and withdrew his niece from the institution, Abbott came to Hutchins' defense. The controversy involved teaching which, Walgreen charged, had a Communist slant. Hutchins held that the function of a university was to inquire into all fields of knowledge and place such inquiries at the disposal of mature students. Meantime Governor Pearson of the Virgin Islands had visited Abbott and persuaded him of the righteousness of Hutchins' position. Late one night he summoned Lochard to write an editorial supporting Hutchins. The editorial duly appeared on page one, for, says Lochard, Abbott felt he was protecting the whole concept of academic freedom.

This liberal position occasionally led him into support of Communists—indeed, he had planned an extensive tour of the Soviet Union in 1930 and only his health deterred him. Incidentally, the fact is repeatedly referred to in letters written to him by friends, mostly warning him not to go. Like most liberals, Abbott began by publicizing the infamous Scottsboro Case, which involved four Negro boys being charged in Alabama with rape of two white girls—Ruby Bates and Victoria Price. Abbott afterwards carried a series, called "Behind the Scottsboro Scene!", in which Ruby Bates, one of the girls supposedly raped, made a confession clearing the boys. The first installment bore this typical head:

RUBY BATES WRITES FOR FIRST TIME THE FULL
STORY OF WHAT HAPPENED ON FREIGHT
TRAIN THREE LONG YEARS AGO

WOULD GLADLY UNDO THE PART SHE PLAYED

REVEALS FACTS ABOUT HOW
VICTORIA PRICE LIED

The publisher was distinctly impressed by the vigorous manner in which the Communists fought for the lives of the Negro boys involved. He afterwards ran stories like WHY WE DON'T HATE REDS. A feature article, signed by a Bishop William M. Brown, extolled Russia in this manner: SAYS COMMUNISM NEAREST APPROACH TO IDEAL STATE. As late as 1939, the *Defender* ran a story with this head: THERE IS NO BLACK AND WHITE ISSUE OR RACE PROBLEM IN SOVIET RUSSIA. And the sub-head read: "Census Proves Nationality Not Chosen On Physical or Color Characteristics: Whether Black or White, One Enjoys Full Rights Under Its Laws."

Thus one year the Young Communist League applied for permission to march in the *Defender's* Bud Billiken parade. Abbott's Bud Billiken editor, David W. Kellum, threatened to resign if the Reds were allowed to parade. He was supported by Abbott's nephew, John. Abbott opposed them both with, "If there is a Bud Billiken parade, these young white people will march!" Even when the Negro chapter of the American Legion withdrew in protest, refusing to march with Communists, Abbott still would not relent.

"Mr. Abbott," says Lochard correctly, "had little vision beyond the Communist boast that they believed in the equality of races."

To be sure, Abbott was no Communist. But, after all, his mistake was common to liberals during the period—indeed, the professors at the University of Chicago had planned a trip to Russia to determine the exact status of the races, and determine as well whether or not there was racial discrimination, segregation or proscription, and had invited Abbott to send a reporter along! They perhaps wanted a Negro in the junket because his presence would undoubtedly provide the acid test. Abbott declined the invitation, although his noisy liberal policy had helped to fix the reputation of the *Defender* in the popular mind as a "radical" paper. But it was a *racial* radicalism not an *economic* radicalism which Abbott espoused. Moreover, he advocated the use of constitutional processes as the only means of social emancipation.

Bud Billiken was Abbott's proudest possession.

Back in 1923, the publisher came up with the idea there should be a column in the *Defender* for children. The reason was twofold: he was probing for a method by which he could enlist newsboys and maintain their interest in the paper; and he felt the paper needed reading matter of interest to young people in general. He brought his idea to his city editor, Lucius C. Harper, who agreed such material should be an integral part of the paper. While talking, Harper's eyes strayed to a squat Chinese statuette on his desk, which was contrived in such a way as to form a pen-wiper. It was called a Billiken, which, according to a Chinese legend, is the guardian angel of little children. Abbott quickly seized the statuette as symbolic of what he wanted, and Harper suggested "Bud

351

Billiken." There and then they jointly decided the young people's page should be called Bud Billiken. From this modest beginning, Bud Billiken developed into a gigantic project that involved more than a quarter of a million participants, perhaps the largest gathering of Negroes anywhere in the world.

A bright, bespectacled, ten-year-old youngster, Willard Motley, later to author *Knock On Any Door*, was selected as the first Bud Billiken editor. His picture was published in horn-rimmed glasses and an editor's eye-shade. The page ran a masthead, similar to that on the front page, with the name "The Defender Junior" and the slogan "Children's Greatest Newspaper." The layout was simple enough: cartoons, jokes, puzzles, folk stories, and the exchange of letters among Billiken "pen pals." Essay contests were conducted in which the kids competed for prizes. A Bud Billiken Club was formed and membership cards and identification buttons were distributed free. The idea proved immensely popular, and the *Defender* was soon deluged with letters from as far away as Africa.

Motley, who was attending elementary school, complained that his column was interfering with his school work and begged to be relieved of the responsibility. David W. Kellum was handed the job and told to develop Bud Billiken into a two-page feature. His bumptiousness had gotten him the job. He had become the first Negro to be commissioned a major in the Reserve Officers Training Corps in Chicago, and the *Defender* had published his picture. But he afterwards complained to City Editor Harper because only a half-column cut was used on the inside page. "I protested," he says laughingly, "because he had put René Maran, a distinguished French author, on the front page with a three-column picture. I felt my achievement was more important, and in my innocent youth said so." From this amusing incident a friendship developed between Kellum and Harper.

Soon afterwards Harper hired Kellum to clip newspapers but, before the latter could settle in the job, "Bung" Thornton, who had quit in a fit of pique, returned. Harper then made an offer to Phil Jones: "Kellum can drive an automobile. Why not let him be Mr. Abbott's chauffeur." He was given the job but two weeks later he side-swiped a passing automobile while taking Helen Abbott to a card party, and his career as a chauffeur came to an end. He returned to the *Defender* where he again was juggled around from one job to another. Finally, he was given the Bud Billiken pages to edit. He was to remain at this post for the next twenty-five years and to contribute significantly to the development of Bud Billiken as a national institution among Negroes.

By 1929, Abbott decided the Bud Billiken program needed perking up. So Kellum approached the late Edgar G. Brown, president of the National Negro Council, and George T. Donoghue, now general superintendent of the South Park Board, with the idea of setting up a "Bud Billiken Day" to be observed yearly on the first Saturday in August. "The purpose," according to the parade marshall, Lawrence Vernon Blanchet, "was to give underprivileged children, who are never seen or heard, a chance to be in the limelight for one day by wearing costumes, marching in a parade, and being seen." By a stroke of luck, Freeman Gosden and Charles Correll, of "Amos and Andy" radio fame, were the guests of honor.

Before this, however, the Pittsburgh *Courier,* the *Defender's* chief national competitor, had been crusading against the theme song used by the comedians. The *Courier* claimed it had something to do with the picture *Birth of a Nation,* which was anathema to Negroes. Harper derided the charge in the *Defender,* and in appreciation Gosden and Correll not only made a personal appearance in the first Bud Billiken parade but distributed ten thousand chocolate bars at the picnic afterwards—twin factors that were far from negligible in bringing out the crowds. Abbott led the march in his Rolls Royce limousine, followed by newsboys, boy and girl scouts, and a host of *Defender* readers. The comedians afterwards contributed two thousand dollars to be used for scholarships for Negro youth.

One thousand children and adults participated. From that day on, the parade attracted the support and participation of a wide variety of people, both white and Negro. They ranged from Joe Louis to Tom Mix and Hopalong Cassidy, and from Lena Horne and Roy Rogers to Jesse Owens and Ralf Metcalfe, the Olympic champions. The reviewing stand usually contained dignitaries of the city and state, including the mayor and governor, who perhaps were anxious to be seen by the thousands the *Defender* could gather together. The paraders, often numbering as many as 30,000, marched through the Negro neighborhood. The South Side's two thousand clubs and organizations were present in the line of march, properly attired in costumes and colorful paraphernalia. Floats of every description were included, as well as bands and units from military organizations. The youngsters afterwards gathered for a picnic in Washington Park, where hot dogs, pop, candy, sandwiches, cakes, fruits and milk were distributed free, plus free entertainment by vaudeville acts.

The Bud Billiken Club became the *Defender's* sturdiest institution. Nearly a million youngsters became members, including people like Nat "King" Cole and Lionel Hampton, the bandleader. Practically every state was represented at a "Bud Billiken Parade and Picnic." Moreover, hearty cooperation was received from such groups as the Masons, Elks, churches, social work agencies, civic organizations and, indeed, the city's government. But basically Bud Billiken was a concrete symbol of the childless Abbott's love for children and is today a measure of the *Defender's* extraordinary drawing power and prestige.

I have made an issue of every single situation in which my people were denied their rightful share of participation.—ROBERT S. ABBOTT, Chicago Defender, 1930.

CHAPTER XX

The Search for Tomorrow

ONE EVENING toward the end of his days—so Dr. Charles M. Thompson relates—Robert S. Abbott received an urgent telephone call from a private detective. The man informed the publisher that in his office he had a pregnant woman who claimed Abbott was the father of her expected child. The detective declared he was only calling "to keep down a disturbance," because the woman had vowed to carry her case to the courts. He assured Abbott that for a modest consideration he could hush the matter.

"You say," Abbott inquired, "she says I am to be the father of her child?"

"Yes, indeed."

"Well," said Abbott, "if that's true, she should be in my office, not yours. You tell her to have the baby, and I'll take it, because I would like to have a child."

He hung up the telephone. Then he turned to the young dentist and added, "I'll never hear any more about *that!*"

It had been an obvious attempt at extortion.

Abbott himself was amused. But his remark to Dr. Thompson was a form of wishful thinking. He had wanted a child

355

desperately but for years had believed himself incapable, and perhaps he was. Consequently, much of the love and affection he would have lavished upon an offspring was extended to his very big family—both Sengstackes and Abbotts, who together formed a group of nearly one hundred sisters, brothers, aunts, uncles, cousins and nieces.

The publisher's immediate blood relations were these:

His brother, Alexander, had seven children: Flaurience, Ethel, John, Mildred, Whittier, Frederick and Edith (now deceased); his sister, Mary Thomas, had two: Gwendolyn and Alberta; his sister, Eliza McKay, had two: Marion and Robert. The Abbott branch was equally fertile, perhaps more. His cousin Randolph had three children: Joseph, Thomas and Bristol, who together had twelve children and twenty-one grandchildren. Abbott was, however, partial to the Sengstackes. He even embraced the German family of his stepfather's sister, Elizabeth Sengstacke Bödeker, who had three children: Hennie, Fritz and Georg, who together had eleven children.

Abbott's hope for immortality resided in these people.

He was often charged with being miserly, but he was overly generous with his family. He contributed regularly to his mother's support and even provided her with a few luxuries. He tried for years to persuade her to abandon Woodville, Georgia, and live in a home he would erect in Chicago. One reason she would not move, despite his many entreaties, was, as she said: "When I die, I want to be right here when Shinney [Rev. Sengstacke] comes for me. I don't want him to have to hunt all over the country for me." This produced an impasse they never hurdled, for Abbott himself had vowed, "I'll never put one penny in the South," and therefore he refused to erect a new house in Woodville, though he contributed to refurnishing the old one.

However, he did assume the tremendous financial responsibility of educating the children of his sisters and brother—

ten children in all. He not only contributed to their tuition, but he often sent each money for clothes, insurance and luxuries. But he demanded itemized accounts of monies spent and endlessly cautioned thrift. He carefully watched their progress, even to requesting reports from their schools. When his niece Alberta became ill with pneumonia while at Brick Junior College, Brick, North Carolina, he paused in a busy life to thoughtfully send the matron-in-charge, Minnie Neely, a box of candy. When his two nieces, Flaurience and Gwendolyn, who were attending Fisk University, Nashville, Tennessee, fell behind in their studies he wrote a long letter to the president, Thomas E. Jones, requesting a detailed explanation. He suspected discrimination. "I can say," Jones replied in a two-page letter, "that we all have the highest regard for Miss Sengstacke and Miss Thomas and as far as I have been able to ascertain nothing was done on personal grounds to hinder their fullest and most rapid development."

When they graduated in 1930, as a gift Abbott presented them with a trip to Europe. They stayed abroad nearly a year. Between tours they were the guests of their German relatives, Hennie and Fritz, who lived near Bremen. Abbott was anxious for the girls' visions to broaden, for he was ambitious to create cultured ladies of them. Flaurience once laughingly said, "Uncle hoped we'd marry royalty." He wrote Gwendolyn while they were abroad, "When you get the next money I want you to go to Hamburg, Berlin and Cologne and see the Rhine. You can see all for about $150. Take one of the girls with you from each family. Fritz's and Georg's family if they are large enough to enjoy and learn something of their country. Tell Hennie to let Friedrich go with you. He can speak English." Yet he was also writing his sister Rebecca thus: "Have you ever heard from the girls since they arrived in Germany. I have not. I hope they got there safely. They don't seem to appreciate what I have tried to do for them. I hope I am wrong."

The fact is, he was frequently complaining that his family did not appreciate him or what he was doing for them. "It seems," he wrote Alexander, "as if everyone is trying to ride me for all that they can get instead of trying to help me. . . . I have done unto others as I wanted to be done unto, but you see what it amounts to. I have been stabbed in the back by both blood kin and supposed friends." He created a dependence in them he himself was unable to recognize. Moreover, what he seemingly never quite grasped was the undemonstrative character of the Sengstackes, who, no matter how much they appreciated his generosity, could never have gushed. His family was also somewhat awed by his spectacular success and wealth. His nephew, Frederick, explains his own feelings this way: "I was uneasy when I first went to stay at Mr. Abbott's home, because I had heard he was a 'millionaire.' For instance, I was used to making my own bed, but Mr. Abbott had *two* maids for this purpose."

The Abbotts, however, were emotional and made no bones about expressing their feelings and opinions to him, but his experiences were identical in money matters, though he hardly lavished as much money on them as he did on the Sengstackes. He did provide considerable sums to financially back two Abbotts in business enterprises and was sorely disappointed in each instance. Following an appeal for more money, he wrote one thus: "I am in just as deep distress as you are. Although, I have been nice and kind to everyone, [you] like the rest of them have tried to bite me in the back. Do you know that I had to pay Levy a thousand dollars on your account and had to credit him for $3,500 that I gave you. You admitted that you used the thousand dollars because you were in debt. You knew that the money wasn't yours. I have lost everything trying to be a good fellow. If I had anyone to give me the opportunity that I gave you, I certainly would have made money for them but instead, you want me to do this and do that. The time has come that if you are going to be on good terms with me, some effort must be made to repay that money."

He was of course never repaid.

The appeals for help were endless. Sometimes the requests, though modest, were spelled out in this fashion: His cousin Hattie Butler, a principal of an elementary school in Birmingham, Alabama, wrote him that "a very close friend of mine received his Master of Arts Degree from Columbia University last summer. We are desirous of having his picture and a 375-word article in the *Defender*. He has been very nice to me in my work and I feel that if I can be of any service to him in this way I should try to do so." When she arrived in Chicago for a visit and suddenly became so ill she had to be removed to a hospital, Abbott naturally was expected to assume responsibility for her. While she was a patient at Provident Hospital, he paid all her bills and covered her expenses during convalescence.

Whenever a crisis developed he was expected to interrupt his own affairs and look to the matter—and he usually did. There was the time, for example, when Abbott's boy nephew, Joseph Abbott, ran away from his home on St. Simons Island. His disappearance naturally alarmed his family. They appealed to Abbott for help. He promptly retained a detective agency to trace him. He was finally discovered somewhere in New Jersey working as a cook in the Barnum & Bailey Circus. Abbott had him brought back, and at his own expense sent him to Hampton Institute to learn the printing trade. When he graduated, Abbott brought him to Chicago and put him to work in his plant, where he is employed today.

The publisher was no less generous with the Sengstackes' German relatives—Hennie Hasselbach, and Georg and Fritz Bödeker. They were married and with their children formed a family of twenty persons. Each of the three had at least one child seemingly a throwback to their Negro ancestry, for they possessed crinkly hair and heavy features reminiscent of the

Negro. This fact caused considerable difficulty when Hitler came to power and trumpeted his race theories. At any rate, until that time, Abbott sent money to Hennie, Georg and Fritz for the upkeep and education of their children. The sums were often lavish, for among Abbott's effects are memorandums of $1,000 checks sent them—that is, a thousand dollars to each family at a clip.

When Abbott made his tour of Europe back in 1929, one of the places he visited, perhaps in memory of his stepfather Rev. Sengstacke, was St. Magnus. There he made the acquaintance of Hennie, Georg and Fritz, who indeed laid out the red carpet for their millionaire relative from the United States. He himself was equally proud to have German relations. Thus the publisher somehow came to regard Germany as a sort of racial Shangri-la and afterwards often spoke of the country sentimentally. He came away with the opinion that "Though avowedly militaristic, German culture, passing through successive stages of refinement, has produced the most perfect type of womanhood."

Upon his return to the United States, it appears he attempted to trace the Sengstacke antecedents and employed an attorney for this purpose. One was discovered in Mexico. George P. Shaw, an American consul in Mexico City, informed him that a Herman Sengstack had operated a dry-goods business at Zacatecas back in 1888, had had financial reverses, and had finally committed suicide. "Mr. Sengstack," he wrote in 1933, "came of a good family and was a decent chap, highly esteemed in Zacatecas due to his pleasant, unobtrusive character. His age at the time of his demise was 30 years. He left relatives in Germany." Abbott never pursued this tantalizing bit of information further, presumably because of the pressures of his own affairs about this time.

Until now, his German connections, who believed him to be very rich and influential, enjoyed a feeling of security and well being to have a millionaire relative. But the rise of Hitlerism clouded Abbott's relations with his German cousins. Fay Hershaw, Flaurience's Negro girl friend who visited the families in 1935, reported to him that the Hasselbachs had enthusiastically embraced Nazism but the Bödekers had not. "Georg," she wrote, "was forced to stop school on account of the color question. He says that as he is not pure Aryan he is not allowed to attend school in Bremen. He hasn't been in school at all this year or last. It was difficult for me to understand, because we have colored students over there right now. Maybe Hitler is more lenient on other nationalities than he is toward Germans of mixed blood."

The boy, Georg Bödeker's son, told her that he had not reported the unhappy facts to "Uncle Robert" because of his fear that his letters would be opened and read by the authorities. Friedrich, Fritz's son, asked that Abbott discontinue sending them the *Defender*, "because the Germans don't like unfavorable comments about their people." They both, she added, "told me to ask you to try and get them a job [in the U.S.]. And they say if you need even a furnace man in your home or office, please give them a chance, as there is no future for them in Germany. They can never hold a civil position as a teacher, policeman, etc. They can't even wear the brown shirts as the Nazi men wear."

Flaurience, while on a world tour in 1936, revisited her German relatives. Her report added new details. The families had finally been labeled "non-Aryan," and consequently were denied the privileges of Aryans, including the denial of adequate food allowances. While not denying their Negro ancestry, they nevertheless removed all obvious evidences, such as photographs of their mother, Elizabeth Sengstacke Bödeker, and a photograph of Uncle Robert which hung in the parlor. Their problem was complicated by the fact that each was married to a pure-blooded German. Their discomfort was especially manifested during Flaurience's brief visit. Every night they fearfully locked the doors and windows, constantly alert that someone might listen to their conversations and report them to the Gestapo. Heinz, Hennie's son who somehow became a member of the Nazi party, was only spoken of covertly. At any rate, Abbott's wealth and influence was no help to them during the Nazi regime—indeed, it only served to humiliate and embarrass them.

The publisher could only shake his head sadly.

Robert S. Abbott symbolized the father figure for a white family of quite a different sort—the Stevens people of St. Simons Island, Georgia, who were direct descendants of the white man, Captain Charles Stevens, who had held Abbott's father, aunts and uncles in slavery. The family comprised six persons—a mother, two daughters, and two grandchildren, plus a husband. During the depression, they appealed to Abbott for financial help. Not only did he respond generously, but he afterwards helped to educate their children. He contributed to their upkeep for nearly six years, and, in the process, a warm personal relationship was reestablished. For like his father, Thomas, he felt a loyalty and sense of responsibility to these people when they were faced with extreme difficulties.

His was extraordinary behavior.

He placed his giving on a methodical basis, however. Consequently, they regularly sent him itemized accounts of their debts. For example, one month the grandmother's medicines amounted to $29.45. At one point, the balance on their mortgage came to $240, which they confessed they were only able to reduce with his assistance. When the youngest girl was about to graduate from high school, she needed dental work which came to $60, and to obtain work the husband also paid $60 for a denture. The married daughter became ill and her hospital bill came to $7 a day. When the girl afterwards decided to attend business college and become a stenographer, Abbott purchased a typewriter and sent it to her. No wonder they exclaimed in one letter, "Words are most inadequate to express to you our sincere appreciation for all your help to us. You certainly saved our lives." Abbott apparently cautioned them to spend the money wisely, for one daughter replied, "Yes! I'll spend it carefully for God only knows when I'll be able to make anything." Finally, to give dignity to the relationship and lift his generous contributions out of the category of charity, he employed the man in the family to maintain the monument he had erected to his father on St. Simons Island on a salary basis.

Virginia Stevens concluded that "Everything was white about him but his skin!"

Now nearly seventy-two years old, Robert S. Abbott began thinking of immortality. He had already chosen his heir and successor, his nephew John. For more than twenty years now, Abbott had watched the growth of the boy and considered him a bright and eager youngster. John's teacher, Sophronia M. Thompkins, who had observed him as a student in the Woodville elementary school, regarded him as "a lovely child." When he had completed his schooling there, he enrolled at Knox Institute, and finally entered Hampton Institute, a fact that delighted the publisher no end. Abbott carefully encouraged his development, so much so that John confided to him: "I am reading books on journalism, newspaper work, and taking a course in advertising. I am going to do some research work on the topic: 'Problems Confronting the Advertising Managers of Negro Newspapers.'"

When John graduated, Abbott immediately brought him into the business—though his foreign editor, Metz P. T. Lochard, had urged him to send the young man to Ohio State University's School of Journalism. Abbott opposed this idea because he felt a newspaper plant was the place to learn the business. Eventually, though, John entered the Chicago School of Printing and studied business administration at Northwestern University. Meantime, in his headlong drive to prepare his successor and thus assure the *Defender's* future as an institution, he almost forgot that John was his brother's son and not his own.

There was indeed a certain poignancy about Alexander's reactions to these developments involving his son. He wrote Abbott, "I am much pleased to know that John has graduated, but I was very much hurt to see later that you did not give me any credit for doing anything for him. I could have kept him here and had him out of college sooner. When John left me he was in second year high school. You asked me to let you send him to college. You know I gave up all my opportunities to take care of the children when John's mother died. Now I am not cross with you, but you did not treat me right." Alexander added this postscript, "Please, Please do not encourage him to change his name. That is all I can give Papa. 'A *Living Monument.*' I want him always to have papa's name—John Hermann Henry Sengstacke."

John, though young and inexperienced, studiously applied himself to the problems of the *Defender*. But Abbott was not to witness his total development. Consequently, a few weeks before he died, he turned to his old friend, Mary McCloud Bethune, a distinguished Negro leader, and said: "John is my nephew. I am depending upon him, Mamie. I am committing my unfinished task to him. Mamie, do you think he can do it?" Patting him reassuringly, she replied: "Rest, Abbott, my big brother, he can do it. He will do it. He will carry on!" Her prophesy was correct. When, after Abbott's death, John Sengstacke assumed leadership he successfully extricated the paper from litigation and financial difficulties. He ultimately bought out Edna's heirs to secure sole control of the paper. Moreover, he extended the *Defender's* influence, stabilized it financially, and, in the process, developed a chain of newspapers which now include—besides the Chicago *Defender*—the Gary *Defender*, National *Defender*, Tri-State *Defender*, Michigan *Chronicle*, Louisville *Defender*, and New York *Age De-*

fender. They represent a total circulation of nearly 300,000.

The evening of December 19, 1939, Robert S. Abbott signed his last will and testament in the presence of George S. Harris, C. N. Langston and Thomas P. Harris. He bequeathed his estate in this fashion: one-third to his wife, Edna; and two-thirds to John, with his sisters (Rebecca and Eliza McKay) subsidiary shareholders. He made no bequest to his old employees, though John was to keep them on the payroll beyond their years of usefulness. But Abbott himself had not become resigned to death. He still presumed he would recover and return to the *Defender.*

His secretary, Agaliece Westbrook (Miller), described his end. According to her, during his last days he was alone a great deal. By this time he was confined to bed almost constantly, except for occasional "sitting up" periods. "Although," she says, "I was no longer working at the *Defender,* at Mrs. [Edna] Abbott's request in Mr. Abbott's behalf, I came to the house every Saturday and sometimes on Sunday to work with Mr. Abbott in answering his correspondence, taking care of his checks and other personal matters."

As he grew steadily weaker, he began to realize for the first time that he would not recover and that perhaps there was not much time left. "One Saturday," she reports, "as I sat in his room typing letters by the window, he announced that he wanted to write his autobiography. It was a day like many others when that big house was completely deserted except for us on the second floor in the master bedroom. I remember vividly because when he spoke of writing his autobiography, I realized with somewhat of a shock that for the first time he was resigning himself to the end of life. Until then, his talk was always of the future and what he wanted to do to expand when he was able to get back to the office. He had not accepted the thought of death."

Thus was his autobiography started.

"I would sit by his bedside and he would talk of the past.

It was never like dictation—instead, it was a sort of reminiscence. With eyes closed, he would recall bits of information about his life and struggles in the old days, his family and friends. There was little continuity to his talk because as his strength ebbed, he became forgetful. Sometimes in the midst of a sentence he would stop talking and when I looked up I would see that he was asleep. I would return to my work and when he awakened, he'd give a little laugh and say, 'Guess I dropped off to sleep. Where were we?' "

The preparation of this autobiography became terribly important to him as the days passed, and he soon became impatient with his own inability to recall the sequence of events. But he kept determinedly at the project, often with Edna encouraging him. She, too, felt there was a story that should be told about his life and work that might not get told unless he tried to remember the past. He now developed a desperate need to see his work live. He related how he had put his personal fortune into the *Defender*. "I think," says Agaliece Westbrook, "he lived with the fear that the paper might not weather the storm with which it was then beset, and if it failed there would be nothing left of all his struggles and sacrifices. It all would have been in vain. So he wanted the story told. But as the days passed, his 'naps' became more frequent and the autobiography was never done."

He died in his sleep February 29, 1940.

When his secretary returned the next day, she found the bed covers turned back as though he had merely gotten up for a brief "sitting up" period. His table beside the bed looked as though work had been only temporarily interrupted, and he would soon resume. He had simply gone to sleep and hoped to awaken to carry on the fight the next day.

He never prepared for death.

He prepared only to live and fight.

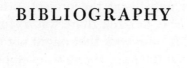

BIBLIOGRAPHY

Selected Bibliography

Abbott, Helen Thornton. *Diary* (unpublished).
Abbott, Robert S. "Making Good," *Southern Workman,* February 1919.
Bontemps, Arna and Conroy, Jack. *They Seek a City,* 1945.
Brazeal, Brailsford R. *The Brotherhood of Sleeping Car Porters,* 1946.
Chicago Commission on Race Relations, *The Negro in Chicago,* 1922.
Detweiler, Frederick G. *The Negro Press in the United States,* 1922.
Drake, St. Clair and Cayton, Horace R. *Black Metropolis,* 1945.
Durr, Robert. *The Negro Press* (pamphlet), 1947.
Gordon, Asa. *The Georgia Negro* (unpublished).
Franklin, John Hope. *From Slavery to Freedom,* 1947.
Gosnell, Harold F. *Negro Politicians,* 1935.
Jones, Dewey R. "Chicago Claims Supremacy," *Opportunity,* March 1929.
Kerlin, Robert T. *The Voice of the Negro,* 1920.
Lochard, Metz P. T. "Robert S. Abbott—'Race Leader,' " *Phylon,* Vol. VIII, No. 2, Second Quarter, 1947.
Moon, Henry Lee. *Balance of Power,* 1948.
Myrdal, Gunnar. *An American Dilemma,* Vols. I and II, 1944.
Ottley, Roi. *New World A-Coming,* 1943.
———, "The Negro Press Today," *An Anthology of American Negro Literature,* 1944.
———, *Black Odyssey,* 1948.
———, *No Green Pastures,* 1951.

Young, Consuelo C. "Reader Attitudes Toward the Negro Press," *Journalism Quarterly*, June 1944.

Young, Frank. *The First Twenty-five Years of the Defender* (unpublished).

Sengstacke, Herman. *Last Will & Testament*, 1860.

Sengstacke, John H. H. *Diary*, 1873-1900 (unpublished).

INDEX

Index

374